WHY WE READ WHAT WE READ

A Delightfully Opinionated Journey Through Contemporary Bestsellers }

Lisa Adams and John Heath

SOURCEBOOKS, INC.
NAPERVILLE, ILLINOIS

Published by Sourcebooks, Inc.
P.O. Box 4410, Naperville, Illinois 60567-4410
(630) 961-3900
Fax: (630) 961-2168
www.sourcebooks.com

Cataloging-in-Publication Data is on file with the publisher.

Printed and bound in the United States of America.
DR 10 9 8 7 6 5 4 3 2 1

CONTENTS

Chapter 7

To J and L,
whose lives really were changed by a book

ACKNOWLEDGMENTS

We are much obliged to Cindy Adams, Nora Chapman, Victor Davis Hanson, Erin Lee, Rick Maze, and Michelle McKenna, who read portions of our early drafts and provided invaluable feedback and advice. We are grateful too for the countless illuminating discussions we had with other friends and associates about their thoughts on books and bestsellers and on our findings in this project.

We are greatly indebted to our agent, Sharlene Martin, for believing in this book and for representing it with her trademark gusto. We wouldn't be here without her. Equally essential were the folks at Sourcebooks, especially Peter Lynch, Erin Nevius, and Heather Moore, who had faith in two authors in search of a platform. Now it's up to us.

And finally, a special shout-out to Emma for putting up with our tottering stacks of books and endless yakking with such enthusiasm and good humor.

WHAT WE'VE DONE AND
WHY WE'VE DONE IT

Okay, we've got a bar bet that can't be beat. We'll wager fifty dollars you can't name the title of the book we're about to summarize. We'll even give you a hint: it roosted in the highest echelons of the bestseller list for three straight years, from 2003 to 2005, and it was still going strong throughout 2006. Ready? There are plenty of details here, so pay close attention—you get only one guess!

Professor Robert Langdon, a middle-aged Harvard art historian and symbologist (great work if you can get it), is interrupted late at night to assist in solving a hideous crime—the mysterious murder and mutilation of a well-known European scholar and researcher. In his reluctant pursuit of answers, Langdon soon finds himself aligned with a young and brilliant beauty who was raised by the murder victim. Because she has followed in her pseudofather's intellectual footsteps, her technical knowledge becomes essential as she accompanies Langdon through many of the most important European museums, churches, and artistic monuments in search of the murderer—and the answer to a much greater puzzle of earth-shattering significance to Western Christendom.

The murderer is (or so it appears) an assassin deeply impressed by, and devoted to, the leader of a highly secretive society. Indeed, the two protagonists are led deeper and deeper into the mysteries of an underground society that has been dedicated for hundreds of years to combating the Catholic Church (and vice versa). The members of this covert circle (associated with the Masons—will no one cut the Masons some slack?) have been among Europe's most important artists, scientists, and writers. Indeed, one of the leaders of the society was the most famous and talented Italian of his era, having left messages in his works that reveal clues to the secrets the society keeps.

Our heroic couple (and they become increasingly couple-esque over the few hours they are thrown together on their quest) must uncover and solve the riddles posed by this society before they, and others, lose their lives. These puzzles involve a series of symbols centered on obelisks, deltas, pyramids, and dualities that, fortunately, are subjects of Professor Langdon's research.

In initial opposition to their search, but eventually crucially cooperative, is a crusty, veteran security officer. But in even stronger opposition to the couple's progress is the staccato pacing of the novel itself: dizzyingly short chapters dart back and forth between heroes and villains, each culminating in a breathtakingly gripping pronouncement designed to keep the reader in heart-stopping suspense.

Finally the saltatory narrative settles down as the good guys solve the riddles and catch up to the bad guys, only to discover that the most helpful individual in their quest is actually the evil genius behind the entire plot! The dramatic climax comes with the exposure of the criminal mastermind and the "great revelation." The exhausted couple is left with each other and with the single greatest (and potentially devastating) secret about the Roman Catholic Church—a secret they will just have to keep to themselves.

And your answer is . . . ?

As with any good bar bet, there's a gimmick. In this case, however, it's not ours but Dan Brown's. You see, he actually wrote the same thriller *twice*. The description just provided outlines the characters, plot, style, themes, and structure of both his smash hit *The Da Vinci Code* and his previous dud *Angels & Demons*. Honest. After *Angels & Demons* came out in 1999, Dan Brown published virtually the same book four years later. So no matter what your answer, you're wrong. (Well, yes, you're right too, but that's not the way these bar bets work. Unless you're bigger and meaner than we are, of course.)

Riding Coattails

Not one of Dan Brown's books prior to *The Da Vinci Code* came even close to becoming a bestseller on its own. But after the *Da Vinci* boost, all of them subsequently found new life on the bestseller list. *Deception Point* and *Digital Fortress* became *Publishers Weekly*'s #4 and #8 mass-market paperbacks in 2004, each selling over one million copies in 2005. *Angels & Demons, Da Vinci*'s doppelganger, did even better. Going nowhere for four years after its 1999 publication, it dashed up the bestseller lists in *Da Vinci*'s tracks, becoming the #8 mass-market paperback in 2003, the #2 mass-market paperback and the #5 hardcover fiction book in 2004, the #4 mass-market book in 2005, and the #10 mass-market book in 2006. Don't people notice they're reading the same book?

According to Dan Brown's agent Heide Lange, she "had to convince his publishers to look beyond the sales of his three previous books" in order to get *Da Vinci* published at all. But as we all know, her coaxing seriously paid off: *Da Vinci* has sold sixty million copies and counting. How did *Da Vinci* achieve such a different reception from its twin?

Sure, there are a few important differences between the two books—we'll come back to *Da Vinci* in our concluding chapter—but the similarities are so remarkable and so thorough that no one could have predicted the titanic success of *Angels & Demons* redux. Indeed, it appears that almost no one did.

How can we account for this triumph—or for the success of *any* of the most popular books in recent years? Clearly publishers can't always predict what will sell. We've all heard the lush tales of writers drowning in rejection slips before becoming wildly successful authors—urban legends in some cases, but true for many prominent bestselling writers such as James Patterson and Mary Higgins Clark. As devoted readers of books both popular and eccentric, fiction and nonfiction, we've long been curious about the bestselling lists. What do American reading habits—or at least our book-buying habits—say about our current values, desires, and fears? Are top-selling books merely flukes, or is there something that links them, certain persistent themes that resonate these days in the American psyche?

Over two million new books have been published in the United States in the past sixteen years. The year 2005 alone saw the birth—and usually the short, lonely life on the shelf—of more than 172,000 freshly minted titles. We're rolling in choices at the local bookstores, even as the local bookstores have gotten bigger and fewer and less local. We don't even need to go *out* to get books: Thanks to online shopping, books are never more than a few clicks away, as easy to acquire as a home mortgage or a Russian bride.

Would it be surprising, then, if recent bestselling books revealed similar themes—if our favorite .01 percent of all books bought in the United States shared similar concerns and preoccupations?

Well, they don't. Not all of them, anyhow. But we've found some clear trends that crank open a provocative window into America's soul.

Our intention here is to provide a glimpse into the current state of the national psyche by looking closely at the books Americans buy—specifically, at those books they have bought in the greatest numbers since 1990. Bestsellers, we must note, do make up only a very small percentage of all books sold—but still, their success is determined solely by audience demand. More than any others, these books resonate with broad segments of the reading public, and we're out to catch the vibe.

WHOSE VIBE?

Our concentration on books means we're not claiming to analyze every pulse and shudder of the American psyche—just the yens and fixations of the book-buying public. The National Education Association (NEA) recently reported that the number of American adults who say they've opened even a single book of fiction in the past year has dropped 14 percent in the last ten years to less than half, representing a "general collapse in advanced literacy," according to the NEA chairman. And the most recent National Assessment of Adult Literacy Survey reveals that 50 percent of adult Americans may simply be unprepared to read any complex texts whatsoever. But that leaves the *other* 50 percent of Americans available for indirect scrutiny. That's still a whole lot of people—and, thanks to their patronage, overall book sales hold pretty steady, with net sales of more than twenty-five billion dollars in 2005, according to industry sources.

BUT ISN'T IT ALL RIGGED?

Sure, a lot of books these days are sold on reputation alone. A glance at the top sellers in the mass-market paperback category, for example—which covers the kind of small, less expensive paperback you see in supermarkets and airports—reveals the same names year after year: Clancy, Grisham, Clark, Patterson, Steel, Roberts, Cornwell, King. Michael Korda ends his survey of the bestsellers of the twentieth century with this bleak observation:

> At the end of the day, the bestseller lists of the nineties made for relatively depressing reading, except to accountants. In fiction, it became enormously difficult to break through the sheer weight of numbers generated by perhaps two dozen, or fewer, top writers, who virtually dominated the list, and in nonfiction, a range of celebrities, merchandise, and self-help books that made it equally hard for all but the most exceptional book to get on the list. (*Making the List: A Cultural History of the American Bestseller 1900–1999*, 199)

Excuse Me, Mister, Have You Seen My Platform?

Platform is a snazzy new buzzword, usually functioning as a noun, but sometimes (alarmingly) as a reflexive verb. It refers to a built-in audience that virtually guarantees a certain number of book sales before the book is even written—and without any effort on the part of the publisher. Do *you* have a platform? Here's how to find out: Bestselling authors, radio talk-show hosts, and newspaper columnists have one. Regular folks, on the other hand, must try to develop a platform, or even "platform themselves"—which sounds terrifically painful—to have a better chance of getting published.

That gravy train is pretty exclusive. To hop aboard its cushy compartments, publishers increasingly seek out writers with a platform—that is, with a built-in audience and a way of reaching it. And of course the national and international marketing machine can help to create (as well as satisfy) audience demand. Nearly three-quarters of all bestsellers so far in the twenty-first century have been published by one of only six corporate publishing houses, a situation lamented in the recent memoirs of such industry titans as Jason Epstein and Andre Schiffin.

But the marketing machine doesn't have all the muscle. The editors and agents surveyed in 2005's *The Making of a Bestseller* (Brian Hill and Dee Power) feel that publicity, advertising programs, and the size of authorial advances are less important to bestseller-brewing than topic timeliness and writing quality (26). Nineteen first novels made the extended annual bestseller lists in 2002 and 2003 alone (15), and the triumphs of such first-time novelists as Alice Sebold (*The Lovely Bones*) and Charles Frazier (*Cold Mountain*) suggest that books can and do beat the odds if they strike readers the right way. (This is increasingly true even in such unlikely places as socialist China, where, as Shuyu Kong demonstrates in 2005's *Consuming Literature: Best Sellers and the Commercialization of Literary Production in Contemporary China,* the commercial ethic and the search for bestsellers are winning the war against party ideology.) Ultimately, for both the surprise smashes and the foreseeable favorites, the fact remains that people purchased these particular books more than any others.

Of course, we know there is not always a simple one-to-one connection between the sale of a book and the significance of its message. People may buy a book for reasons other than its themes. Maybe it was part of a book club order, or a gift. Maybe a friend, or Oprah, recommended it. Some books have sold well after they were seen on the President's desk. A few of the books on the lists were required reading in schools. Was a book bought but never read? We still don't believe that more than a few dozen readers actually got past the first chapter of Brian Greene's recent bestselling explanations of super-stringy things (*The Elegant Universe: Superstrings, Hidden Dimensions, and the Quest for the Ultimate Theory*, New York, 2000), much less Jacques Barzun's encyclopedic *From Dawn to Decadence*. Tens of millions of Bibles are bought each year, and even more are given away. Ninety-two percent of Americans own at least one Bible, and the average household has three. But how often are they opened? A Gallup survey revealed that fewer than half of Americans can name the first book of the Bible, and only one-third know who delivered the Sermon on the Mount. Twelve percent of American Christians think Noah's wife was Joan of Arc.

Nevertheless, it is still reasonable to assume that most books become bestsellers because readers like what they find—or what they have been told they will find—inside. And those are the books we will analyze: the ones that people actually buy instead of those sitting on the shelves or the ones reviewers recommend. Sometimes, of course, bestsellers gain critical acclaim and become classics (Dickens, for example); more often they disappear faster than those *Magic Eye* books—you remember them: stare at this garbled image for long enough and you'll see a schooner!—that were all the rage in '94 (#4, #6, and #10 in *Publishers Weekly* hardcover nonfiction). As another voyager through popular books has observed, "The time-bound nature of the best seller is of course precisely what makes it a suitable medium for an exploration of the values that are current in a specific era" (Erik Löfroth, *A World Made Safe: Values in American Best Sellers, 1895–1920,* 15).

It's not our primary job, then, to engage in the time-honored debate about *literary* versus *commercial, highbrow* versus *lowbrow,* or worse, what some critics are now calling *middlebrow* (closely related, we think, to the unibrow), but rather to look at what sold and to try to figure out what links these books thematically. Of course we have by necessity categorized the books we reviewed, and we have our opinions about what's good and bad, but we're not just snots out to trash popular culture. (If you need further proof, we saw *Mission: Impossible III* and *Must Love Dogs* in the theater.) We read a wide variety of books, including many bestsellers. Of our own volition we have bought and read self-help books, Oprah recommendations, formula fiction, political screeds, and, of course, *The Da Vinci Code*.

But What, Exactly, Is a Bestseller?

There have always been flutters of controversy in certain circles over what criteria should determine any bestseller list. *Publishers Weekly* produces the most pedigreed of the bunch, a list first published in 1912 and still followed closely by those in the publishing industry. The *New York Times Book Review*, which published its first bestseller list in 1942, is the most name-droppingly prestigious. *USA TODAY* began publishing lists in 1993; these note the top 150 sellers each week. And the baby of the family is the Book Sense list, which has been generated weekly by independent bookstores since 1999.

Despite the acrimony of this debate, there is in fact a tremendous degree of overlap among the lists. Our choice—determined primarily by ease of access to the numbers over the past sixteen years—is the annual list of bestselling books from *Publishers Weekly*. This particular list sets aside almanacs, atlases, and annuals, sorting the remaining bestsellers into four categories—hardcover fiction, hardcover nonfiction, trade paperback (which includes both fiction and nonfiction), and mass-market paperback (fiction only). Though we'll cite these categories along with book rankings, for the purposes of analysis we make a more general division between fiction and nonfiction.

We also know, however, that if we limit ourselves to annual bestsellers, we might overlook some very popular authors and books. Even in his day, Mark Twain never made it onto any list at all, and many fashionable authors never had a number one (see the list on page 134 of John Bear's book *The #1 New York Times Best Seller*). An author might write a book that sells very well for a number of years but never quite earns a spot on any one year's list of top titles. So we have supplemented the yearly *Publishers Weekly* lists with *USA TODAY*'s list of the one hundred bestselling books for the decade between 1993 and 2003 (no other list-maker has compiled such a study). And we have also on occasion made use of *USA TODAY*'s searchable online database of weekly top sellers, which facilitates the study of the relative positions of books and authors over time. In fact, for political bestsellers, we took advantage of the presidential election year by reading all the books (about forty . . . sigh) to make it onto any of the weekly lists in 2004. All of these lists are reprinted in the appendix at the back of this book, though we advise you not to worry too much about the relative rankings—ultimately we just want to provide a basic idea of the popularity of the books and authors we cover.

WHY THIS TIME PERIOD?

To probe the current state of America's psyche, we naturally needed to analyze recent bestsellers. But what exactly qualifies as *recent* in our disposable society? Five years? Twenty? To offer any real insight, we knew we needed two things: enough books to make reasonable generalizations and enough time to witness the ebb and flow of trends. In short, we needed somewhere between fifteen and twenty years of bestsellers. Electing not to plunge back into the '80s—our hair alone shows how much has changed since then—we decided to cover those bestsellers that have hit the shelves since 1990, giving us sixteen years of material for our study. (We won't be reviewing *every* book to have made the lists during that period—that would be over a thousand books, and you would hate us—but just enough to sketch an accurate picture of what's been going on.)

What We Found

We came to this project curious and cautious, knowing what we liked, but not knowing at all what we'd find. We had heard of some famously bestselling books—such as *Chicken Soup for the Soul* and *Tuesdays with Morrie*—but knew little about them. We knew about low-carb diets and romance novels, Oprah and Rush Limbaugh and Dan Brown, and literary fiction such as *Life of Pi* and *The Secret Life of Bees* that everybody seemed to be reading—but didn't know whether all those books were bestsellers or what that even meant.

What we found surprised us in every imaginable way. Books whose titles we had never heard had been selling millions of copies under our noses for years, whereas some of the books we had thought most popular had barely scraped the lists. Although genre fiction and self-help thrived as expected, more than one thorny novel was selling en masse alongside killer-thrillers and Dr. Phil's latest. Through our reading, religious movements came to life, and political polarities scarily zoomed forth. Dozens of mediocre books shocked us with their longevity. And many Oprah books revealed themselves as literature, not nearly as cheesy as we had heard they were.

We occasionally found books that even endowed our project with new depth and purpose. One of the most engaging and important bestsellers in recent years is *Reading Lolita in Tehran* by Azar Nafisi (#7 trade paperback in 2004), a "memoir in books" of Nafisi's life as a professor of Western fiction in Iran during the 1980s and 1990s. Her story is a celebration of reading; a reminder of the beauty, complexity, and subversive power of great literature; an exposé of the falseness of education when imposed for an overtly political, social, and religious agenda; and an account of human dignity in the face of undeniable evil. It is also required reading for anyone interested in the realities of an Islamic state and in the experience of women in a truly oppressive society. Here, Nafisi insightfully articulates the "danger" books can possess:

One of the most wonderful things about *Pride and Prejudice* is the variety of voices it embodies. There are so many different forms of dialogue: between several people, between two people, internal dialogue and dialogue through letters. All tensions are created and resolved through dialogue. Austen's ability to create such multivocality, such diverse voices and intonations in relation and in confrontation within a cohesive structure, is one of the best examples of the democratic aspect of the novel. In Austen's novels, there are spaces for oppositions that do not need to eliminate each other in order to exist. There is also space—not just space but a necessity—for self-reflection and self-criticism. Such reflection is the cause of change. We needed no message, no outright call for plurality, to prove our point. All we needed was to read and appreciate the cacophony of voices to understand its democratic imperative. This was where Austen's danger lay. (268–269)

Nafisi's thoughts about the reasons for reading—and her experiences teaching literature to students both thirsty for and hostile toward it—intensified our analysis of our own culture through its reading habits. Do American bestsellers, either fiction or nonfiction, share this "democratic imperative"? Do our contemporary favorites reveal the same interest in self-reflection and self-criticism, in multivocality and the coexistence of opposing voices?

The answer—and you just had to see this coming—is, well . . . No.

On the one hand, recent American bestsellers reveal a searching, energetic reading public not only devoted to escapist fantasies but also deeply interested in life's most complex issues: politics, religion, the law (or at least lawyers), and emotional connection. Our eternal American quest for self-improvement also shows no signs of abating—

fitness celebrities, financial gurus, and spiritual counselors hawk their ephemeral wares in ever-increasing numbers. In our apparently stressed-out and time-starved culture, readers are still making the effort to search for answers. Readers want better government, firmer thighs, and tighter connections with their spouses, emotions, and something out there in the universe.

That's all good news. Books could be there to aid America's explorations of these serious and complicated issues.

Yet our review of American bestsellers, both fiction and nonfiction, suggests that readers are increasingly attracted to simple, univocal reinforcements of hunches, rather than to complex, challenging efforts to search for real answers. For reasons we explore in this book (some of them fairly obvious, others more subtle), readers prefer to be told answers they already know or intuit rather than to ponder different ideas or engage in debates. The books themselves are part of the problem: They often allow, or even encourage, readers to vilify difference without trying to understand it, to celebrate the home team and denounce the visitors without reflection. This cheerleading syndrome is psychologically understandable, of course; people worry that their ideas and beliefs won't stand up to scrutiny.

But we believe that this rejection of other points of view in all aspects of life—family, religion, politics—is extremely dangerous both personally and culturally. Not only do our reading habits undermine the process of gaining genuine insight into the world and ourselves, they are distinctly undemocratic. By refusing to read anything that would surprise or challenge us—by denying the very possibility that other perspectives, interpretations, or conclusions could have value—we remove ourselves from democratic discourse and severely limit our options. Wadding our ears with familiar comforts, we become increasingly imperative and fearful; indeed, we become extremists, unwilling or unable to endure criticism or debate.

Moreover, we do not satiate the hunger for answers that brought us to the bookshelf in the first place. Recent bestsellers are, to a disconcerting extent, empty calories, appeasing the emotions briefly without providing enough real substance to address the underlying issues or genuine needs of the reader.

As lifelong readers of both fiction and nonfiction (and now as teachers of literature and writing), we have experienced the genuine transformative power of great books. We have shared the struggles of many an unfamiliar life; we have discovered and reconsidered our guiding principles because books have compelled us to embrace and process life's complexities, tensions, and ironies. And we see these immensely valuable and fulfilling gifts—these most wonderful aspects of reading—being threatened, being exchanged for the quick fixes and self-satisfied conclusions that can't possibly help or transform anyone in a world as rich and mazy as ours.

So many of us are searching. And so many of us have forgotten, or were never taught, what perilous joys books can bring. And so we hope, in some small way, to redirect the search to a more satisfying end. Looking to books for answers has never been wrong—but books, at their best, help us to come up with our own.

What We'll Be Covering. And Not Covering.

Even after immersing ourselves in the strange new world of the bestseller, we still had to impose a few limits that would make for a more insightful study. Thus we decided to skip certain categories, such as reference works and books that owe their sales spikes to popular movies (*The Lion, the Witch, and the Wardrobe* and *In Cold Blood*, for example).

We also omit most biographies and memoirs, mainly because the themes of the writing seem to have little bearing on the books' rankings. Athletes, politicians, and personalities—people with platforms!—hop the bestseller lists with ease, finding captive audiences for their thoughts on themselves, their peers, their sand-wedge secrets, and their vanishing menses. Since the '90s, Americans have devoured the life stories and wisdom of authors as disparate as Suzanne Somers, Tom Brokaw, Tiger Woods, Pope John Paul II, Joan Didion, Howard Stern, Bill Gates, the Beatles, the Dalai Lama, Bill and Hillary Clinton, Tommy Franks, Clay Aiken, Paris Hilton, and professional wrestler Mick Foley (yup, his memoir was actually #13 in 1999)—as well as books feeding national obsessions with the civil war, the British royal family, and the O. J. Simpson trial. Very occasionally, a memoir by a regular dude hits the charts, such as Frank McCourt's poignant *Angela's Ashes* (#4 trade paperback in 1999), but raging success of the unplatformed variety is so rare for biographies and memoirs that we feel justified in skipping them all.

We bypass cookbooks as well, another venerable genre of popular reading. According to Alice Payne Hackett and James Henry Burke in *80 Years of Best-Sellers,* by 1975 the three all-time hardbound bestsellers were cookbooks (*Better Homes and Gardens, Betty Crocker's,* and *The Joy of Cooking*). Many new cookbooks have sold well over the past sixteen years, from the slow-cooking atavism of *The Fix-It and Forget It Cookbook* line (#1 trade paperback in 2002) to the revised edition of the Rombauers' masterpiece (*The Joy of Cooking,* #5 in hardcover nonfiction in 1997). The only cookbook to break into the top one hundred for the entire 1993–2003 decade, however, was *In The Kitchen with Rosie* (#21), a slim volume of recipes from Oprah's personal chef. Books concocted by celebrity chefs from the Food Network now dominate the list: in 2006, Rachael Ray sold over three million of her various cookbooks—including the #4 title on the *Publishers Weekly* trade paperback list—and Ray's colleagues Paula Deen and Giada DeLaurentiis also made strong showings, each with multiple titles.

Just a few years back, however, people were much more interested in what *not* to eat. We'll take a peek at this starving society in the next chapter, which covers the category of books we call the *Obvious:* those that promise to shrink waistlines and super-size wealth and well-being. Transparent and perpetual as their allure may be, though, these best-selling guides to diet, financial success, and personal inspiration offer a distinct slant that reveals the purest essence of American desires during the past sixteen years. We explore the success of diet-related best-sellers such as *Dr. Atkins' New Diet Revolution* and Arthur Agatston's *South Beach Diet;* business guides including *The 7 Habits of Highly Effective People* by Stephen Covey, *Who Moved My Cheese?* by Spencer Johnson, and *Good to Great* by Jim Collins; and priority-straightening jump-starters such as Richard Carlson's *Don't Sweat the Small Stuff,* Sarah Ban Breathnach's *Simple Abundance,* Mitch Albom's *Tuesdays with Morrie,* and the *Chicken Soup for the Soul* megaseries. The candor, sincerity, and underlying assumptions of these books reflect an America endlessly seeking change, success, and spiritual growth—yet finding its solace not in change itself, but in the comforting if short-lived experience of reading about it.

We next explore the nature—and the function—of good and evil as presented in popular works of fiction and nonfiction. The epic of this period stars Harry Potter, but soaring nearly as high are the Muggles who rule the mystery, suspense, and thriller genres: John Grisham, Tom Clancy, Stephen King, James Patterson, Mary Higgins Clark, Patricia Cornwell, and Dean Koontz. With stunning regularity these authors satisfy an audience hungry for messy stories with tidy resolutions. And not very different, surprisingly, are the proliferating "nonfiction" political diatribes that sound more like schoolyard taunts and tattles than reasoned efforts at national improvement. Many of these bestselling observers—including Rush Limbaugh, Al Franken, Newt Gingrich, Michael Moore, Bill O'Reilly, Ann Coulter, and Michael Savage—have an Enemy-Who-Must-Be-Named, a Voldemort to blast with *crucios* and *avada kedevras.* Whether personified in Bush or Clinton, or discovered in the war in Iraq or the "liberal elite," evil is increasingly simplified and associated with one side of the political aisle.

In surprisingly similar ways, both fiction and nonfiction offer neat definitions of evil—specific, irredeemable, and entirely separate from you and me—that allow readers to classify and confine this nettling problem and reaffirm their allegiance to the good guys. Political groupies smugly blaze forward, existing beliefs reinforced, without having to consider other points of view. Just as psychically gratifying, both genres also engage their readers in battles of vast importance, connecting them—either through vicarious crime-fighting thrills or real if intangible networks of like-minded people—to the larger world and its (real or imagined) life-and-death struggles, of which disconnected Americans rarely feel a part.

No subtler are the bestselling books on love, sex, and relationships. Though the authors of popular relationship-revival guides differ in their approaches to conquering marital unhappiness, all the nonfiction bestsellers of this genre—including *Men Are from Mars, Women Are from Venus* by John Gray, *The Proper Care & Feeding of Husbands* by Laura Schlessinger, and *Relationship Rescue* by Dr. Phil (McGraw)—deliver emphatic instructions for marriage-mending that spring from the same rigid views of gender roles and relationships. Discontented spouses are advised to take comfort in an unbridgeable gender divide—and to, with practice, learn to accept and even celebrate those differences. For the most part, these guides promise relatively quick and easy solutions to complex marital problems, even as their premises may ironically undermine the possibilities for genuine compatibility and change.

On the other side of the tracks, today's popular romance novels—including selections from Nora Roberts, Danielle Steel, Janet Evanovich, and other bestselling if lesser-known authors—likewise offer sanguine yet surprisingly constrained visions of romantic love. Though the definition of an ideal relationship differs gigantically between the romance novels and the self-help manuals, both genres cleverly manage to sketch out dreamy scenarios in which happy relationships require little effort. Drawn from a different and in some ways more obvious template, the novels of Nicholas Sparks (*The Notebook; Message in a Bottle*) and Robert James Waller (*The Bridges of Madison County*) concede that lifelong happiness isn't inevitable, but passionate love can swell and last forever. Far more subtle than these books' assertions, however, are their effects on searching, unhappy readers, who find comfort and catharsis, but few lasting solutions, in these bestsellers.

But nowhere is the American thirst for answers more apparent than in our religious and spiritual reading. We do love our epic battles, and this time, it's not just God and Satan duking it out for our immortal souls. Despite the innate insolvability of the biggest mystery of all, sincere gurus of various persuasions clamor to join this Capitalization Club, profitably instructing sincere seekers on the secrets of God, the Savior, the Universe, Love, the Light, the Spirit, the Soul. The bestselling spiritual books of the recent past reveal an America divided between two spiritual camps—fundamentalist Christian and New Age—neither of which can quite let the other alone. Confident that their time-honored theology will trump any pipsqueak of a religion, the Christian titles— Bruce Wilkinson's *The Prayer of Jabez*, Rick Warren's *The Purpose-Driven Life*, Joel Osteen's *Your Best Life Now*, Joyce Meyer's *Approval Addiction*, and Tim LaHaye and Jerry Jenkins's *Left Behind* series— attempt to win, maintain, and encourage Christian souls by using promises, guidance, and even terror to keep readers on the narrow road. Hiking a different path entirely, Don Miguel Ruiz's *The Four Agreements*, Neale Donald Walsch's *Conversations with God*, James Redfield's *The Celestine Prophecy*, and Gary Zukav's *The Seat of the Soul* provide four distinct takes on New Age thought that all counter Christian beliefs, either indirectly or heatedly.

How each group responds to the other is often more culturally interesting than are the religious particulars. In our analysis of these bestsellers, we uncover a conservative Christian population that feels righteous, yet dismissed and mocked, one that can't extricate itself from its struggle between faith and reason. We also discover a passel of seekers, probably both Christian and non-Christian, looking for more freedom than a jealous God has to offer, more opportunities for growth and choice, and entirely new (but not necessarily more believable) explanations of the universe. Yet despite the animosity and the sometimes enormous theological gaps, each camp dangles before readers an equally irresistible nugget of cultural salvation: the Christian titles provide comfort with their clear, unchanging, black-and-white answers, and the New Age books offer endless and expansive opportunities for betterment and second chances. Although these two perspectives might not blend well in any one real-life religion, they are linked by their constant appearances in our bestselling books: no matter how many hurt feelings they may have caused in the spiritual arena, they are the yin and yang of today's culture, in religion and beyond.

We then turn to the bestseller lists' highest class: the literary books, non-genre titles that tend to offer more complex language and themes. Beginning with a visit to Oprah's famous book club, we examine her most popular selections as well as other top-selling literary works— about fifty in all—unearthing the themes that literary readers can't put down. In books such as Jon Krakauer's *Into Thin Air,* Wally Lamb's *She's Come Undone,* Barbara Kingsolver's *The Poisonwood Bible,* Khaled Hosseini's *The Kite Runner,* Sue Monk Kidd's *The Secret Life of Bees,* Jacquelyn Mitchard's *The Deep End of the Ocean,* and Charles Frazier's *Cold Mountain,* we find a near obsession with human triumph over adversity; unlike bestsellers of other genres, these books never make the claim that life is simple or that problems are easy to fix. Indeed, the trials the characters face (abandonment, slavery, addiction, disease, poverty, exile, deception, loss of family, relentless labor) are experiences so wrenching that they actually place the eventual victory in sharper, more cathartic contrast. Again and again, literary readers seem to enjoy descending vicariously into the depths of misery in order to feel the characters' resilience and taste their redemption.

Though the bestselling literary novels often present a fairly realistic picture of life—leaving readers with mixed feelings and without clear answers, with a deeper awareness of life's ability to wrench as well as to shield—they also tend to circle the same subjects, focusing almost exclusively on issues of home and family. In stark contrast lie most of the nonfiction books—such as Eric Schlosser's *Fast Food Nation,* David McCullough's historical blockbusters, and Malcolm Gladwell's cultural investigations *Blink* and *The Tipping Point*—which are focused primarily on history, culture, and science. In light of these fairly stark differences (and one rather staggering similarity), we explore not only what gets read but *how*—and by whom—showing how greater diversity in topics, reading methods, and even denouements can help us expand our thinking and use books to their fullest.

Finally, in our concluding chapter, we return to the headstrong, disconcerting life of Dan Brown's *Da Vinci Code,* a mystery novel that has mysteriously sold sixty million copies and managed to remain at the top of the bestseller lists for over four years (still the #1 trade paperback in 2006). Much has been made of (and made off) *Da Vinci's* longevity. Among fans, the novel has inspired a swell of interest in church history and Christian theology, impelling critics of various persuasions to skewer the book for its faulty assertions; it's also prompted fleeting but intense sales of at least four more books that critique its claims. In response to the hoopla, others, blasé, have defended the novel as a harmless, fun piece of fiction. But though many have tried, none can quite account for its raging popularity.

We do little, alas, to end the drama or to solve the mystery as decisively as a work of detective fiction would do it. But we do have yet another interpretation to throw into the mix. *The Da Vinci Code* is, in many ways, the crowning example of our findings in this project. It's speedy, simple, full of secrets. It drop-kicks its characters into a hair-raising search for truth of worldwide, if not otherworldly, significance. It's not only about sex and religion, but about sex *in* religion! And, come on, it has a *killer albino*. In the final chapter we discuss *The Da Vinci Code* as a representative work of today's bestselling literature, a novel of suspense, struggle, sides, and paranoia (a surprisingly common feature in bestsellers)—and ultimately, answers, reassurance, and redemption.

And finally, we make a long-term suggestion about how to improve the situation, about how to make Americans demand more from their reading. Our solution is so conventional, so traditional, so unlikely to find fruition, it's probably not worth more than a paragraph. But we never met a paragraph we couldn't turn into several pages, and so we do.

Our perusal of recent bestsellers takes us first to the psychic pick-me-up section of the list, a shelf hopping with stimulants for a sluggish American soul caught in the quagmire of competing urges: How can we get rich without getting guilty? How can we get happy without getting rich? How can we shed pounds without sweating, or at least without sweating the small stuff?

Welcome to the world of American can-do-ism at its most rhapsodic, an inspirational land of fables, foibles, and feel-good fowl, of affectively effective people and inner peace, where there is always a simple abundance of cheese, and it's never too late to learn "life's greatest lesson."

THE OBVIOUS: DIET,
WEALTH, AND INSPIRATION

I have always loved mayonnaise and am glad to see that this plan
allows Mayo to be used liberally.
Amazon.com reviewer of *The South Beach Diet*

Never underestimate your power to change yourself.
No. 284 in H. Jackson Brown Jr.'s *Life's Little Instruction Book*

We begin our study by examining diet, financial, and inspirational titles. Though these categories are timeless and obvious—*of course* everyone wants to be slim, rich, and motivated, and always has—in and between the lines of individual books lies a distinct spin on these topics that illuminates the specific concerns and desires of Americans in the recent past.

Before we look more closely at these bestsellers, however, it will be helpful first to discuss briefly the endurance of these and other categories in the cultural landscape.

In *Making the List: A Cultural History of the American Bestseller 1900–1999*, Michael Korda enumerates Americans' habitual literary preferences during the twentieth century. Diet and self-help guides, celebrity memoirs, sensationalist scientific and religious speculation, stories about pets, medical advice (particularly concerning sex, longevity, and childrearing), folksy wisdom and humor, and the Civil War have all sustained America's interest over the past one hundred years (xii). How well do recent bestsellers fit into the patterns of a century?

Very well, it turns out. But there are two noticeable deviations. First, stories about pets have been hard to find. If ever there were a sign of a crisis in American culture, this would be it. Where are the puppies, people? Even books about Barbara Bush's dog Millie and Bill Clinton's cat Socks failed to grab lasting readership. *All I Need to Know I Learned from My Cat* made it to #4 in trade paperbacks in 1991, *The Hidden Life of Dogs* was #9 in hardcover fiction in 1993, and *James Herriot's Favorite Dog Stories* snuck in at #14 three years later, but for a decade following, the lists were relatively critter-free. The only bestselling animal in *USA TODAY's* final one hundred for 1993–2003 was a racehorse, *Seabiscuit: An American Legend,* hurtled down the backstretch by the release of the movie. All that most animals got during this period were a few supporting roles in other bestsellers: there's a horse, of course, in Nicholas Evans's *The Horse Whisperer,* revelations of insect mysteries in *The Secret Life of Bees,* entire flocks of anonymous fowl stewing in the *Chicken Soup for the Soul* books, and adaptable mice in *Who Moved My Cheese?*

Decades of Bestselling Trickery

The title of Harper Lee's perpetually bestselling novel (#25 on *USA TODAY's* 1993–2003 list) was clearly a desperate marketing ploy to cash in on the century-long animal-loving trend and hoodwink the unwary reader. It worked on us, unfortunately, so a word to the wise: We've scoured the book several times—it was required reading in ninth grade, for god's sake (and must still be)—and there's not one real mockingbird to be found, dead or otherwise. Consider yourself warned.

But in the past couple years we've seen some signs that animals might be taking back the stage. In 2005, Jim Edgar's *Bad Cat,* a collection of 244 photos of strange and deranged cats, scored *Publishers Weekly's* #11 spot for trade paperbacks. And two dog books ruled in 2006: John Rogan's funny tale of life with a problem Labrador (*Marley and Me: Life and Love with the World's Worst Dog,* #3 nonfiction) and the book he perhaps should have bought in response (*Cesar's Way: The Natural Everyday Guide to Understanding and Correcting Common Dog Problems,* #8 nonfiction).

The success of *Bad Cat* and *Marley and Me,* along with Billy Crystal's recent hit *700 Sundays* and Nora Ephron's *I Feel Bad About My Neck,* may also indicate that we are getting our funny bones back. Humor—at least of the intentional variety—has been in short supply during much of this time period. Comedians climbed the charts in the early and mid-nineties: Howard Stern, Jerry Seinfeld, Tim Allen, Paul Reiser, and Ellen DeGeneres all made the annual bestselling lists, and the comic-strip collections of Gary Larson, Bill Watterson, and Scott Adams were bestsellers eighteen times just between 1992 and 1996. But then things changed. With the exception of the acerbic treatments of politics in *Rush Limbaugh Is a Big Fat Idiot* (#13 in 1996) and *Lies and the Lying Liars Who Tell Them* (#6 in 2003), both by Al Franken, and *America (The Book)* from Jon Stewart and the Daily Show (which earned *Publishers Weekly's* "Book of the Year" for 2004), few books of humor made it onto the annual lists over the past decade.

Overall, American readers during this period seem to have been in an unusually somber mood. Are our humorists less funny—who doesn't miss *Calvin and Hobbes* and *The Far Side?*—or are we just grimmer in the twenty-first century? Maybe we've been searching for humor in different places (even Dave Barry has abandoned his column). Did crank emails and parodic websites replace funny books? Or was this just one of those periodic swings in preference, like television vacillations between sitcoms, drama, and reality shows?

Perhaps it's not such a coincidence that humor books began disappearing from the annual lists just as readers were turning to *Tuesdays with Morrie,* the multiple offerings of *Chicken Soup for the Soul,* and other sincere inspirational titles. Did written humor, dependent as it so often is on irony, inversion, and critique, lose some of its appeal in our pursuit of confirmation and comfort?

Or perhaps the answer is much simpler. It's just not easy to chuckle when your brain is starved for carbohydrates and you've sworn off chocolate cake, french fries, spaghetti, pancakes, and apple pie for life. Or even for a few months. Because for most of the last decade we have been on a diet . . . and a most peculiar diet at that.

Low Carb and Lovin' It

Diet books have been happily ensconced on bestseller lists since Lulu Hunt Peters topped the charts with *Diet and Health* for several years in the mid-1920s. The constancy of bestselling diet books has traditionally been their inconstancy—every year a new book and a new fad. One nutritionist has written that he has seen at least fifty "famous" diets rise and fall over the past thirty years. Remember Stillman? Pritikin? The Scarsdale diet? In the ten years from 1972 to 1982, for example, there were at least 103 different popular diet books with almost as many approaches, nearly enough for a new diet every month of the decade (Steven Starker's *Oracle at the Supermarket* has a complete list in an appendix). Grapefruit today. Cabbage soup next. Then "eating like a caveman" to become *Neanderthin* (yes, actually published in 2000). Dieters have been nothing if not fickle in their book selection.

The startling difference about the past few years' successful diet books is that the very *best* sellers share a single theme: protein good, carbohydrates bad. Very bad (well, except for the good ones—duh!).

Variety appears only in the style and extremity of the advice. A book market that for scores of years has been a wide-open field for both pedigreed dieticians and panacea-peddling quacks has become increasingly monolithic. Since *The T-Factor Fat Gram Counter* ran through its few years of fame (1991–1994), the annual lists have been dominated by low-carb gurus. This "brand loyalty"—readers appear to hop between different manifestations of the same diet, choosing between recipes and degrees of severity but not approaches—is something quite novel.

Back in the 1970s, for example, when Dr. Robert Atkins's no-/low-carb *Diet Revolution* was published, dieticians and physicians scoffed at it as dangerous and unproven, and it quickly went to #1 on the *New York Times* bestseller list. It got lost, however, in the variety and competition—there was always another bestselling method of trying to lose weight back then, a Russian Air Force diet ready to take its place in the pantheon. But twenty years later, Dr. Atkins was back with his *New Diet Revolution,* and this time America was even fatter and more desperate, making this the second bestselling book of 1993–2003, with over ten million copies in print (in 2004 it was still the #9 mass-market paperback). Only *Harry Potter and the Sorcerer's Stone* outsold it over that period, and we think that's at least in part because the young magician became a secret hero to the low-carbers. Sad, gaunt little Harry was locked in a closet most of his life by his evil relatives and thereby deprived of many of the fruits, cereals, breads, grains, starches, baked goods, dairy products, sodas, and sweets that send most kids right off the obesity chart. Heck, just look at his carb-scarfing cousin Dudley. Look at him! Now tell us there's not a nutritional lesson to be learned there! So irresistible was low-carb reading that *Dr. Atkins' New Carbohydrate Gram Counter*—not exactly a page-turner—came in at #37 for the same decade, and we don't doubt that if there had been a *Dr. Atkins' 101 Party Games with Meat,* it would have skewered its way into the list. All told, Atkins-related books have sold over twenty million copies.

And Atkins wasn't the only one. *The South Beach Diet, Protein Power, The Zone,* and *Sugar Busters!* are also high-protein, low-carb plans to reduce girth that dominated the diet market from 1998 to 2003 (numbers 23, 59, 69, and 76, respectively, in *USA TODAY*'s top one hundred). In fact, *The South Beach Diet* eventually edged out Atkins. In 2004 *The South Beach Diet* was on the *Publishers Weekly* bestselling list for fifty-one weeks (apparently, America took one week off during December for carb indulgence), spending sixteen of those weeks in the #1 position. That year it ended up #2 in hardcover nonfiction; in 2005 it was the #7 mass-market title and the #9 trade paperback. *The South Beach Diet Good Fats/Good Carbs Guide* claimed the #1 spot in trade paperbacks in 2004. Hilariously, *The South Beach Diet Cookbook* (#5 in hardcover nonfiction in 2004) yielded to *The South Beach Diet Dining Guide* in 2005. Why avoid good food at home when you can pay someone else not to cook it?

Carb reduction became a cultural phenomenon. In a 2004 AC Nielsen survey, 17 percent of U.S. households reported that someone in their residence was on a low-carb diet. Atkins Nutritions made over $100 million in 2003, and the global low-carb market was estimated at $10 billion, almost a third of the $33 billion commercial diet industry. Atkins developed formal partnerships with T.G.I. Friday's and Subway, and Kraft Foods began selling products bearing the South Beach Diet trademark. We're cautiously hopeful that Chips Ahoy and Cheez Whiz will get the seal of approval.

This cultural phenom even changed the book market. With the rise of low-carb living, Americans began to read diet books with the same genre loyalty the book industry has come to expect from the romance, Western, mystery, and sci-fi faithful. "Low-carb" on the cover carried the same clout as the names Grisham or King or Steel.

This trend makes a certain sense in fiction—if a reader likes the formula and style of one Dean Koontz thriller, then the next Koontz book is unlikely to disappoint. And especially because there appears to be an overwhelming number of choices in the bookstore and such little time, there's a certain comfort in settling for the safety of the familiar. But what's especially revealing about the protein fetish is that—unlike the subjective satisfaction to be found in a Dean Koontz novel—there is an objective element to a diet book: does its advice work better than that found in other diet books? The most popular diet books, theoretically, should be the ones that help the most people lose the most weight in the most sustainable way.

But according to the studies, the low-carb diet has not been proven to be any more effective than any other low-calorie diet, including the more traditional low-fat approach, in keeping weight off in the long-term. And there are many possible negative health effects associated with the low-carb regimen, including hyperactive pastaphilia, a humiliating concatenation of symptoms that includes uncontrollable drooling and whimpering when in the vicinity of an Italian restaurant. *Then* there's the medical report on the deceased Dr. Atkins, which noted that the diet doctor had had a history of heart attacks and congestive heart problems and was himself medically obese at 258 pounds when he died in 2003. Michael Bloomberg, the mayor of New York, was overheard saying—and later apologized to Atkins's widow for it—"the guy was fat and the food was inedible."

The truth of Bloomberg's observation may be dawning on us, for there are signs that the low-carb phase in our reading and dieting cycle may be passing, or at least slimming down. Atkins Nutritionals filed for bankruptcy in July of 2005. Few mourned, and some, like the chief of the Idaho Potato Association, claimed farmers would be "jumping up and down in the potato fields." The owner of OB Macaroni, which nearly went out of business after sales slumped, was quoted as simply saying "Ha ha ha." (Indeed, Interstate Baking Corporation, makers of such brands as Hostess, Dolly Madison, and Wonder, reported that the low-carb trend contributed to its own Chapter 11 filing in 2004.) Even *The South Beach Diet* slipped to #46 in trade paperbacks in 2006. Recent studies indicate that currently only 2 percent of the population is cutting carbs.

Of course, many dieters never did. Even in the midst of the low-carb craze, a few bestselling diet books touted other approaches. Bill Phillips's *Body-for-Life* program came in at #15 on the 1993–2003 list (and was also #11 in 1999, #3 in 2000, #8 in 2001, and #10 in 2002). He's a bit vague on what exactly you're supposed to eat, although he does want you to exercise twenty minutes daily and buy his nutritional supplement. Bob Greene's books rode Oprah's popularity (he was her personal trainer and coauthor—and she was the "best man" at his wedding) to the charts in 1996 (#1), 2002 (#15), and 2006 (#7) with a weight-loss approach based on rigorous training programs and gradual dietary changes. And holistic health guru Andrew Weil (also a favorite of Oprah—he coauthored a cookbook with her personal chef) took his *Eating Well for Optimum Health* to #10 in 2000 with a sensible, research-based diet.

Dr. Phil's *The Ultimate Weight Solution* also topped the charts (#4 in 2003) without emphasizing carbohydrate reduction. Of course, this might say more about Dr. Phil's cultural omnipresence than about his dietary sapience. At this point the guy could write a book on monkey training or do-it-yourself surgery—*Seven Get-Real Strategies for At-Home Appendectomies*—and it would likely be a blockbuster. (In fact, Dr. Phil's *son* wrote a diet book for teens that made it into *USA TODAY*'s top 150 for three weeks in 2004, and his wife—Robin McGraw—climbed the charts in 2006/2007 with *Inside My Heart,* a woman-focused inspirational book aggressively promoted by Captain Get-Real himself.)

Mireille Guillano also rose to the top (#11 nonfiction in 2005) with her *French Women Don't Get Fat: The Secret of Eating for Pleasure.* One

gets the feeling this book is all about style (and a catchy if disingenuous title) rather than the advice itself, which is hopelessly old-fashioned.
She advocates a healthy, reasonable diet (it includes soy, and even
chocolate, although only a couple bites at a time) and reasonable exercise (taking the stairs). Good advice, sure—but will it be enough to
prompt Americans to trade in their Twinkies for tofu?

Most encouraging, *You: The Owner's Manual,* a surprisingly entertaining survey of current knowledge about the human body, was the fourth
bestselling nonfiction book in 2005. The two physician authors make recommendations "that will make you healthier and younger" (the book
seems to be aimed at the aging, health-conscious boomers) and include
many recipes for improving various bodily functions. A significant part
of the book's appeal is that it focuses on achieving and maintaining health
in a variety of ways, not diet alone; the follow-up companion book *You:
On A Diet* offers a witty, science-based plan for "waist management" that
was the second bestselling nonfiction book in 2006. Perhaps the *You* series
represents a new, more positive trend in diet reading—though we have to
suspect that a lot of people bought the first book for the sex statistics.

So what does this low-carb carnival tell us? First, perhaps most obviously, the buying of diet books is not tied to any ultimate reality about
long-term weight loss. In fact, during the same period that readers were
buying every low-carb book, guide, and Mad Lib to hit the local bookstore, Americans were growing fatter. The two factors most closely
associated with obesity—poor dietary habits and physical inactivity—
now cause 400,000 deaths each year, making obesity the second-leading
preventable cause of death (smoking is first). Sixty-five percent of adult
Americans—about 127 million people—are overweight or obese, an
increase of nearly 10 percent in just the last six years of the twentieth
century. Since 1976, obesity has doubled in the adult population and
tripled in the youth population. One in fifty people is seriously obese,
up from one in two hundred in 1986.

So it's no surprise that we are clamoring ever more for a miracle diet. And there *is* one thing that distinguishes the (failing) low-carb diets from all their (failed) predecessors: the immediate result. Sending a body into carb-starvation mode results in quick weight loss (much of it in water loss) over the first few weeks and even months. Forget that these are very peculiar, perhaps even unhealthy, regimens to maintain; ignore that the science suggests that they won't work over an extended period; dismiss the only studies to follow dieters for an entire year that show no long-term benefits over traditional diets. No. The most important truth is that within weeks—days, even—the scale in the bathroom has become a friend once again. The quick, even if short-term, success delivers an immediate sense of accomplishment.

These diet books provide a sort of parallel reality. We feel better about ourselves—we're taking some responsibility and doing something about our problems (and it's a pretty difficult something). We're also part of something, a cultural phenomenon, like wearing Air Jordans or watching *Survivor*. And perhaps most comforting—and obvious—of all, we don't actually have to break a sweat. In a year, studies suggest, most low-carb readers are back to struggling with lumpy thighs and searching for answers once again. But interestingly, readers have been saying not that the Atkins diet failed them, but that *they* failed the Atkins diet. Rather than look at the underlying issues, or even challenge the efficacy of the textbook, readers have hopped on the next low-carb train—like the more palatable *South Beach* (giddily subtitled "The Delicious, Doctor-Designed, Foolproof Plan for Fast and Healthy Weight Loss")—to the promised land. Sure, we're all vaguely aware that not even Moses made it there, but then he didn't have a carbohydrate gram counter, now did he?

It's not that we reject the idea of working per se. After all, Americans on average work more hours than citizens in any other industrialized nation. The low-carb diet is *not* easy. In fact, it's a pain—even those versions that allow all the steak and mayo one can eat. But although the low-carb books challenge us physically and psychologically, they do not challenge any of our basic preconceptions. We accept that we must somehow change our eating habits to be thinner—and we are willing to go through enormous contortions to do that—but most of us do not want to pay for a book that tells us that we have to eat a lot less (of most everything), that we must exercise (the U.S. government now recommends sixty to ninety minutes each day to sustain weight loss), that it will take a long time, and that we will have to live like that for the rest of our lives. Who wants to be reminded that losing a single pound will require us to burn 3,500 more calories—thirty-five *hundred* more calories—than we consume? With its cookbooks and counters and trademarked foods, the low-carb diet *seems* complex, all the while masking the underlying complexity of the genuine change required for most of us to lose weight for the long term.

Ultimately, the low-carb craze was about instant results, cultish devotion, overly simplistic answers to complex psychological and physiological issues, and self-imposed insulation from critique and alternative voices. It was, in other words, a perfect representative of our general reading habits over the recent past.

Help Me, Ronda

Our burgeoning bellies are one thing—six months of clogging the arteries with a high-fat diet may help some and will probably not kill many—but what have Americans done in the recent past to shape up their souls?

At the beginning of this chapter, we listed the types of books that have endured throughout the twentieth century, according to *Making the List: A Cultural History of the American Bestseller 1900–1999* by Michael Korda. One of Korda's categories—"folksy wisdom"—may describe the most titles on recent bestseller lists. The "wisdom" imparted in these books changes over time, of course, but in the last few decades we have been in search of spiritual wisdom, of connections with ourselves, our spouses, our communities, and something bigger, bigger even than our expanding tushes. We want to be inspired to be something more, to be not just thinner and richer (although those are a good start), but happier and more content with what we have. The idea that money and business should take a back seat to love, family, friends, and inner contentment may not be novel, but we have been turning to such reassuring reminders in astonishingly enormous bestselling numbers.

There's nothing new about self-help in American reading, of course. Current self-improvement guides have their roots in the so-called Protestant ethic and Puritan New England, which culminated in works such as Cotton Mather's *Bonifacius: Essays to Do Good* (1710). Since then, each generation has had its own bestselling vision of what's wrong and how to fix it, from Franklin's *Poor Richard's Almanac* through Transcendentalism, New Thought, Mind-Cure, John Dewey, and the modern model of self-actualization, the "prodigiously ordinary" pronouncements of Norman Vincent Peale's *The Power of Positive Thinking* (1952).

Pundits have not much liked the last half-century of self-help manuals—and they are an easy target—faulting the books' over-simplicity, redundancy, egoism, and promise of everything with a minimum of effort. Tom Tiede's witty and bitter rant against modernity in general and self-help of the 1990s in particular, for example, is a charmingly wrathful book (*Self-Help Nation*, 2001) that self-avowedly sets out to be "the long overdue, entirely justified, delightfully hostile guide to the snake-oil peddlers who are sapping our nation's soul." The self-help genre is also mocked brilliantly in the 1998 novel *God Is My Broker,* in which financially strapped monks break into sectarian wars between devout followers of Deepak Chopra, Napoleon Hill, the Coveyans, and their nemeses, the (Tony) Robbinites. As the fictitious author, a "monk-tycoon," states in the last of the "7 1/2 laws of spiritual *and* financial growth," "The only way to get rich from a get-rich book is to write one . . . or buy this one."

But such criticism is ultimately useless and is certainly beside our point: the genre is immortal. Self-help acolytes are addicts, and nothing short of an apocalyptic intervention is going to stop them. Like Jason in the *Friday the 13th* movies, the books keep coming back, selling in bigger and bigger numbers. (A glance at the Amazon.com reviews of Tiede's caustic *Self-Help Nation*—the book was given two stars the last time we checked—quickly reveals the disjunction between believers and critics.) That these books won't go away says something about American culture, and the particular instruction offered by the most recent incarnations reveals a land of readers searching not so much for instant wealth or self-gratification as for reassurance, inspiration, simplification, and nourishment for ailing psyches. In the last decade, we Americans have downed a lot of chicken soup for our souls.

That's not to say we don't want to get rich too. But what's interesting is that many of the "how to succeed in business" and "get rich now!" books have been written to appeal, however casually, to the spirit. A few of the books are fairly old-fashioned—"Look, son, here are some rich people: do what they did. See those guys? They have to work for a living, the poor schmucks; don't do that"—such as the offerings of Charles Givens (#2 nonfiction in 1991, #13 in 1992), *Rich Dad, Poor Dad* (#20 in *USA TODAY*'s top one hundred for 1993–2003), *The Millionaire Next Door* (#75 in the top one hundred), and David Bach's bestselling (and trademarked) "Automatic Millionaire" system (#12 in 2004). But most financial guides during this time period added at least a veneer of soul-searching to their more practical advice. Note the subtitle of Suze Orman's *The 9 Steps to Financial Freedom* (#1 nonfiction in 1998), for example: *Practical and Spiritual Steps So You Can Stop Worrying.* If you actually read the book, though, it's clear that she's more interested in the psychology of the investor—it turns out that becoming very wealthy will set your mind at ease! It certainly couldn't hurt, and we hope to try it someday. In general there is nothing especially spiritual about her approach other than a recommendation to follow one's "inner voice" (which, we seem to recall, led to Socrates's conviction and death). Orman's 1999 bestseller (#6 in nonfiction), *The Courage to Be Rich,* carried a similarly slippery subtitle: "Creating a Life of Material and Spiritual Abundance."

The strongest feel-good leanings, however, emerge not in the personal-finance books but in those dealing with business success—and these have been the *most* popular books of this genre during the past sixteen years. The top-selling book was Spencer Johnson's brief *Who Moved My Cheese?* (#7 on *USA TODAY*'s top one hundred, #1 in hardcover nonfiction in 2000). Johnson is the coauthor of the bestselling *The One Minute Manager* and the rest of the "One Minute" line, which includes *The One Minute Father* (we haven't read that one, but we hope it's not about *being* a dad, but only how long it takes to become one). Johnson was recently inducted into Amazon.com's Hall of Fame as the bestselling business author of all time, the number one nonfiction author, and number two bestselling author ever (after J. K. Rowling). This pin-up boy for recent bestselling nonfiction deserves a closer look . . . at least for one minute.

Everything is fast in Johnson's world, and so is *Who Moved My Cheese?* It tells the story of the Cheese, a parable of no more than 8,000 words. Even with big fonts, wide margins, and over a dozen little cheese drawings, it still doesn't make it to one hundred pages. Here's an even briefer synopsis of Johnson's bestselling tale:

Two mice (Sniff and Scurry) and two "littlepeople" (Hem and Haw—you'll get the humor in a moment) are looking for Cheese in a maze. Sniff and Scurry find Cheese using their "simple brains" by the trial-and-error method. Hem and

Haw, we are told, apply their "complex brains with beliefs and emotions" to their task. These sophisticated minds make life in the maze "more complicated and challenging." Hem and Haw "relied on a more sophisticated method of finding Cheese that depended on their ability to think and learn from their past experiences." Both the mice and the wee people eventually discover Cheese—lots of it, piled high in a room. The wee people get comfy, then confident, and finally arrogant. They don't even notice that they're eating all the cheese until one day it's gone. The mice, single-minded little buggers that they are, realize the supply is dwindling and quickly race out to find more. They are too dumb to "overanalyze" things, not "burdened" with many complex beliefs. Hem and Haw, however, are paralyzed. "It's not fair," they whine. "We're entitled to Cheese," they cry. Will they never stop analyzing and lamenting the Lost Cheese, and go out to find some New Cheese? Will they ever get over their fear and head back into the maze? Or will they wait too long, until weak with hunger and stress, they turn on each other like the Donner party and begin nibbling on each other's sophisticated brains?

For those who struggle with allegory, Johnson supplies the moral of the story in a helpful outline at the end of the book:

- Change Happens: They Keep Moving the Cheese
- Anticipate Change: Get Ready for the Cheese to Move
- Monitor Change: Smell the Cheese Often So You Know When It Is Getting Old
- Adapt to Change Quickly: The Quicker You Let Go of Old Cheese, the Sooner You Can Enjoy New Cheese

- Change: Move with the Cheese
- Enjoy Change!: Savor the Adventure and Enjoy the Taste of New Cheese!
- Be Ready to Change Quickly and Enjoy It Again: They Keep Moving the Cheese (74)

Hey! It turns out to be about change and not really about cheese at all! And even though Johnson tells us "cheese" can stand for whatever we want—good health, spiritual well-being, a loving family—the parable doesn't really make sense unless "cheese" means business success. The blurb on the book notes that the story has been "hailed by men and women in leading organizations" such as Exxon, General Motors, Goodyear, Kodak, Marriott, Whirlpool, and Xerox.

Interestingly, the story doesn't quite make sense even in the business context, at least on a symbolic level. The whole reason for introducing the mice, it would seem, is to contrast their behavioristic search for cheese with the littlepeople's cognitively "sophisticated" thinking. But the mice and the littlepeople find cheese exactly the same way: they get hungry and go room to room until they bump into another pile of the stuff. Never once are we shown any actual sophisticated thinking from the littlepeople, or any thinking at all—neither are they paralyzed because of their big brains nor do they learn a thing from their mistakes. Hem and Haw are dolts, to tell the truth. They are outsmarted by rodents and deserve whatever ugly fate awaits them. And when Haw finally sets off to find cheese, he does it the same way the mice do, stumbling through the maze. If Hem and Haw represent those of us who have trouble confronting change and suffer for it because we have big brains, who are the triumphant mice? Does one survive better in business by being a "mouse," randomly (if fearlessly) heading off in another direction, indiscriminately developing new products, haphazardly searching for new customers, using the power of scent and hormones to increase market share?

Now, we know it's futile to demand logic from a myth and silly to look for airtight metaphorical consistency from a book that advises us to "smell the cheese often so you know when it is getting old." (The same technique works on people, by the way.) The real power of this book is that it fishes out the underlying assumption of all self-help books—change is what we all need and crave—and makes it explicit. It takes the traditional American belief in infinite malleability, the confidence that with a bit of effort everyone is redeemable, and turns pliability into a necessity. Because readers have sensed the need for change all along, *Who Moved My Cheese?* confirms what we already know and galvanizes us to get moving.

Or does it? There is no advice here on *how* to change, only a story suggesting that one must. This ur-manual on self-improvement offers no solutions or directions. "Change!" it shouts. "They" are always moving your cheese! Life conspires; you must adapt! But how? To what end? What if you're tired of cheese—what if you want to find some bacon? Or—most likely of all—what if you don't know what you want? How do you figure out what to search for? These questions are not addressed. In a business manual, perhaps they don't really need to be—it is, basically, a boardroom pep talk with cheese-sketchings instead of pie charts. The book cautions us to keep moving, cheering us on to keep searching for new products, novel services, and unexplored markets. The details can best be left to the folks in marketing and R&D.

Anyone who has ever worked for a corporation, large business, or sprawling institution knows how difficult it can be to implement change and how necessary change can be. But anyone who has been employed in these environments also knows that even more frustrating are the frequent and seemingly random changes imposed from the top that inevitably impede rather than increase one's productivity. There are few things less appetizing than the thought of a battalion of middle managers armed with Johnson's parable, endlessly scheduling meetings to spread the cheese on the bread of company profitability.

But *Who Moved My Cheese?* is a perfect book for the contemporary American business reader with little free time. It is short. It tells a cute story with some animals in it. It takes a hugely complex issue—the tension between adaptability and flexibility on the one hand, and between stability and long-term planning on the other—and reduces it to an easily memorizable mantra: change. It advocates a "one size fits all" approach to corporate life and beyond. Whatever is wrong, change is the answer; to be any more specific would reduce the book's applicability and thus its widespread appeal. The logic is clear and easy to follow: things could be better, and even if they are fine now, they could be worse soon; so change.

Playing yin to Johnson's yang is Stephen Covey's detailed *The 7 Habits of Highly Effective People* (#12 on the top one hundred in 1993–2003), the second bestselling financial *vade mecum* of the past sixteen years. In the time it takes Johnson to eat dinner, finish dessert, and taxi back to his hotel, Covey has barely opened the menu. There are over 350 densely written pages here, an average of fifty per habit. Seven, of course, has been a significant number for millennia (days of the week, deadly sins, dwarves), and numerous self-help books have drawn on its magic. In fairness to Covey, he has moved *Beyond the 7 Habits* (on audio cassette) and graduated to *The 8th Habit: From Effectiveness to Greatness* (2004). But it is with his bestselling seven habits that we must deal here.

The Magic of 7

One may remember Deepak Chopra's *The Seven Spiritual Laws of Success* (in the top ten in 1995), but the Pythagoreans have come out in full force over the past fifteen years. Some of our favorite titles:

- *The Seven Principles of Making Marriage Work*
- *Seven Secrets of Successful Work*
- *Seven Principles Every Teenager Needs to Know*
- *7 Amazing Exercises that Slim, Sculpt, and Build the Body in 20 Minutes a Day*
- *The Seven Stages of Money Maturity*
- *Seven Weeks to Sobriety*
- *The Seven Sacred Rites of Menopause*
- *The Seven Secrets of Successful Catholics*
- *Seven Stages to Heaven: How to Communicate with Your Departed Loved Ones in Seven Easy Steps*

Covey's subtitle suggests he's after bigger and better things than mere "change" or even financial success, namely "restoring the character ethic" (e.g., integrity, humility, fidelity, temperance, courage, justice, patience, industry, simplicity, modesty, and the Golden Rule) to corporate management. This is a book meant to help the reader act right and feel happy about success, to inspire his or her better self to move from "dependence to independence to interdependence," working with people in a "synergistic paradigm" in order for business to grow. Whatever these things may mean, the book has been wildly successful, endorsed by dozens of other self-help authors (including Norman Vincent Peale himself); the presidents of corporations such as Procter & Gamble, Black & Decker, and Amway; and both Marie Osmond and the U.S. Ambassador to Sweden. And it has sold over fifteen million copies, inspiring its own "habit" line of hot-selling successors.

What accounts for this popularity? Covey's seven habits are not particularly revolutionary in the larger self-help world, but he does shake things up by applying the concepts to business. As he brings these touchy-feely ideas to corporate America, Covey reminds readers of things they already know but may have been afraid to talk about in the boardroom. In the briefest outline, the seven pillars of effective and ethical management are (1) take responsibility, or as he puts it, "be proactive"; (2) figure out what you want ("begin with the end in mind"); (3) "put first things first"; (4) "think win/win"; (5) listen ("seek first to understand, then to be understood"); (6) "synergize," which means, well, you know, synergize; and (7) "sharpen the saw," that is "renew the four dimensions of your nature—physical, spiritual, mental, and social/emotional."

His treatment of each habit can be monumental; for instance, his presentation of the fourth habit, "Think Win/Win," reaches nearly mock-epic proportions. To the uninitiated, this practice would appear to need little defense, but Covey spends thirty pages arguing that win-win is generally superior to other possibilities, such as, for example, lose-lose. There are charts listing all the possible permutations, with analyses of the pros and cons of each. Clearly, Covey often doesn't quite know when to stop (he is the father of nine, in case one is looking for further evidence). And he's got graphs and pictures. This is a project born for the boardroom, with enough diagrams to inspire even the most ineffective middle-management wannabe.

Stylistically, this is no easy read either. Covey combines common-sense management discussion with a quasi–New Age patois of "paradigm shifts" and "rescripting" and "stewardship delegation." This book is not for skimming. To follow Covey's discussion, the reader must buy into his terminology from the beginning, or else paragraphs such as the following are likely to be impenetrable:

> To do this [exercise all four dimension of our nature], we must be proactive. Taking time to sharpen the saw is a definite Quadrant II activity, and Quadrant II must be acted on. Quadrant I, because of its urgency, acts on us; it presses

upon us constantly. Personal P/C must be pressed upon until it becomes second nature, until it becomes a kind of healthy addiction. Because it's at the center of our Circle of Influence, no one else can do it for us. We must do it for ourselves. (89)

Despite the length and stylistic awkwardness of his book, Covey seems to have inspired readers by tapping into a vein of human kindness pulsing in the middle of the machine. No single institution has come to symbolize the hard, cold, selfish modern world more than the corporation. But Covey comes out and tells us that managing people is different, or should be, from organizing inventory. Workers shouldn't feel like cogs in the machine. It's just plain refreshing to hear that we can work in an environment that encourages and rewards, and (even more remarkably) is rewarded *by*, the decent treatment of all the little cogs.

Covey, like Johnson, has put the responsibility squarely back on the reader's shoulders. Organize, prioritize, synergize, and above all—habit *number 1*—take responsibility. The systematic approach, with its semi-technical jargon and PowerPoint graphics, smoothly merges common-sense management advice with pop-psyche, feel-good ethics. Reading *7 Habits* provides a sense of control, as well as positive feelings about the workplace, to energize burned-out managers and employees alike.

And like Johnson, Covey says little directly about how to run a business. Whether these authors' suggestions have actually led to better management skills, happier employees, or greater profitability is difficult to determine. The success of a guidebook, as we learned in our discussion of low-carb reading, may have little connection with long-term results. But the success of the approach suggests that American business readers wanted to feel *good* about their profits in the '90s; the 1980s "greed is good" vision gave way to a spiritually imbued bottom line.

There are signs, however, that cold, hard facts may be climbing back into the spotlight. Hitting the charts in 2002 (#14) and 2003

(#11) was the data-driven and purely pragmatic *Good to Great,* Jim Collins' follow-up to his bestselling *Built to Last. Good to Great* is basically the opposite of both *Who Moved My Cheese?* and *7 Habits* in every way. Collins identified the companies that "made the leap" from fifteen years of average performance to a minimum of fifteen years of exceptional performance (measured by cumulative returns at least three times the market). Then he looked for similarities in the eleven companies he found that met these specifications. Stuffed with facts and case studies, *Good to Great* offers a mix of common sense (e.g., hire the right people first) and mild surprises (the leaders of these companies are not the celebrity CEOs that everyone knows; they are refreshingly humble behind-the-scenes types that channel their ambition into their companies).

There is nothing even vaguely spiritual in Collins's approach. One of his conclusions, for example, is that a great company must "understand its passion." A passion like, say, cigarettes! And a great company like, well, Philip Morris! It turns out that most of the top executives at Philip Morris were passionate consumers of their own products—they just *loved* to smoke, and they wanted to spread their addictive joy across the world. Collins contrasts Philip Morris's globalizing enthusiasm with competitor R. J. Reynolds, whose shortsighted money-grubbing executives began to diversify away from tobacco. Collins sees this move as a lack of passion for the product, but one-time heir (and now anti-tobacco advocate) Patrick Reynolds might beg to differ: half of his closest relatives—including his father, R. J. Reynolds Jr.—have died of tobacco-related illnesses.

Collins, for his part, claims that he doesn't necessarily like what his research reveals, but he's not going to let ethics get in the way of his analysis. Although that's a debatable stance, it may indicate a new trend in the world of business books. Even Suze Orman, whose latest "book" is an insurance kit on CD-ROM, seems to have given up on the spiritual subtitles, opting instead for the catchy *Evaluate Your Personal Insurance Policies On-Line—Instantly!*

But don't get discouraged. No matter how times change, there's one genre out there that will *never* lose its comforting shimmer. Indeed, the past sixteen years have been nothing if not inspirational.

Soothing the Soul

By 1992, motivational speakers Jack Canfield and Mark Victor Hansen had spent two years collecting over one hundred of their favorite inspirational stories and were ready to find a publisher. They contacted thirty-three publishers; within a month, thirty-three had turned them down. Less motivated individuals would have taken the hint. The can-do spirit of their project, however, wouldn't quit—and neither would they. They tracked down more publishing houses, but met with similar results: eventually, they were rejected by 140 publishers.

Their agent gave up.

Most people at that point would have found less humiliating pursuits, such as mime or mascot work, but not Canfield and Hansen. (Indeed, they often tell this story in their own lectures and have posted it on their website.) They packed up their spirit-rekindling tales and headed to the American Booksellers' Association Convention, where they personally hawked their book booth to booth, until finally one publisher decided to take a chance.

And thus began the cornucopian *Chicken Soup for the Soul* franchise. Once that original book, *Chicken Soup for the Soul: 101 Stories to Open the Heart and Rekindle the Spirit* (1993), got a foothold, it quickly stomped the publishing world into submission. So successful were the authors in opening the hearts of American book-buyers that they have gone on to brew (sometimes with the aid of a sous-chef) scores of *Chicken Soup* books, five of which made it into *USA TODAY*'s one hundred bestselling books of the decade from 1993 to 2003: *Chicken Soup for the Soul* (#16), *Chicken Soup for the Teenage Soul* (#26), *Chicken Soup for the Woman's Soul* (#50), *Chicken Soup for the Mother's Soul* (#70), and *Chicken Soup for the Teenage Soul II* (#85). A quick glance through the yearly bestsellers in *Publishers Weekly* for the same decade reveals that various offshoots of the original *Chicken Soup* appear twenty-five different times, including (in addition to the titles previously mentioned) *Chicken Soup* books for Couples, Golfers, Teenagers (III), Mothers (II), Women (II), and Christians, as well as *A Second Helping of Chicken Soup for the Soul*, *A Third Serving of Chicken Soup for the Soul*, *A Fourth Course of Chicken Soup for the Soul*, and a *Chicken Soup for the Soul Cookbook*.

In 1998—the *annus mirabilis* of chicken soupdom—six of the top nine trade paperbacks were separate mutations of *Chicken Soup for the Soul*. Canfield and Hansen won the title "The Best-selling Authors of the Year" from *USA TODAY* for both 1997 and 1998, selling more books during these two years than any other writers in America. Their website notes that they also hold the record in the *Guinness Book of World Records* for having the most books on the *New York*

Chicken Soup Books We'd Like to See

Chicken Soup for the Indicted CEO Soul
Chicken Soup for the Man-Whore Soul
Chicken Soup for the Killer Albino Soul
Chicken Soup for the Aryan Nation Soul
Vegetable Soup for the Chicken's Soul
Empty Bowl for the Anorexic Soul
Chicken Soup (and Pizza, and Chips, and Brownies) for the Pot-Lover Soul

Times bestseller list at one time: seven books on May 24, 1998. Lumped together into one pot, there are more than ninety million copies now in print. That's one helping of *Chicken Soup* for every person in France and Canada combined, or more than enough for every family in the United States.

The chefs in the *Chicken Soup* kitchen continue to ladle bestselling inspiration for every niche. Whether you have a Grieving, Preteen, or NASCAR soul—whether you are a Veteran, Fisherman, Bride, Nurse, Grandparent, or Prisoner (seriously)—whether you love Oceans or Horses—there's a volume for you. Recent additions include *Chicken Soup for the African American Soul, Chicken Soup for the Latter Day Saint Soul,* and *Chicken Soup for the Father and Daughter Soul* (for all those mutant two-souled folks running around). In 2005, seven *Chicken Soup* volumes sold over 100,000 copies each! The last we checked (it's a little like counting rabbits), there were fourteen new volumes in 2006 alone.

What's the authors' secret? Well, first, they aren't really the authors. They are the editors, collectors of 101 short (one- to three-page) inspirational stories. For the first book they claim to have culled "the best of the best from our 40 years of combined experience"—that experience being as motivational speakers—but apparently there was a lot more of the best of the best than they first imagined . . . about one hundred books' worth, in fact.

The tales, grouped into chapters such as "Learning to Love Yourself," "Live Your Dream," and "Overcoming Obstacles," have been selected for their ability to uplift droopy souls. They are motivating anecdotes with titles such as "Who You Are Makes a Difference," "Puppies for Sale," "I Love You, Son," "I Think I Can," "Abraham Lincoln Didn't Quit"—well, no, he was *shot*—and "Yes, You Can." Most of the stories are a bit (but *just* a bit) too long to reproduce here completely. This sample, however, captures the feel of the rest. It's titled "The Magic Of Believing":

I'm not old enough to play baseball or football. I'm not eight yet. My mom told me when you start baseball, you aren't going to be able to run that fast because you had an operation. I told Mom I wouldn't need to run that fast. When I play baseball, I'll just hit them out of the park. Then I'll be able to walk. (187)

The original book contains stories about acts of kindness that prevent suicides (21, 36), crippled children (25, 65, 171), children dying from leukemia (40–42; 61–63), and a woman who imported 400 children from Vietnam: "I visualized all those babies growing up in good Christian homes in America" (270). And always in the background is a chorus of familiar self-affirmations such as "I am me and I am okay" (76).

The cumulative effect of the book is not unlike reading a 300-page rendition of Robert Fulghum's essay "All I Really Need to Know I Learned in Kindergarten." In fact, that's in here too (130–131). (Actually, Fulghum *did* expand his famous essay into a book that went to #1 on the *New York Times* bestseller list for thirty-four weeks in 1990.) It's cute, sure, but is it true? Is it helpful? Is it even inspirational? According to cynic Wendy Kaminer (in her book *I'm Dysfunctional, You're Dysfunctional*), "only people who die very young learn all they really need to know in kindergarten" (7). But these stories have meaning for millions of readers—what's the key to the success of the *Chicken Soup for the Soul* series?

Chicken Soup provides an opportunity to listen to dozens of different motivational speakers at once, without having to go to the luncheon. The editors suggest that "reading a book like this is a little like sitting down to eat a meal of all desserts. It may be a little too rich. It is a meal with no vegetables, salad or bread. It is all essence with very little froth" (xvi). (And we like any diet that describes "all desserts" as "essence.") But these confections provide not just some sweetener for the heart, but also a heavy sugar rush for the general outlook. The testimonies to human courage and decency offer hope; they are reminders of the spark of goodness that is said to lie latent in us all. It's not that readers aren't aware that this is but one small side of the human experience. But *Chicken Soup* enables them to quiet the cacophony of voices—good people don't always triumph, bad people frequently flourish, natural evil strikes randomly and often quite thoroughly, there are usually too many choices with perplexing consequences—and drown out some uncertainty and complexity with the gentle crashing of wave after wave of little but decisive human victories. The stories, quite simply, make readers feel good, but (we have to say) at the expense of a realistic picture of human experience. There is no such thing as tragedy in this kitchen (except, perhaps, for the chickens).

The authors of the stories need not provide any extended exegesis of their texts—the tales are so patently inspirational that it would take a record-breakingly insensitive soul to fail to get the message. But in *Don't Sweat the Small Stuff . . . and It's All Small Stuff,* lecturer and stress consultant Richard Carlson takes another approach. Instead of offering lengthy narratives, he provides a list of maxims and accompanies them with direct, practical spiritual advice for becoming "a more peaceful and loving you." *Don't Sweat the Small Stuff* was even more popular than any single edition of *Chicken Soup*—this little volume was the tenth bestseller of all books in the decade from 1993 to 2003 (and #1 trade paperback in 1997 and 1998).

Carlson gives advice on how to stop stressing out, one hundred "simple ways to keep the little things from taking over your life." His premise is that the reader has the "goal of being kind and gentle," of finding an "inner peace," or of leading a "contented life": "regardless of who you are or what you do, however, remember that *nothing* is more important than your own sense of happiness and inner peace and that of your loved ones" (19–20). Groovy, man. The basic philosophy here is a blend of Stoicism (something of which Carlson seems unaware) and trendy Buddhist principles: we have fallen into the habit of insisting that things should be other than what they are. The key to inner peace is to align your expectations with the way life is rather than attempt the reverse. As the Stoic Epictetus cautions, "Don't demand that things happen as you wish, but wish that they happen as they do happen."

And so Carlson sets out one hundred suggestions to help us find that inner peace. It's an aphoristic approach to change, a list of individual suggestions that could be placed on desk calendars and bumper stickers . . . and actually have been. His one-page explications flesh out the bare bones of the pithy sentiments. Most of these fall into three basic categories (our divisions, not his)—Be Nice, Let It Go, and Relax—and include titles such as "Once a Week, Write a Heartfelt Letter," "Spend a Moment Every Day Thinking of Someone to Thank," "Adopt a Child through the Mail" (that *has* to be illegal), "Praise and Blame Are All the Same," "Choose Being Kind over Being Right," "Become a Less Aggressive Driver," "Acknowledge the Totality of Your Being," and "Lighten Up."

In terms of structure, then, it is very similar to *Chicken Soup for the Soul*—tablespoons of psychic inspiration or reflection-worthy thoughts that are best digested a few doses at a time. And—as in *Who Moved My Cheese?*—the assumption is that readers desire to change, or at least that someone else desires them to change. Our own copy of *Don't Sweat the Small Stuff* is a "previously owned" model (by the enigmatic "E.G."), and has asterisks, underlining, and comments scribbled throughout—the original reader was taking these apothegms to heart. Perhaps most interesting, though, is the note inscribed on the chapter titled "Be Patient." There, in the margin, with three asterisks and an exclamation mark, in big letters, is written "Yes, Russell!" Indeed, how much more peaceful it would be for us all if Russell, and all the

Russells we know, would read this book. We strongly suspect that this little tome was frequently acquired as a gift.

It's not that Carlson is completely unaware of how hard it will be to adopt some of his simple suggestions, to change one's perspective so completely. At one point, when he observes that a goal of the spiritual life is to learn to love unconditionally, he admits that "people and dogs are hard to love unconditionally." But he has an answer: "A plant, however, is easy to love just the way it is" (208). Practice makes perfect: start on the road to inner peace by opening your heart to a fern.

So much of this advice is both absolutely simple and sensible (well, maybe not the stuff about the plant) but also—as with the other bestselling soul-books—remarkably hard to follow without a tremendous commitment to serious spiritual practice. Although Carlson's program claims to offer an alternative to the stressful hustle and competitiveness of American life in one hundred short lessons, the real attraction is the simple reminder that we have it in our own power to change the world merely by changing how we look at it. We suspect it is the actual process of reading the book—much more than attempting to follow its advice—that brings a needed sense of order, control, and calmness to a harried America. At any rate, like *Chicken Soup,* it is a fix that requires a return to the dealer for increasingly specific bestselling doses: *Don't Sweat the Small Stuff at Work* (1998), *Don't Sweat the Small Stuff in Love* (1999), *Don't Sweat the Small Stuff with Your Family* (1999), *Don't Sweat the Small Stuff for Teens* (2000), *Don't Sweat the Small Stuff for Men* (2001), and *Don't Sweat the Small Stuff for Women* (2001), as well as a *Treasury* of not-sweating (1999).

Sarah Ban Breathnach's *Simple Abundance: A Daybook of Comfort and Joy* (#22 for 1993–2003 and #4 in 1996 and #2 in 1997 for hardcover nonfiction) is attractive for many of the same reasons, although her lessons are more concerned with self-love than cozying up to steadfast flora. And she knows it's going to take more than one hundred different shots. More like 365. Her volume is designed to rescue exhausted, overworked, and frustrated women from their frazzled lives and nagging discontent, reacquainting them with their authentic selves and teaching them to live more simply and happily. (She continues digging into the issue in *Something More: Excavating Your Authentic Self,* which ended up #7 for nonfiction in 1998. Dr. Phil's *Self Matters,* #1 in 2002, also focuses on the reclamation of the "authentic self" from the conformity and expectations of the world around us, but his down-home, "get real" approach is not nearly as full of comfort and joy.)

Despite the self-help world's obsession with magic numbers (seven steps, seven laws, 100 tips, 101 stories), Breathnach wisely opted for "daybook" over "365 lessons," which probably would have been a bit too daunting even for the number crunchers. Still, the book is just that—a collection of page-long musings, one for each day, plus a list of suggested "Joyful Simplicities" for each month. Although the entries are discrete, the lessons build on each other, taking the reader on a year-long journey to self-awareness and peace.

Simple Abundance lies somewhere between traditional wisdom and *Victoria* magazine. Its premise—that today's women need to "reconcile [their] deepest spiritual, authentic, and creative longings with often-overwhelming and conflicting commitments"—is surely true. And Breathnach's methods for getting there are definitively folksy:

> At the heart of Simple Abundance is an authentic awakening, one that resonates within your soul. . . . A deep inner shift in your reality occurs, aligning you with the creative energy of the Universe. Such change is possible when you invite Spirit to open up the eyes of your awareness to the abundance that is already yours. (January 3, "Simple Abundance: The Inner Journey")

Luckily for the reader, her "silent companion [that is, authentic self] has lit lanterns of love to illuminate the path to Wholeness," a path that, for the author, includes "working with my illustrated discovery journal, writing my daily dialogue, in prayer, playing with my treasure map collage, embarking on the golden mirror meditation, planning my day, and then just sitting in silence. Listening attentively. Waiting expectantly" (January 5, "The Woman You Were Meant to Be"; January 26, "Simple Abundance: The Basic Tools"). Breathnach explains each of these techniques, but the basic formula involves meditation, collages, and self-pampering as you burrow deep inside to find "the beautiful mystery that is *you*" (February 1, "Creative Excursions: The Gift of Time"). The path to Wholeness, it turns out, involves a great deal of lace.

It's an interesting, if slightly weird, blend. On the one hand, the book's back-to-reality lessons are right-on: you don't need everything you want (there's that Stoic thing again); you should form your own opinions; material objects can't fulfill your true longings. On the other hand, it can be difficult to take a book seriously that contains lessons called "Making Peace with Your Hair" (April 17) and "Secret Passions: Scented Linen Closets" (June 12) and that encourages the reader "to strike up a reciprocal relationship with your guardian angel" (November's list of Joyful Simplicities). Nonetheless, if one has to choose a transformative program, it's not hard to see why people would pick one that reinforces the importance of self. For the overextended, self-sacrificing woman, even reading this devotional-style volume can be a positive step toward remembering her own needs and dreams for her life—whether or not she ever chooses to enact significant change.

MAGNIFICENT MORRIE

By far the best written of all the inspirational, heart-tugging nonfiction guides is Mitch Albom's memoir *Tuesdays with Morrie: An Old Man, a Young Man, and Life's Greatest Lesson*. On a series of Tuesday afternoons,

Mitch Albom listened to his former professor, now bedridden and dying quickly of MLS, expound on the "meaning of life." Morrie Schwartz indeed died a remarkable death. Brave and witty to the end, he reached into the cash- and status-hardened chest of a former student and found a heart. Over time we watch the yuppie snap out of his midlife crisis as he learns to tend to, and admit his love for, the spunky patient.

Although not *quite* as good for a cry as *Extreme Makeover: Home Edition,* Mitch and Morrie's story comes awfully close. And American readers, as we will see more thoroughly in our chapter on literary fiction, want to be touched (emotionally, at least). So it's no surprise that *Tuesdays with Morrie* was the eighth bestselling book of the decade from 1993 to 2003 (#4, #1, and #3 in nonfiction in 1998, 1999, and 2000, respectively). It remained in *USA TODAY*'s top 150 for 354 weeks—almost seven years! But has it really changed "millions of lives," as it says right there on the paperback cover?

While Morrie's courage in the face of death is truly inspirational and touching—while Mitch Albom is a good writer—and while Morrie's words of wisdom are heartfelt and fairly indisputable— for all their emotive power, the lessons here are not exactly revolutionary. Morrie discusses topics such as "the world," "regrets," "death," "family," "money," and "marriage," but the essence of his position can be gleaned from a paragraph on page 43:

> So many people walk around with a meaningless life. They seem half-asleep, even when they're busy doing things they think are important. This is because they're chasing the wrong things. The way you get meaning into your life is to devote yourself to loving others, devote yourself to your community around you, and devote yourself to creating something that gives you purpose and meaning.

Even the cynical narrator realizes at this early stage that Morrie was right. "The most important thing in life is to learn how to give out love, and to let it come in" (52).

Professor Dumbledore says pretty much the same thing to Harry Potter at the end of the first book. So did Jesus, come to think of it (but not in any of the *Harry Potter* books). By the end of Morrie's life, the lesson hasn't changed, nor have the important questions: "As I see it, they have to do with love, responsibility, spirituality, awareness" (175).

We are, according to Morrie, too wrapped up in our daily lives, too spiritually deficient even to ask, "Is this all? Is this all I want? Is something missing?"(65). But we sense it, and we read Mitch Albom's memories and discover that yes, we, like the author, have been missing something. We are reminded of some basic sentiments we have always known but keep forgetting: that our power boat isn't a substitute for love (although both can really mess up our hair); fame won't fill the void the way children will (although it will get you a much better table at a restaurant); and giving can be more satisfying than receiving (especially if it's a sassy one-liner).

And Morrie has another familiar, comforting thesis that also runs through much of America's search for itself: we don't lead genuine lives because our culture teaches us to value what we shouldn't. For the most part, the enemy is our passive acceptance of everything around us. Take responsibility, these books say. You can't change the world, but you can change yourself. Morrie's subversion is healthy and simple enough: "But the big things—how we think, what we value— those you must choose for yourself. You can't let anyone—or any society—determine those for you" (155). He's right, of course, but there's also something revealing here: determine your own existence, be independent, think for yourself, make your own decisions, discover for yourself what's truly important—and do it by following the words of therapists, seminar hosts, and yes, the writers of bestselling books.

Millions have. Morrie's lesson is both to think for yourself—to shake yourself from your shallow life—and to *think like Morrie*, who will deliver both inspiration *and* answers.

We doubt the book actually changed millions of lives in any long-term way, but we are certain that millions were moved by the death of Morrie and affected by his courage and homiletic message in much the same way a good sermon can shake one's lethargy for a few hours. Ruth Elson ends her study of the *Myths and Mores in American Best Sellers 1865–1965* with the observation that formulaic novels "are satisfying because they tell you what you want to think you know already" (319). *Tuesdays with Morrie*, though not a formulaic novel, offers precisely this comfort.

The Importance of Being Earnest

One often hears laments from cultural critics that we live in a "cynical age." Our recent reading habits suggest the contrary: we live an age searching for sincerity, no matter how heavy-handed. These self-help and inspirational books are *earnest*, and they evince all the benefits and burdens of that weighty Anglo-Saxon word.

The bestsellers offer much-needed hope. But their sincerity can be so overpowering that it edges out almost all opportunity for critique or teasing or self-deprecation or any kind of sense of humor at all— the kind of irony that makes provocative reading and independent thought possible. Harold Bloom puts it this way in his book *How to Read and Why:*

> Irony demands a certain attention span, and the ability to sustain antithetical ideas, even when they collide with one another. Strip irony away from reading, and it loses at once all discipline and all surprise. Find now what comes near to you, that can be used for weighing and considering, and it

very likely will be irony, even if many of your teachers will not know what it is, or where it is to be found. Irony will clear your mind of the cant of the ideologues, and help you to blaze forth as the scholar of one candle. (27)

Ironic we are not. It's not cant we mind—it's "can't." In fact, the two things most of these books very carefully do *not* demand is an "attention span" or "the ability to sustain antithetical ideas." The books are designed for short bursts of reading, a few minutes at a sitting. Reading in such bits and bites makes it virtually impossible to keep track of antithetical ideas, much less to hold them in equilibrium. These are books with one point to make, over and over. Almost all of them could be read backward, or randomly, or one section a week over many years, without forfeiting any meaning or comprehensibility.

What we do not get from these books, then, is the "multivocality" discussed in *Reading Lolita in Tehran.* The bestsellers reviewed in this chapter adamantly promote change, but not by means of thinking carefully and reflecting on many points of view. Instead, they help us momentarily conquer and control a large and chaotic world by reducing rather than expanding our options. They allow us to rule out competing perspectives by tuning in to a single blaring voice. They allow—indeed, encourage—us to feel that our aspirations (some of which we have forgotten in the rush through life) are within reach: a slimmer body and a fatter portfolio, to be sure, but also a world where change is easy, inner peace a mere page in the distance, and love just a Tuesday away.

Despite their focus on the necessity of change, however, they almost never present an authentic picture of what profound, long-term change actually requires. Instead, they provide good feelings about the concept: reading about change becomes a substitute for change itself. We feel better about our bodies when we read about the possibility of better bodies, more positive about life when we read about positive people, and more hopeful about business when we read about better business practices. Reading this way—even self-help reading—ironically can become a proxy for effective *doing*.

But of course it doesn't cure what ails. So when the glow wears off, we remember the feeling and move on to the next lexical drug of the hour. *Atkins* gives way to *South Beach. Chicken Soup* #1 becomes *Chicken Soup* #46. The more we seek this kind of "help," the more we need it; because these bestsellers provide good feelings but no lasting change, the reading experience actually perpetuates the very need for new self-help and inspirational books.

There is a whole school of thought that argues that all media, including books, have an explicit agenda to create an uncritical conformity to the status quo, to "preclude an oppositional consciousness." We're not that paranoid. We believe, rather, that honest thinking about life is hard and uncomfortable—genuine change even more so—and Americans often prefer their reading like their malt beverages and suspension systems: smooth and easy. We love the idea of change as much as we avoid facing its hardest truths. And so a book claiming to have "changed millions" becomes an enduring bestseller—though probably not a real solution.

And perhaps this points to a more radical conclusion: that we are choosing to read these particular books because we are reading for the wrong reasons. Are books capable of doing all we are demanding of them these days? Is reading actually supposed to make us slimmer, richer, more content—indeed, *happier?* Or does it serve a more limited but deeper purpose—to expand our sensibilities, for example, or to sharpen our vision, challenge our preconceptions, and deepen our empathy for the human condition? It is to the connection between bestsellers and compassion that we now turn.

BLACK AND WHITE AND READ ALL OVER: GOOD AND EVIL IN BESTSELLING ADVENTURE NOVELS AND POLITICAL NONFICTION

What would be the cost of not having an enemy? Who could you
strike for retribution other than yourself?
Cold Mountain

That man is truly good who knows his own dark places.
Beowulf

Good and evil are concepts with which we are intimately familiar. We all talk about them, read about them, and watch them
play out on TV. We all assume that we know what the terms mean
and probably that others agree with our criteria. But how do we define
them, really? How do we weigh good against good or evil against evil,
creating the ethical hierarchies that guide our choices?

If we turn to bestselling books for these answers, we're bound to get
some conflicting guidance. Is "goodness" loyalty to a person no matter what? Is it telling the truth? Fighting crime? Being religious?

Supporting democracy?

And is "evil" the opposite of those things? Does it lie in the terror-ist, the sociopath, the ghoul in the closet, the errant choice? Does it lie, simply, in the lying?

In *Reading Lolita in Tehran,* Azar Nafisi offers a compelling hypothesis:

> This respect for others, empathy, lies at the heart of the novel. It is the quality that links Austen to Flaubert and James to Nabokov and Bellow. This, I believe, is how the vil-lain in modern fiction is born: a creature without compas-sion, without empathy. (224)

Nafisi's thesis in fact applies to both fiction and nonfiction and serves nicely to launch our own inquiry into the nature of good and evil as presented in bestselling books of the past sixteen years.

In the fiction realm, we cover the very top series of this period, *Harry Potter,* as well as the leading authors of bestselling thriller, mys-tery, adventure, and horror novels. For nonfiction we examine the tidal wave of political books published in the last decade and especially during the 2004 election year.

Fiction's regular bestselling authors on the annual lists play a dom-inant role in this chapter, including Dean Koontz, Stephen King, Mary Higgins Clark, James Patterson, and Patricia Cornwell. J. K. Rowling, John Grisham, and Tom Clancy also make the annual lists, but have surpassed even these to make *USA TODAY*'s top one hun-dred for the decade from 1993 to 2003—all with multiple titles!

The nonfiction books follow a slightly different pattern. Although we maintained our general practice of analyzing only the very top books from 1991 to 2006, we handled the 2004 titles slightly differ-ently. Throughout that extraordinary election year, nearly 40 percent of *all* the hardcover nonfiction bestsellers on the weekly *Publishers Weekly* lists were political titles! That's a total of forty books—eight of which hit #1 at some point in the year. To understand the tenor of the political scene more comprehensively, we decided to review all of those forty. Besides, where else could we read about the "dogs of hate" pounding out the "drumbeat for lesbianism," or find the President referred to as the "Idiot-in-Chief" of "the dumbest nation on earth"?

But first to the fiction. Let us see how America's most popular authors of our most popular genres approach these age-old questions.

Dark Arts and Brave Hearts

THRILLER NIGHT

Upon initial consideration, Nafisi's emphasis on empathy seems an odd, limited way of dividing the good from the evil. Even if the rule applies to a few works of great literature, it couldn't possibly hold true for the whole industry of genre fiction, could it?

Astonishingly, it seems that it does. In all of the books we reviewed whose villains are living and breathing (or in Voldemort's case, floating and leeching), this definition is accurate. The villains vary—yappy terrorists, supernatural beings, assorted sickos—but what they all share is an essential impenetrability, an inability to absorb, much less be moved or changed by, the experiences of their victims or antagonists. (Interestingly, evildoers are everywhere nowadays, in contrast to Karen and Barbara Hinkley's findings in their survey of American bestselling fiction from 1965 to 1985, where "villains are . . . scarce." *American Best Sellers: A Readers Guide to Popular Fiction*, 187. Even authors who formerly loved to dwell in morality's murky grays, such as Anne Rice and John LeCarre, began to pen increasingly black-and-white works throughout the '90s and into the twenty-first century.)

For the terrorists—featured, for example, in Tom Clancy's *Rainbow Six* (#86 for 1993–2003), Patricia Cornwell's *Cause of Death* (#9 hardcover fiction in 1996), and James Patterson's *3rd Degree* (#5 mass-market in 2005)—coldness is the necessary side effect of the passion they feel about their political or religious beliefs. To take a successful stand, they must put aside normal emotional connections. In *Rainbow Six,* Domingo Chavez—a member of an elite international terrorist-fighting team known as Rainbow—tries to understand the terrorist mentality with the help of Dr. Bellow, the team psychologist:

> "What the hell is a good terrorist?"
> "He's a businessman whose business is killing people to make a political point . . . almost like advertising. They serve a larger purpose, at least in their own minds. They believe in something, but not like kids in catechism class, more like reasoned adults in Bible study." (87)

But despite their "reasoned" approach, the terrorists become engulfed by their visions. Though they don't necessarily take pleasure in killing (some do), their fanaticism deranges them, enabling them to justify gross acts of carnage. The soldiers of Rainbow respond and save the day, puzzled by the terrorist mindset but concluding that "all you really needed to know about these people was how to put steel on target" (424).

We also find terrorists in the Cornwell and Patterson novels, though these are more briefly depicted. *Cause of Death* features a religious cult whose lusty dreams of world domination lead them to sell nuclear materials to the Libyans. In *3rd Degree,* Patterson's Charles Danko claims to take life for radical political reasons, though this is actually just a cover for revenge killings in the name of his butchered brother. With his self-absorption and personal motives, Danko strays from the terrorist archetype and more clearly resembles the disturbed individuals who make up another popular category of killers: the sick bastards.

James Patterson: The Next Grisham?

James Patterson is an author on the rise. Or perhaps you could say he's a bunch of authors on the rise. He must not run at Nora Roberts's supernatural pace because he's needed to enlist several other people to write (excuse us, *coauthor*) most of his recent bestsellers. And there are many. In 2005, Patterson and friends had four books in the top fifteen in *Publishers Weekly* fiction—an all-time record! That doesn't include his two 2005 mass-market hits. In 2006 he hit the #1 slot on the *New York Times* list with nine different books! *Ay carumba.*

This sort of villain is a seemingly upstanding member of society who is actually, at heart, a sociopathic, homicidal maniac. In Dean Koontz's *False Memory* (#15 mass-market paperback in 2000), Dr. Ahriman is a perverted psychiatrist who brainwashes his patients and their associates, implanting bizarre disorders and desires and forcing his victims to perform lewd and gory acts at his bidding. The killer in Mary Higgins Clark's *On the Street Where You Live* (#6 mass-market paperback in 2002) is a charming real estate agent who strangles young women, believing himself to be the reincarnation of a murderer who lived a hundred years before. And the husband-and-wife team in James Patterson's *1st to Die* (#9 mass-market paperback in 2002) lives out a twisted game of abuse and control, killing several brides and grooms on their wedding days.

It doesn't take a genius to figure out why terrorists and psycho killers show up so often in formula fiction. They are obvious, scary choices:

but they are scary not only because they are violent, but also because they are *unreachable*. With few exceptions (one batch of terrorists in *Rainbow Six,* the IRA gang, is successfully talked out of its mission), these villains will not respond to reason, to emotion—to anything. They are without empathy. If anything, they *enjoy* the distress of their victims; they do not relate or relent.

The fascinating element of these books, however, is not so much the mere existence of the empathetically challenged, but the way in which they are presented to readers. All of these books to some degree take us into the minds of the villains, and several weave antagonists' thoughts and experiences throughout. Yet these intimate passages are *not* intended to cultivate our empathy. They serve the opposite function: plunged into the perverse pleasures of these villains, we are repelled by and alienated from them, more convinced than ever of their evil and their fundamental difference from ourselves. Sneakily, in the guise of empathy, these books harden our hearts.

Still, although it's not intended, or really possible, for the average sane reader to relate to these villains, some authors take more pains than others to make their bad guys seem like real, if disturbed, people. Koontz's game-playing psychiatrist gets almost as much page-time as the main characters, and his personal beliefs, desires, and diabolical plans are lavishly described. Clancy gives his villains more of a fair shot than anyone, even making his ex-KGB, terrorist-abetting character turn around and enable the saving of the world (though, really, we know that's going to happen, given the amount of time Clancy spends on this character; the true bad guys only get a paragraph, or a page at best). At the other end of the spectrum, Clark's murderer in *On the Street Where You Live* could scarcely be less distinctive. From the first pages, we see that there's nothing to this villain save a hackneyed propensity for evil cackling:

Along the way, he realized he had become one with the author, sharing his sense of supremacy over his victims, chuckling at his playacting as he grieved with the grieving. (6)

It had been announced that the prosecutor was holding a news conference at eleven. It was five of eleven now.

He reached over and turned on the television set, then leaned back and chuckled in anticipation. (56)

That's not to say that every book of this nature should dwell with believable, clinical detail on the inner workings of sociopaths and madmen—such renderings would probably be tedious and would certainly stray from the genre. But shadowy figures with evil laughs? Isn't this a little too predictable, bordering on ridiculous? One can hardly avoid recalling the unsustainable cackling from a self-conscious Dr. Evil and his cohorts in *Austin Powers*. Why do we bother with such a false intimacy, entering into an evil mind only to reduce it to a dull, single dimension?

The irony of focusing on these one-note, grotesque characters is that although the most bizarrely, indisputably evil people can theoretically do us the most damage, in reality they are the least likely to affect our lives. So although the horrible *ideas* in these books might be scary, the *structure* is quite soothing. Evil exists in *them*—the psychos, the freaks—not in us. It's not in life's mundane and unpredictable injustices, or in the painful, infinitely varied choices and circumstances that for most of us will cause more heartbreak and destruction than homicidal maniacs. Through these heightened experiences of horror, we learn that evil is incredibly simple ("he's nuts") and comfortingly alien ("he's nuts")—which is almost as reassuring as the genre's standing promise that the good guys will triumph every time.

On Pantsuits

A mystery novel is supposed to have a tidy, satisfying resolution. Everything is supposed to be explained. But nothing in Mary Higgins Clark's *On the Street Where You Live* reveals why the female characters dress themselves so horribly. Consider these disturbing excerpts:

> She was wearing one of her favorite outfits, a dark green winter-weight pantsuit and white turtleneck sweater. (26, of Emily)

> When she'd gotten dressed that morning, she'd been pleased with her new red wool pantsuit, but now she wasn't so sure. It didn't hold a candle to the cut and fabric of the dark green pantsuit that Natalie Frieze was wearing. (264, of Pat Glynn)

One pantsuit we could let slide. Even two on a good day. But three different pantsuits? On three different characters? Pantsuit-sparked *jealousy?*

Personally, we think the psycho killer is just a front for the *true* evil lurking in this novel.

It's also telling that we do not demand the same simplicity or uniformity from our protagonists. The good guys aren't superheroes; they are multidimensional, flawed, and human (at least more so), all the better to trigger our empathy. And they come in different forms. Martie and Dusty, the main characters of Dean Koontz's *False Memory,* are optimistic, in-love types. Patricia Cornwell's serial heroine, on the other hand, is generally cynical and glum. Lindsay Boxer, the leading character of James Patterson's *1st to Die* series, is a hot-blooded police officer fighting her way through a debilitating disease and several personal losses. (As a side note, Patterson's technique in *3rd Degree*—the third book in the *1st to Die* series—serves as a handy good-and-evil primer: while the villain gets his point of view across throughout the book in third person, only Lindsay gets to speak in first person—just in case we weren't sure to whom we were supposed to relate.) These characters are by no means perfect—they have professional and personal problems and weaknesses—but their allegiance is firmly on the side of right.

This is fair. One might even call it "good characterization." But it's a bit unfairly subtle, given how rigidly evil is defined in the very same books. Is it accurate to be expansive when defining goodness and narrow when defining evil? Probably not, but on an emotional level, it makes sense. By expanding the definition of good and limiting the definition of evil, we give ourselves more leeway to fit into the former category. These protagonists might be messed up in some ways and

A Touch of Gray

Of all the thriller-type books we read, only one deliberately messed with the good-versus-evil dichotomy: Nelson DeMille's *Wild Fire* (#13 in 2006), the story of a kook who plans to detonate nuclear bombs in American cities, thus triggering a response that will annihilate the Muslim world. The protagonist of the book—a wisecracking renegade, kind of a dick—finds the idea tempting, though ultimately immoral, and repeatedly admires the mastermind's charm and man's-man values, feeling the guy might have made

(continued)

> a good friend under other circumstances. And he's not the only one lured by the promise of a world without Islamic terrorism—the CIA knows about the plan and hopes it will succeed! DeMille claims in the introduction that this is a "scary book for scary times." But what makes it so unsettling—the plot alone, or also the notion that the ethical barricades we erect are not as sturdy as we'd like to believe?

might make mistakes, but they're not, you know, *bad people*. They aren't, you know, *murderers*. And neither, of course, are we. This flexibility allows readers to dabble in empathy without muddling the genre's required boundary between good and evil.

THE HEIGHT OF HORROR

Stephen King is in some ways the primary adherent to this half-empathetic style. King's bad guys are generally supernatural, so (for reasons of taste if nothing else) he avoids subjecting readers to their perspectives. We even see most of his human wackos, such as Annie Wilkes in *Misery*, through the eyes of the protagonists alone.

Curiously, though this technique sounds like a recipe for absolute moral simplicity—and even more extreme than the other books we just reviewed—for two reasons, King's novels actually tend to be more complex than the other books we reviewed here.

First, he is a master of characterization. King brings his average-Joe protagonists to life with instant personality and arrestingly visceral interior monologues. More than any of these other authors, he picks his heroes from among the masses; they're not so much diamonds in the rough as chunks of colorful gravel. And they're almost always on the side of "good" not because they're crime-fighters by profession or even especially swell people, but simply because they are being pursued by aliens or vampires or possessed trucks or some other rapacious hell spawn, and you really can't help but sympathize.

King doesn't bother to pretend that he is giving his antagonists a voice. What he does is make us care about his characters, and we care not because the characters' thoughts are being juxtaposed with those of horrific criminals and we have no choice, but because they are actually interesting and relatable people whom we don't want to see smooshed by possessed trucks. And one of the reasons his characters are interesting and relatable is that, more often than not, they are just sorta normal and not particularly exemplary.

Second, though Stephen King's books are firmly ensconced in the good-versus-evil genre, with evil often depicted as an external, impenetrable force, King is also clearly interested in exploring the evil within. Classics such as *The Shining, Carrie,* and *Firestarter* deal with *internal* powers, forces, or tendencies that dish out horrible consequences when unleashed (justifiably or not). The villain in *The Dark Half* is actually an evil alter ego—the hero's "dark half"—that larks about killing people. Though King writes in the same morally simplistic framework of all these authors, he defines evil less narrowly and locates it less specifically; in addition to an external source of evil, there is often an internal one, and sometimes the two are one and the same.

Though not one of his best or most famous works, *The Girl Who Loved Tom Gordon* (#8 hardcover fiction in 1999) illustrates this two-layer evil perfectly. It tells the tale of nine-year-old Trisha McFarland, who must fight for survival when she gets lost during a hike on the Appalachian Trail in New Hampshire. Watching, following, and toying with her is the obligatory Thing in the Woods, also known as the God of the Lost, which makes itself known to the hapless wanderer by leaving half-eaten deer in her path and carelessly ripping out the vegetation. In addition to this supernatural but very real beast, Trisha must battle the dark voice within that is bubbling up to push her toward resignation and terror:

> *Besides, you may never get to be Pete's age,* that disquieting inner voice said. How could anyone have such a cold and scary voice inside them? Such a traitor to the cause? *You may never get out of these woods.* (35)

> *Yes, but what about the special thing?* the cold voice asked. Trisha was frightened by that voice all over again. The stuff it said was bad; that she should have discovered such a dark girl hiding inside her was even worse. (119)

The Thing in the Woods serves as both a tangible enemy and a metaphor for Trisha's instinct to run, to give up and die. In the final confrontation with this nightmarish creature, Trisha understands that she can triumph only if she holds her ground and her courage:

> She stood in the set position and let the stillness spin out around her. . . . Let it eat her; let it beat her. It could do both. But she would not beat herself.
> *And I won't run.* (209)

In this and other ways, *The Girl Who Loved Tom Gordon* is also a coming-of-age novel in which Trisha collects (generally unpleasant) life lessons as she struggles to survive. She begins the journey as an angry kid with an angry brother who's angry about an angry divorce, and she ends the ordeal with the mature and generally accepted reflection that life really isn't fair:

> Life could be very sad, it seemed to her, and mostly it was what it could be. People made believe that it wasn't, and they

lied to their kids . . . so as not to scare them or bum them out, but yeah, it could be sad. The world had teeth and it could bite you with them anytime it wanted. She knew that now. She was only nine, but she knew it, and she thought she could accept it. She was almost ten, after all, and big for her age.

I don't know why we have to pay for what you guys did wrong! That was the last thing she had heard [her brother] say, and now Trisha thought she knew the answer. It was a tough answer but probably a true one: just because. And if you didn't like it, take a ticket and get in line. (141)

At nearly ten, Trisha has pondered life, death, God, and the universe, and she knows what's what. But the fascinating thing about her conclusions is that, however true, they sneakily undermine the genre in which the book is written. The whole point of picking up a good-and-evil book is the topsy-turvy ride on the way to a promised happy conclusion. Though Trisha lives—and is glad for it—hers is not exactly a happy conclusion. If the world has "teeth"—as surely it does—no one can count on a happy ending. So even though the book delivers on its promise, King is telling us that the real world operates differently. Is that, if anything, perhaps the true definition of "horror"?

It's revealing that the two bona fide "horror" writers we reviewed— Stephen King and Dean Koontz—are the ones that touch on internal sources of evil. Koontz's *False Memory* has a standard happy ending— and uses the "false empathy" technique described earlier to differentiate the heroes from the bad guy—but the book's premise belies just how scary the idea of internal evil is. Dr. Ahriman is a psychiatrist who wickedly hypnotizes people and implants images, ideas, and impulses into their minds. The main character is Martine "Martie" Rhodes, who is just going about her business one day when she's suddenly overwhelmed by visions of herself mangling her husband with a variety of seemingly innocent household objects. "Within her was some Other Martine," she senses, "the deranged personality she feared, a creature who was capable of any atrocity" (181). (Ahriman's bag of life-ruining tricks also includes implanting disorders and false memories in his victims and causing them to kill themselves or others.) Between agonizing panic attacks, Martie and said husband put together the clues and solve the mystery, which is just the beginning of a long quest to vanquish the deadly doctor. It turns out, of course, that all that evil stuff doesn't *really* come from the protagonists' minds—so there's not really an internal evil present—but it's worth noting that the *idea* of having a dark side is terrifying enough to build an entire novel around it.

It seems that, despite the premises of the thriller and mystery books, psycho killers are as comforting as they are scary—and our own sketchy insides might be the spookiest things out there. The highest-selling author of these genres would seem to agree: he has a similar take on this conclusion, legal-style.

HEY, I GOT A SOCIAL DISEASE!

John Grisham is a book-selling god. Although the authors previously discussed in this chapter are unbelievably successful, making the top ten just about every year, Grisham blows them all out of the water with *twelve* books in the top one hundred of the 1993–2003 decade. That's, you know, more than 10 percent. And he's not slowing down: in 2005 he had the #1 hardcover fiction seller; in 2004 he had the #3 hardcover fiction, as well as the #2, #3, and #5 mass-market paperbacks (#1 and #4 went to Dan Brown). His first nonfiction book, *The Innocent Man,* came in at #1 in 2006. After picking up a Grisham, one understands how this possibly could have happened: the man is just astoundingly readable. You open a book, and suddenly you're on page 150; it's magic, or osmosis, or a damn sneaky print-size, combined with an undisputed storytelling gift.

Grisham's novels are different from thrillers, mystery stories, military adventures, and horror novels. There are no psycho killers. There are no terrorists. There are no slavering creatures of the night. Instead, there are lawyers, whom some might consider the scariest villains of all time, but who, in Grisham, are just regular guys trying to do the right thing in a world that makes it very, very difficult.

Of course we are obliged to note that not all of Grisham's protagonists are lawyers. He has written a handful of small-town, down-homey kinds of novels devoid of any courtroom drama. But certainly he is best known for his legal thrillers, and perhaps he is even at his authorial best when writing them. He's especially good at describing the worldly lures that trap and nearly destroy the well-meaning, as he displays with unapologetic candor in works such as *The King of Torts*, #3 fiction in 2003 and #80 of all books for the 1993–2003 decade.

The eponymous protagonist is Jarrett Clay Carter II, who starts out an overworked and underpaid public defender in the scum district of Washington, D.C. He represents an endless supply of thieves, sexual offenders, murderers, and crack-addicted kids who never had a chance. Clay is a likeable guy; he believes in his work but yearns to escape the long hours and low wages. He defends the poor and detests greedy, name-dropping snobs like his girlfriend Rebecca's father—nicknamed Bennett the Bulldozer—who makes his living slashing Virginia countryside into malls and subdivisions and then brags about it at the Potomac Country Club (to which Clay would never be accepted for membership even if he wanted to apply).

Clay's fortunes shift when he is approached by the mysterious Max Pace, a self-described "fireman":

> I get hired by big companies to put out fires. They screw up, they realize their mistakes before their lawyers do, so they

hire me to quietly enter the picture, tidy up their mess, and, hopefully, save them a bunch of money. (85)

Max is currently working for an unspecified pharmaceutical company, manufacturer of an anti-addiction drug called Tarvan that was, thanks to some Washington big shots and FDA sidestepping, being tested in federally funded rehab clinics. Unfortunately, trouble with Tarvan has come to light. Though the drug is a miracle cure for most addicts, 8 percent go nuts and kill. The company has pulled the drug, but it has also linked six deaths to Tarvan, including one caused by one of Clay's clients. The company wants to pay off the families of the victims and keep the story from getting out. Clay's mission, should he choose to accept it, is to approach the families, convince them to take a $5 million settlement and keep quiet, and collect his own compensation: $15 million.

Clay thinks it over. He'd be abandoning his client and switching sides. But the client, he thinks, wouldn't have a case anyway; he did commit the murder, and drug influence is not a sufficient defense. Further, any lawsuit against the pharmaceutical company would be impossible, considering he doesn't even know its name. The victims were killed in a city where street violence is a daily reality; their families would never suspect there was anything behind these deaths but a theft, a roving thug. In fact, this would be their only chance to be compensated, and with a sum that would get them out of the very neighborhoods that had cost the victims their lives. And, well, it wouldn't be so bad for him either.

He does it. Then Max brings him another case, and so Clay is introduced to the dirty world of what they call "mass torts"—and is inducted into the company of mass tort lawyers, a band of obscenely wealthy litigators always sniffing out the next bad product and those damaged by it. These lawyers get 20 to 30 percent off the top of any settlement—

millions and millions of dollars, which they spend on ludicrous toys—and they justify their wages by presenting themselves as "those down in the trenches who were unafraid to attack big business on behalf of the working people, the little people" (164).

Clay is revolted by their illusions, their "frenzied orgy of consumption," vowing that "he would not, under any circumstances, waste his money on jets and second homes" (158–159). But before long, Clay is more concerned about competing with his cohorts than about leading a reasonable lifestyle or defending his clients properly. In the end, a series of unfortunate events costs him his fortune, but he walks away with his integrity, red-faced but clear-headed.

We have to admit some discomfort with a fantastically famous author *tsk-tsk-tsking* us about greed when he's been hogging the best-seller lists for over a decade, but we suppose it's not entirely his fault. At any rate, what Grisham seems to be haranguing is not wealth (and certainly not success), but selfishness, the loss of concern for others, blindness to the things that really matter—and especially, if one is a lawyer, disregard for one's clients. (And according to interviews we've read, Grisham does commit his own resources to family and community, so he doesn't seem to be laughing all the way to his private jet.)

There's not much subtlety to *The King of Torts,* but the book is nonetheless compelling as a study of a man's transformation into his greatest enemy. Though Clay never explicitly makes the connection, in his heyday he fits his own description of Rebecca's family: "[they] worshipped money and were obsessed with salaries and net worths" (52). Yet it doesn't take much to turn this champion of the underdog into a money-grubbing creep. Clay's transition, though a bit hasty, is still pretty believable, mainly because he never actually changes his values, but simply decides that his new world demands a different set of expectations and rules. Intimidated by the other lawyers in his circle, Clay compares himself to them: "Youngest lawyer. Smallest jet. No war tales. Weakest liver. Clay decided it was time to grow up" (226). Clay never realizes that he's coming to resemble his loathed Bennett the Bulldozer, even as he fantasizes about Rebecca's family's reaction to his well-publicized riches.

Playin' with the King of Torts

Okay, we couldn't help ourselves. Here's our fully singable parody of Juice Newton's "Queen of Hearts," dedicated to the legendary John Grisham.

Midnight
I'm already on page 205
Caught up in another legal thriller that I can't put down
Grisham
How do you do it every time?
Is your secret all the "the's" in all your titles followed by a short noun?

CHORUS:
Playin' with the King of Torts
See him settle out of court
Another lawyer's gonna fall
So weird that we care at all.
Playin' with the King of Torts
Now he's feeling out of sorts
But there's not time for doubts
The movie is coming out.

> Jarret—
> Are you really gonna take that cash?
> You know that the drug is making addicts go berserk and kill
> Millions
> Yes, I see I was a wee bit rash
> When you help the little people, someone's got to pay the bill.
>
> REPEAT CHORUS—and don't forget the awesome key change!

So in Grisham we get this interesting combination of social ills and personal weakness, an evil waiting within that can be triggered by the larger world. Clay isn't a madman by a long shot; he's just a guy who lost his way, a guy who could have used some Tuesdays with Morrie.

Another top-seller by Grisham, *The Brethren* (#1 fiction in 2000, #27 for 1993–2003), offers the same social uneasiness without the redemptive conclusion. A darker and more expansive novel, *The Brethren* follows two distinct stories that eventually merge. First, we meet a trio of judges—the Brethren—serving time in a minimum-security prison. They've invented a clever blackmail scheme: by placing "pen pal" ads in gay magazines, pretending to be young men in rehab clinics, they begin to correspond with older men. They identify those who are rich and closeted—and using real names—and then demand money in exchange for silence. The victims, desperate to keep the sexual secret from their wives and communities, start to pay up.

The other, very different storyline follows Aaron Lake, a squeaky-clean congressman chosen by Teddy Maynard, the director of the CIA, to be the nation's next president. Wait, chosen? That's right. Teddy knows that with the right marketing and gobs of cash, public opinion can and will be bought:

"Listen, Mr. Lake, don't worry about the money. Shortly after you announce, we'll scare the hell out of the American people. They'll think you're half-crazy at first, some kind of wacko from Arizona who wants to build even more bombs. But we'll jolt them. We'll create a crisis on the other side of the world, and suddenly Aaron Lake will be called a visionary. Timing is everything. You make a speech about how weak we are in Asia, few people listen. Then we'll create a situation over there that stops the world, and suddenly everyone wants to talk to you. It will go on like that, throughout the campaign. We'll build tension on this end. We'll release reports, create situations, manipulate the media, embarrass your opponents. Frankly, Mr. Lake, I don't expect it to be that difficult." (27)

And why is the director of the CIA selecting a president? Well, apparently some Russian big shots are secretly stockpiling arms, and America isn't militarily prepared. So Teddy wants to put a man in office who will double defense spending, priming America to avoid a big confrontation: "If we are unprepared, then we could well have a war. If we are strong, we avoid war" (23). The American people don't sense the impending danger, so "situations" have to be created to convince them to get behind a more defense-happy presidential agenda.

The two plotlines come together when the CIA people discover Aaron Lake's secret post office box, which somehow eluded their earlier investigations, and a gay pen-pal letter inside from the-Brethren-in-disguise. By this time, Lake is well into his campaign, and it's impossible to pick another man. The CIA has no choice but to keep Lake's little secret from getting out, and they do this by tracking down the Brethren, granting them immunity, and paying them $2 million each for their silence.

We'll just come out and say it: this is a weird book, and an especially weird book for John Grisham to have written. It technically has a happy ending, in that all the protagonists get what they want: the Brethren get out of jail and get rich; Aaron Lake gets to be president; Teddy Maynard gets to run the country the way he sees fit; and various frightened gay men get to keep their cash and their closets. But there's not much to love in any of these characters, and their success is also the success of less-than-noble values. Essentially, this is a cynical book about the triumph of power: money's power over public opinion; fame's (and Teddy's) power over Aaron Lake; and the Brethren's power over their victims. It's typical Grisham in that the source of evil is internal, drawn into being by societal opportunity. But what's unusual is that none of these people suffers publicly or personally for his greed; the evil, if it can be called that (and it isn't), walks off with the trophy. We're not sure what Grisham is trying to do here (something different? has he cleared it with the formula police?), but we're pretty sure that this sort of thing is not what made him famous. Amazon.com readers note that the book is odd, as well as oddly devoid of good guys, but still, of course, eminently readable—though not one of Grisham's highest rated.

Quirks aside, what *The Brethren* does illustrate is a characteristic as vital to these genres as the good/evil dichotomy itself: the underlying assumption that the choices and actions of the characters have vast, even global, importance. These are not books about overcoming depression, getting along with family members, or making the cheerleading squad. They are books about saving lives, nations—the planet. *The Brethren* illustrates this quality in the unusual form of CIA director Teddy Maynard. The guy is so bomb-hungry that we half-expect him to be revealed as a lunatic who's invented all these deadly international threats himself, but nothing in the novel contradicts Teddy's assertions. For him, getting Aaron Lake elected is a matter of grave importance: the future of the United States is at stake! Every move *matters*.

This obsession with the critical, the heart-pounding, the life-and-death cannot be overemphasized. We Americans are so deeply accustomed to associating formulaic entertainment with guns, bombs, bloody hospital beds, and the like that we forget there is no inherent connection between "good and evil" stories and over-the-top dramatics. In fact, the persistence of this link once again reveals our unwillingness to accept evil as an everyday, mundane presence in our everyday, mundane lives. In these books (and in most other popular entertainment), evil has to be *huge,* to threaten life or even civilization, so that we can distance ourselves from it ("he's nuts") and at the same time vicariously experience a breathless and exciting world.

There seems to be a real longing in us to be holy warriors in some magnificent epic, to take brave, significant, and indisputably good action against indisputably evil foes. When we "escape" into the latest thriller—and remember, these books are often considered "beach reading," "just for fun," and happily escapist even by their devoted readers—we leap into far more difficult lives than our own (no one said terrorist-snuffing was easy). But they are lives with clear social purpose, clear *moral* purpose, lives unencumbered by the complexity that tends to crop up when situations become a little less life-and-death, a little less grand.

HARRY POTTER AND THE BIG FAT BESTSELLER

We've probably all heard the amazing story of J. K. Rowling. Her rags-to-riches tale is so extraordinary that it sounds like an urban legend proliferating among the hopeful in writers' groups. And actually, it is. Rowling was not a welfare mother on the brink of starvation who scribbled some notes about Harry Potter on a napkin and became a bazillionaire. But she was a hardworking single mom who did get some public assistance over the years to supplement her income from teaching and clerical work. Like many writers, Rowling spent years pouring her spare time into a manuscript, and finally, with the help of an agent, she found a publisher. One thing about the legend is indisputably true, though: she is definitely now a bazillionaire.

She is also arguably the absolute bestselling author of the recent past, having sold over 250 million copies of the *Harry Potter* books worldwide. The first five books earned numbers 1, 3, 4, 5, and 6 of the top one hundred books sold from 1993 to 2003 (Dr. Atkins revolutionized his way to #2). The sixth *Harry Potter* book wasn't out when that list was compiled, but it was by far the top book of 2005, selling over thirteen million copies. With both kids and grownups helplessly addicted, the series has sold more than *The South Beach Diet,* more than *Chicken Soup for the Soul,* more than *The Da Vinci Code.*

And what's more, it's really good. As of this writing, six books have been published; they are as follows:

- *Harry Potter and the Sorcerer's Stone (Philosopher's Stone* in the UK)
- *Harry Potter and the Chamber of Secrets*
- *Harry Potter and the Prisoner of Azkaban*
- *Harry Potter and the Goblet of Fire*
- *Harry Potter and the Order of the Phoenix*
- *Harry Potter and the Half-Blood Prince*

But for the sake of brevity and clarity, we'll refer to them by book number in this chapter.

In many ways, the *Harry Potter* saga aligns perfectly with the other books discussed here. This sweeping septet covers the adolescence of scrawny Harry Potter, a malnourished orphan who learns on his eleventh birthday that he is actually a wizard, destined to join a whole magical world that just happens to exist alongside the regular (or "Muggle") one. What's more, he is actually one of the most famous wizards of all time: the evil wizard Voldemort ("You-Know-Who") tried to kill Harry as a baby, only to have the spell rebound and reduce the Dark Lord to a powerless, ghosty sort of thing. The only trace of the battle remains etched in Harry's forehead, a scar in the shape of a lightning bolt that broadcasts Harry's unlikely invincibility to the entire wizarding world. Though Harry doesn't know it at first, he learns soon enough that the Dark Lord is struggling to return—and that he himself must play a vital role in vanquishing the evil wizard once and for all.

At the time of this writing, alas, only six of the seven books have been released. The seventh and final adventure, *Harry Potter and the Deathly Hallows,* won't hit the bookstores until July 2007, but with an initial print run of 12 million, we're guessing it will be a pretty big seller. We've resisted reading any books or visiting the myriad of websites dedicated to predicting Harry's ultimate fate, but the trajectory of the series is clear. In many ways, *Harry Potter* is the perfect good-versus-evil story, a classic battle between a demonic villain and an all-too-human, fallible hero. Voldemort is an archetypal enemy, a terrifying creature "whiter than a skull, with wide, livid scarlet eyes and a nose that was flat as a snake's with slits for nostrils" (643, book 4). No longer human, he does not change, or surprise us, and he thoroughly lacks empathy, showing "just as little mercy to his followers as his enemies" (298, book 1). He is as evil as can be—and as simplistic.

Harry, on the other hand, is a regular kid, struggling to get through his course load at the Hogwarts School of Witchcraft and Wizardry, form friendships, play sports, and yes—when the situation arises—fight the ultimate evil. Harry, of course, doesn't have Voldemort's magical might, but the world manages to keep on truckin' because there *is* a requisite good wizard on duty: Harry's mentor, Professor Albus Dumbledore, the headmaster of Hogwarts and possibly the most powerful wizard in the world. There's something of Gandalf and Frodo in this pair: Dumbledore's might and wisdom combine with Harry's luck and bravery to form one bad-ass evil-fighting machine.

But Harry spends most of his time being a kid and, more importantly, a complex character. Harry and his cohorts are rich, distinctive, and relatable, in large part because much of the series playfully documents their daily lives as students at a magical school. Within the serious framework of a good-and-evil story, Rowling has invented an often hilarious and always charming universe that places the joys and difficulties of every reader's educational experience in a wonderful magical context. The humor alone distinguishes Rowling's novels from all the other good-and-evil books we've discussed here, which may elicit a few chuckles, but that's it.

But what also separates the *Harry Potter* series from other good-and-evil stories is its increasing ethical (and narrative) complexity. Whereas the other novels—even other series—don't expand or complicate the definitions of good and evil as they go, Harry's moral world becomes less straightforward, less easily navigated, as he grows older and more experienced.

Initially, the ethical landscape is quite simple. We quickly learn about the dormant battle between good (Harry, Dumbledore, etc.) and evil (Voldemort and his followers) and about Voldemort's attempts to return to power. This pending grand conflict underscores all the books. But there's also a related, everyday tension that's a more constant and predictable source of angst for Harry: the regular conflicts and rivalries between students.

Hogwarts is arranged in the fashion of the British public school system; students are assigned to one of four "houses," which compete for school acclaim. Members of the same house share classes and a dormitory, so it's rare that deep friendships emerge between students in different houses. On the night students arrive for the first time, they are mentally probed by a magical, singing hat, which determines their house placement based on their core characteristics:

You might belong in Gryffindor,
Where dwell the brave of heart
Their daring, nerve, and chivalry
Set the Gryffindors apart;
You might belong in Hufflepuff,
Where they are just and loyal,
Those patient Hufflepuffs are true
And unafraid of toil;
Or yet in wise old Ravenclaw,
If you've a ready mind,
Where those of wit and learning
Will always find their kind;
Or perhaps in Slytherin
You'll make your real friends,
Those cunning folk use any means
To achieve their ends. (118, book 1)

Harry and his soon-to-be friends become Gryffindors, and Harry's schoolyard nemesis, Draco Malfoy, whose father was a Voldemort devotee back when the Dark Lord ruled the roost, becomes a mean and snooty Slytherin. We quickly learn that the Slytherin House is for bad students—"There's not a single witch or wizard who went bad who wasn't in Slytherin. You-Know-Who was one," reports Hagrid, the groundskeeper (80, book 1)—and the other three are for good students. This fundamental conflict between Slytherin and the other houses, especially Gryffindor, dominates much of the six novels.

(Okay. It's hard not to be critical of Rowling's decision to stuff all her villains into a single Hogwarts House and to portray the Slytherins as pretty universally crummy and hyped up on racial purity—could there be a clearer indication that we are supposed to dislike these people? Although Slytherin characteristics have long been viewed with suspicion—and not unjustly—the Slytherin House could have been the most morally interesting of them all, exploring the differences between ambition and ruthlessness, resourcefulness and exploitation, clever minds and cutthroat ones. Likewise, courage and intellect and loyalty (the principal traits of the other houses) can mask and even spawn grave flaws of their own. Rowling's neat categories make it easy to confine the problem of evil in one form, one place, one type of person—and it's surprising, given the trend of the series, that a really splendid Slytherin hasn't emerged in the later novels. Maybe that's a treat she's saving up for the last book.)

Though these house lines remain firmly drawn throughout the six novels published at this writing, good and evil begin to get more complicated in the later books, which also deliver messier endings. In *Harry Potter and the Prisoner of Azkaban,* the third book, we learn that appearances are not always what they seem: escaped convict Sirius Black, accused of killing Harry's parents, turns out to be innocent— and Harry's devoted godfather— while their supposed avenger is the actual traitor. The bad guy, indeed, gets away. But things really take a dark (and genuinely jarring) turn in book four, when an innocent classmate dies at the hands of Voldemort. More death follows in books five and six, priming the pump for the grand battle sure to take place in the last novel.

There's nothing remarkable about sinister developments, however, in a good-and-evil epic. More interesting is that Rowling begins to introduce new, less predictable, dare we say *real life* forms of evil in books four and five. *Harry Potter and the Goblet of Fire,* book four, introduces us to the questionable morality of the media. "Special Correspondent" Rita Skeeter employs a "Quick-Quotes Quill" to invent juicy stories about Harry and his friends and publish them as fact in the wizarding world's primary newspaper, the *Daily Prophet.* Harry's good friend Hermione manages to shut down the sensationalist reporter, but we learn through the experience that people act on a wide range of motivations:

> "So the *Daily Prophet* exists to tell people what they want to hear, does it?" said Hermione scathingly.
>
> Rita sat up straight again, her eyebrows raised, and drained her glass of firewhisky.
>
> "The *Prophet* exists to sell itself, you silly girl," she said coldly. (567, book 4)

Rita wants to titillate the masses; the owners of the *Daily Prophet* want to sell papers. But they're not red-eyed snake beasties; they're not marching around with skulls on their wrists or plotting a reign of terror. We have two side-by-side evils here, one supernatural and ultimate, one human and mundane, both of which must be confronted by the young heroes.

And the world gets even shadier in book five, *Harry Potter and the Order of the Phoenix*. Rita Skeeter's dirty dealings in book four foreshadow the complete deterioration of the *Daily Prophet* in book five, when the Ministry of Magic uses the paper to discredit Harry and Dumbledore and squelch their warnings about the Dark Lord's return. Fear is the motivation here:

> "Accepting that Voldemort's back would mean trouble like the Ministry hasn't had to cope with for nearly fourteen years," said Sirius bitterly. "[Cornelius] Fudge [the Minister of Magic] just can't bring himself to face it. It's so much more comfortable to convince himself Dumbledore's lying to destabilize him." (94)

The paranoia grows, and the Ministry begins to pass increasingly invasive decrees to gain control of Hogwarts, seizing more and more authority until Dumbledore is ousted, the teachers are monitored, and the students are silenced and cruelly disciplined. Only at the book's end, when the proof is absolutely undeniable, does a dazed minister accept the unsavory truth of the Dark Lord's restoration.

All this denial and terror and fascistic behavior, alas, are sadly unsurprising to us grown-ups. But remember, these books are ultimately written for children. Some of the younger set we know had a difficult time grasping the new, muddier evil in the fifth book. Why would anyone not believe the truth? Why would anyone go about censoring newspapers, restricting freedoms, preventing others—the obvious good guys—from speaking out and fighting the bad guys? It's hard to understand if you've been told all your young life that the world is populated with only Harrys and Voldemorts—that people are either good or bad, that they do evil only because they *are* evil. And though some real-life moralists might agree (FOX news analysts, for example), we think most people would concede that a majority of the world's problems are not caused by snakelike demons or their followers, but by regular people making unfortunate decisions. As Harry grows up, becoming acquainted with the Good, the Bad, and the Afraid, so does Rowling's audience.

And just as Harry learns about the weaknesses of good people, he also comes to see that good can exist in generally lousy people. Despite the anti-Slytherin slant, from the very beginning Rowling troubled her categorical world with a thorn named Professor Severus Snape. By far the most morally interesting character in the epic, Snape is a greasy, bitter, grudge-carrying Slytherin who unabashedly hates Harry Potter and his friends and favors Draco and the other Slytherins. As a teacher he's cruel, cold, and pretty downright unethical, humiliating students and tampering with their grades. He also shows a certain disregard for life, as Rowling wittily describes: "Professor Snape was forcing them to research antidotes. They took this one seriously, as he had hinted that he might be poisoning one of them before Christmas to see if their antidote worked" (234, book 4).

However, Snape may not be, in an ultimate sense, evil. Though he once was a "Death Eater"—a follower of Voldemort—he claims to have repented and has earned Dumbledore's trust. Harry and friends suspect Snape of continued allegiance to the Dark Lord, but they are proven false several times (in book one, Snape even saves Harry's life). The end of the sixth book calls Snape's repentance and loyalties into question, but we'll have to wait for the seventh book to get the final verdict.

Even more interesting, Harry discovers that his own father used to humiliate and torment the unpopular Snape when they were students at Hogwarts. Used to idolizing his dead father, Harry is torn between his dislike of Professor Snape and his shame over his father's arrogance and cruelty. He begins to realize that not all human behaviors are related to one's ultimate position on the good-and-evil roster. Even his godfather patiently reminds him, "The world isn't split into good people and Death Eaters" (302, book 5).

Indeed not. But Harry himself is split at times, increasingly so in the later novels, between his finer qualities and the darkness within. Harry, you see, has from the beginning been portrayed as potentially Slytherin; the Sorting Hat, pondering Harry's suitability for each house, even assures him, "Slytherin will help you on the way to greatness" (121, book 1), but Harry is so fervently opposed to the idea that the Hat places him in Gryffindor. Harry *is* without a doubt correctly placed—in his most instinctive moments he is brave and selfless—but he has a significant dollop of Slytherin pride. He is also a Parselmouth—a person who can speak and understand the language of snakes—a talent associated with the Dark Arts in general and Voldemort in particular.

Harry's gift for reptilian communication, however, extends far beyond gab sessions with garter snakes. In book five, he dreams that, in snake form, he strikes, biting the father of his best friend Ron, and he wakes in a panic, knowing the event really happened:

> "No!" said Harry furiously; it was crucial that Ron under-
> stand. "It wasn't a dream . . . not an ordinary dream. . . .
> I was there, I saw it. . . . I *did* it." (464)

Harry is right about his clairvoyance: Mr. Weasley is in grave condition from the bite, which came straight from the fangs of Voldemort in snake form. And so Harry becomes aware of a powerful link to his enemy: he can perceive the thoughts, feelings, and even experiences of Voldemort. He knows when the Dark Lord is happy or furious (such intense emotions cause his scar to burn); at times he shares Voldemort's desires or sees through his eyes. Once, he even yearns to "sink his fangs" into Professor Dumbledore (but then, who doesn't? wink wink), saying, "It was like something rose up inside me, like there's a *snake* inside me" (475, 481).

Harry is not really Voldemort. But nor are his snakish experiences entirely imposed on him. Harry is haunted by his Slytherin tendencies, by the fact that he had the potential to excel in a house he hates. Even though we're not thrilled about the unfair simplification of Slytherin, its association with evil makes for an intriguing struggle inside this epic hero. The more Harry fights to distance himself from the dark side, the more he finds himself personally entwined with Voldemort. This link is caused, yes, because they play opposite roles, one destined to destroy the other (says the prophecy, "*AND EITHER MUST DIE AT THE HAND OF THE OTHER FOR NEITHER CAN LIVE WHILE THE OTHER SURVIVES,*" 841, book 5)—but also because of the qualities they share. As Dumbledore explains to Harry, "He saw himself in you before he had ever seen you" (842, book 5).

Aside from its astounding commercial success, what makes the *Harry Potter* series such a significant work for this chapter is that it succeeds as a captivating good-and-evil story, with heroes we love and villains we hate and a promised happy ending (come on—it's been a great ride, but we know Harry's going to win), while baring the ugly truth that life is actually not that simplistic. Good people have bad qualities; bad people have good ones. We *all* must struggle against the enemy within. And most lives are not distinguished by our inherent righteousness or malevolence, but shaped instead by our choices: between Gryffindor and Slytherin, perhaps, or between fear and truth, or cruelty and kindness. But one thing is certain: without empathy, we are Voldemorts. It is Dumbledore who marches into the forbidden forest to rescue his enemy from a nasty end.

* * *

These books are fun fiction. They are worthy of study because so many of us turn to them so often for our entertainment and escape. And their general presentation of good and evil says much about what excites and comforts us.

But these books are not really intended to be taken seriously. Although Tom Clancy has managed to eke out a semi-political career, no other author has achieved that kind of real-world leverage. Nobody cares what James Patterson thinks about terrorism. Nobody's clamoring to hear Stephen King's views on the yucky creatures invading our nation's forests. And hardly anybody, we hope to god, gets fashion advice from Mary Higgins Clark.

We might find—might expect, in fact—a very different perspective on good and evil from the authors who deal in real life. Let us turn to our nation's guiding voices in the tempestuous political sphere.

Jane, You Ignorant Slut

If we are to believe what we read, nowhere in the past decade and a half has evil lurked more insidiously than in politics. Bill Clinton was pretty evil. G. W. Bush and the neo-cons are wicked and corrupt. Terrorists and liberals are members of the same satanic cult! Of course, the waters of political discourse have always boiled over with epic exaggeration; Demosthenes and Cicero articulated scandalously brilliant caricatures of their political opponents and their policies. But few who have scoured the most popular recent books on politics would deny that we have reached a new level of acrimonious (and hysterical) charge and countercharge.

Are we *Losing America? Running on Empty?* Have we been *Bushwhacked* by *Imperial Hubris* that's *Worse Than Watergate?* Or have we *Misunderestimated* the *Enemy Within?* Can we be *Delivered from Evil, Renew America* and finally *Talk to a Liberal* (if we must) about *The Way Things Ought to Be?*

Something just seems fishy when the titles of some of the best-selling nonfiction books sound more like movies starring Harrison Ford or Bruce Willis.

And the hype doesn't stop with the names. These authors are supposed to be discussing the most serious problems facing today's world. Many of them, however, seem to envision themselves as freedom-fighting heroes in the pages of the fictional spine-tinglers we just discussed. Although great literature, no doubt, can reflect reality—the "epiphany of truth," says *Reading Lolita in Tehran* (3)—it doesn't ring quite as true when nonfiction impersonates already-simplified formula fiction. But that's what we have seen in many of the bestselling political books from the past sixteen years, especially the bumper crop that busted onto the shelves in the election year of 2004.

Unlike a Clark or Koontz or Patterson novel, however, where the enemy loves being the bad guy—devoting many precious hours to plotting and cackling—our political writers have a problem: the "other" side. Indeed, neither the liberals nor the conservatives are willing to 'fess up as the evil ones (plotting and cackling notwithstanding). How can one be a noble freedom-fighter if the enemies actually think of themselves as the good guys?

This highly annoying situation has only one solution: the other side must be accused of lying.

After reading these books, one can only conclude that virtually every major political leader, insider, journalist, and commentator of the past decade is a liar— not just a liar, but a really, really big liar, with his (or more rarely, her) pants on fire. Ann Coulter insists that Al Franken is lying about Rush Limbaugh's lying about Clinton's lying. One book claims Michael Moore is lying about Bush's lying about Saddam's lying. Another is completely dedicated to disproving everything in Hillary Clinton's bestselling autobiography. The Left maintains that the Right lies to stay in power. The Right complains that the Left habitually lies because it rejects the very existence of truth.

It's actually sort of funny. But only sort of—because although it doesn't matter much if there's a psychopathic psychiatrist on the loose in a fictional landscape, it does make a great deal of difference who is president, what policies are enacted, and how we go about determining those choices.

There's a certain satisfaction—if limited and perverse—that comes from pursuing these concatenations of charges through dozens of books. To test your own mastery of contemporary political commentary, we have developed the following brief exam, our Prevarication Measuring System (PMS). Can you match the following authors and works with their accusations?

a. The presidential election of 2000 turned out to be a swamp of distortion, diversion, and brazen deception. . . . Most of us voted for the lesser of two spinners. [Hint: spin is this writer's bailiwick.]

b. Bush misled the people and the Congress, peddled falsehoods to the United Nations, [and] miscalculated the ease of making democracy flourish in a country riven by religious and tribal hatreds. [Hint: a Southern senator old enough to know the verb "to rive."]

c. When Democrats scheme from the White House, it's to cover up the president's affair with an intern. When Republicans scheme, it is to support embattled anti-Communist freedom fighters sold out by the Democrats. [Hint: a blonde bombshell (by GOP standards) who really is arguing here that Democratic lying about sex is very, very bad, but Republican lying about public policy is very, very good. Did you note the bit about freedom fighters?]

d. Why has our government gone to such absurd lengths to convince us our lives are in danger? The answer is nothing short of their feverish desire to rule the world, first by controlling us, and then, in turn, getting us to support their efforts to dominate the rest of the planet. [Hint: a film producer who never met a misleading edit he didn't like.]

e. The ultra-leftist traitors within our borders have unleashed a relentless barrage of words against the war on terrorism with their subversive tongues. These turncoats and their sympathizers spew a web of lies and anti-American hatred with unquenchable zeal. [Hint: an ultra-conservative talk-show host. Yes, we know, this hint is of no help whatsoever.]

f. There can be no justification for [G. W. Bush's administration's] lying, misleading, obfuscation, deceit, and other such secrecy-protecting ploys and tactics. [Hint: someone who has seen such behavior in the White House before and apparently is still pretty darn upset about it.]

g. If *Living History* proves anything, it establishes how willing Hillary is to distort, exaggerate, falsify, fabricate, invent, omit, or obfuscate facts to suit her political ends. [Hint: former chief political advisor to a sex-scandal-ridden president, himself ousted in a sex scandal.]

h. While it might not seem like I'm changing the tone when I accuse my friends on the right of being liars, my hope is that, if we keep calling them on their calculated dishonesty, their dishonesty will lose its effectiveness. Then O'Reilly and company will have to resort to Plan B: name-calling. Which, I think, will expose them for what they are. Stupid bastards. [Hint: someone with a sense of humor, which eliminates nearly everyone else from consideration.]

Answer key:
a. Bill O'Reilly, *The No Spin Zone* (4)
b. Robert C. Byrd, *Losing America* (211)
c. Ann Coulter, *Treason: Liberal Treachery from the Cold War to the War on Terrorism* (178–179)
d. Michael Moore, *Dude, Where's My Country?* (101)
e. Michael Savage, *The Enemy Within* (74)
f. John W. Dean, *Worse Than Watergate* (178)
g. Dick Morris, *Rewriting History* (29)
h. Al Franken, *Lies, and the Lying Liars Who Tell Them* (354)

Yes, this great spewing of accusations is absurd and amusing. But it also cripples the uninitiated and curious reader, making it nearly impossible to disentangle the conflicting claims and analyses of policy—and the evil that is said to underlie it. Anyone actually reading multiple points of view, trying to make decisions based on facts, may be better off giving up and going out for tacos.

Both sides, though, seem to be assuming that nobody is old-fashioned enough to consider diverse perspectives on complex issues. Almost all of these books were written for an audience of the converted, hymnals for those familiar with the tunes and eager for the latest orchestrations. People don't say things like "Al Gore is the Democrats' most esteemed political figure after Saddam Hussein" (Ann Coulter in *Treason,* 206) or that George W. Bush is "an idiot leader of an idiot nation" (Michael Moore in *Stupid White Men,* 87) if they are trying to persuade anybody. A great majority of these authors, after all, are celebrities publicly involved in the political process: familiar politicians (e.g., the Clintons and senators Byrd and Graham), members of various administrations (e.g., Perle, Phillips, Clarke, Hughes, Dean, and Morris), TV and radio commentators (e.g., O'Reilly, Limbaugh, Savage, Buchanan, and Hannity), and nationally marketed journalists (e.g., Ivins, Dowd, Gertz, Woodward, Sammon, and Kessler). Michael Moore's films and books synergize into sales just as neatly. These are folks with *platforms!* The bestsellers are packed with familiar perspectives and material— some are even reprints of previously published essays, columns, and television segments. Readers know what they are going to get before they even open the book.

So it really doesn't matter what the lies are, or if the "proof" is accurate; for the most part these authors are writing to an audience that already believes in the dishonesty of the other side and that simply wants examples and reinforcement, valid or not. Still, a few authors nobly plug away with facts and reasoned argument. But many take advantage of their carte blanche and devote their pages to wild rhetoric instead.

When it comes to accusations of lying, George W. Bush, of course, is the favorite—and obvious—target of the past few years. John Dean details the secrecy, paranoia, and campaign of disinformation perpetrated by the White House in *Worse Than Watergate: The Secret Presidency of George W. Bush.* Kevin Phillips describes two generations of Bush manipulation in *American Dynasty: Aristocracy, Fortune, and the Politics of Deceit in the House of Bush,* which features an appendix on "Deception, Dissimulation, and Disinformation." (Apparently, the propensity for politicians to lie is not merely vocational; it can be genetic as well!) In *Losing America,* Senator Robert C. Byrd states, "This entire adventure in Iraq has been based on propaganda and manipulation" (257). On the venomous side is Michael Moore, whose list of George W.'s "Whoppers" fills an entire chapter of *Dude, Where's My Country?*

But President Bush is by no means the only political figure to find himself labeled a liar and cheat. Vice President Dick Cheney earned that familiar characterization from Calvin Trillin (*Obliviously On He Sails,* 6)—and this one rhymes!

> One mystery I've tried to disentangle:
> Why Cheney's head is always at an angle.
> . . .
> The code is broken, after years of trying:
> He only cocks his head when he is lying.

And much of the Right's condemnation of Bill Clinton is derived from his "truth problem." Rush Limbaugh (*See I Told You,* 46–52) wasted no time in compiling a list of "lies" told by Clinton only one year into his presidency, matching Michael Moore for urgency. (Indeed,

Moore and Limbaugh make unsightly bedfellows in their disgust with Clinton, whom Moore says is just like Bush, although the latter is an "uglier and somewhat meaner version.") These falsehoods listed by Limbaugh were for the most part campaign statements that Clinton had contradicted or not fulfilled in the first year of his presidency.

Wannabe presidents are in season as well, as John Kerry discovered when a fellow commander of a Vietnam swift boat targeted him in the bestselling *Unfit for Command,* the sixth chapter of which is simply titled "A Testimony of Lies" (John E. O'Neill and Jerome R. Corsi; cf. the final chapter of Bill Sammon's *Misunderestimated; The President Battles Terrorism, John Kerry, and the Bush Haters*). And it's never too early to cash in on the possible lies of a potential candidate. Dick Morris, in anticipation of the 2008 presidential campaign, wrote an entire book (*Rewriting History*) trying to unmask Hillary Clinton's lyin' eyes.

But the critiques of political figures go way beyond accusations of dishonesty. It's deeper even than mere policy disagreements. To use the appropriate "preview" language for a movie starring Harrison Ford and Bruce Willis: this time, it's personal.

Consider Bill Clinton. During the '90s, it could be expected that the President and his First Lady would be targets of the Right. At first it seemed to be Clinton's political agenda that drew the anger of his critics—gays in the military, health care reform, and so on. Newt Gingrich's *To Renew America* criticized the Democrats' policies and celebrated the "revolution" of the 1994 election, when the Republicans won a majority of seats in the House for the first time since 1954. His lengthy arguments for Republicans balancing the budget and reducing the national debt—and against reforming Social Security—may bring an ironic smile to a reader in 2007. And more recent conservative books, such as Sean Hannity's *Deliver Us from Evil: Defeating Terrorism, Despotism, and Liberalism,* often blame Clinton's foreign policy for allowing the seeds of terrorism to take root.

Campaign promises were only the tip of Clinton's cigar, however, for waiting in the wings were Gennifer Flowers, Paula Jones, Chinese espionage, midnight pardons, and especially Monica Lewinsky. (*The Starr Report* even made it to the #1 spot on *USA TODAY*'s bestseller list in the fall of 1998.) The Lewinsky affair became a "cultural fault line," as Bill O'Reilly laments (*No Spin Zone*, 91)—how much do we care that someone, especially the President of the United States, lied about having an extramarital affair? Not enough, according to most authors on the Right, who, like Ann Coulter, Michael Savage, and O'Reilly, were scandalized that "millions of Americans were not appalled and some were even angry with people like [O'Reilly] who came down hard on Clinton. Ideology and apathy ruled the day" (*No Spin Zone*, 92).

The animus towards Clinton went—and still goes—way beyond disagreement with his politics; it is downright hatred, and it sells. Clinton remains even now, as Kevin Phillips wryly notes, the Right's leading bogeyman. The cynically hysterical *America (The Book)* from *The Daily Show with Jon Stewart* shows a diagram with one-quarter of the "Partisan Brain: Right" composed of the "Clintonellum," which "sends blood to face at mention of Bill or Hillary" (149).

People are also really steamed at George W. Bush, but for very different reasons. In *Crimes against Nature*, Robert F. Kennedy Jr. claims that Bush "will go down as the worst environmental president in our nation's history" (3). Senator Robert C. Byrd, in *Losing America*, describes how "the Constitution's careful separation of powers has been breached, and its checks and balances circumvented" by the Bush Administration (21). Maureen Dowd's *New York Times* columns, collected in *Bushworld: Enter at Your Own Risk*, frequently try to account for the arrogance of the "Boy Emperor"—"whether he is right or wrong, George W. Bush is a bummer" (523)—in half-joking (we think) Freudian musings. Although many liberal authors clearly respond as viscerally to Bush as conservatives do to Clinton, the specific complaints in their books are overall less personal.

EVIL IS AS EVIL DOES

One of the main reasons these folks get *so* frothy around the gum line is that the two sides define evil—or at least rank the competing evils—so differently. It's clear from the divergent criticisms of Bill Clinton and George W. Bush that we're still squabbling about what defines a bad president. September 11 gave everyone new reasons to don their finest red faces and balled fists: terrorists, the Bush Administration, liberals, conservatives, Islam, and the American Way all got lambasted by someone or other for saying or doing or being something or other. *The 9/11 Commission Report* itself went to #1 on the *USA TODAY* bestseller list and spent twenty-three weeks in the top 150.

But though Left and Right alike are swollen with outrage, or perhaps with too many french/freedom fries, the Right owns evil. The books from the Left do accuse the Bush administration of being arrogant, irresponsible, and frightening. And some of their authors surely hate Bush; Michael Moore's vitriol leads him to gush in purple-faced prose worthy of a blockbuster thriller: "Why has our government gone to such absurd lengths to convince us our lives are in danger? The answer is nothing short of their feverish desire to rule the world, first by controlling us, and then, in turn, getting us to support their efforts to dominate the rest of the planet" (*Dude, Where's My Country?* 101). But one can read most of the liberally oriented books without running across the concept of iniquity. One can't dip a toe into the conservative books without getting it all gummy with evil.

Conservative author Sean Hannity has an explanation for this difference. Although he insists in one of his bestsellers, "I'm not saying that liberals like Bill Clinton and Al Gore and Tom Daschle and Dick Gephardt and many of the elitists in academia and the media are evil"

(*Let Freedom Ring*, 11), he nevertheless believes that Democrats (a word synonymous with "liberals" in this line of thought) are incapable of dealing with the fact that real evil exists in this world:

> It's difficult for liberals to see such moral questions clearly, because most of them are moral relativists. (*Deliver Us from Evil*, 2)
>
> To them people like Saddam and Osama bin Laden are not morally depraved murderers, but men driven to their bad acts by the injustices of Western society. (3)
>
> Indeed, the greatest threat to our resolve today in the War on Terror is the political liberalism—and selfish opportunism—of the Democrats. (5)
>
> George Bush and Conservatives, unlike the liberal appeasers who turn a blind eye to it, grasp the nature of evil. (13)

Indeed, most of the conservative books consistently (and even matter-of-factly) draw on the following dualities:

- Good/Evil
- God/Atheism
- Judeo-Christianity/Islam
- Morality/Moral relativism
- United States/Terrorism
- Conservatives/Liberals
- Republicans/Democrats
- Less filling/Tastes great

Okay, maybe not the last one. This game of dichotomies is hard to stop once you get going.

Some of the authors on the Right, or members of its offshoots—

such as the paleo-con Patrick Buchanan (*Where the Right Went Wrong*), former CIA analyst Michael Scheuer (*Imperial Hubris: Why the West Is Losing the War on Terror*), and Richard Clarke (*Against All Enemies: Inside America's War on Terror*)—disagree with the position that the war in Iraq was the correct way to corral the elusive Islamisist quarry. But the *most* popular conservative books make a remarkable claim: either you are for the President's approach to the problem, or you are for the terrorists.

These books draw an increasingly tight connection between evil and terrorism on the one hand and those who don't agree with the authors—namely liberals or Democrats—on the other. Trolling through Michael Savage's *The Enemy Within: Saving America from the Liberal Assault on Our Schools, Faith, and Military,* for example, hauls in a hearty catch of evil, labeled in a distinctive style: "The old hags, the harridans in the Senate who make a living off the abortion racketeers, get up and scream that we should continue to rip babies out of the womb and sell the skin for women who have wrinkles" (13). Democrats are "maniacs, the psychotics on the Left, who continue to denigrate this great country" (17) and "ultra-leftist traitors," "Dogs of Hate" (123), "hate-filled soul vampires," and "self-loathing moral vagrants" (162). Savage's real enemies are not so much the Islamic fundamentalists themselves, but the "ultra-leftist traitors within our borders [who] have unleashed a relentless barrage of words against the war on terrorism with their subversive tongues. These turncoats and their sympathizers spew a web of lies and anti-American hatred with unquenchable zeal. Their goal? Sabotage President George W. Bush's effort to fight terrorism" (74). Criticism of the administration's policy is identical to supporting, and thus becoming, the enemy.

The doyenne of this Manichaean "Me Right, You Satan" world of political commentary is Ann Coulter. Her *Treason: Liberal Treachery from the Cold War to the War on Terrorism* devotes one hundred pages to the "myth of McCarthyism"—the guy was after *Communists,* people—but it is primarily a compilation of accusations against Democrats. A sampling:

> Liberals have a preternatural gift for striking a position on the side of treason. You could be talking about Scrabble and they would instantly leap to the anti-American position. Everyone says liberals love America, too. No they don't. Whenever the nation is under attack, from within or without, liberals side with the enemy. This is their essence. (1)
>
> Whether they are defending the Soviet Union or bleating for Saddam Hussein, liberals are always against America. (16)
>
> Liberals warm to the idea of American mothers weeping for their sons, but only if their deaths will not make America any safer. (212)
>
> Of course, it is impossible to have 100 percent support for defending America because some Americans are liberals. (221)
>
> There were precisely two groups of people who desperately wanted airport security to be browbeaten into giving suspicious passengers a pass: terrorists and Democrats. (264)
>
> Liberals are appalled by patriotism with an edge of anger because it might lead America to defend itself. (283)
>
> Liberals hate America: they are rooting for the atheistic regimes of Stalin and Mao, satanic suicide bombers and terrorists, or the Central Park rapists. (285)
>
> Liberals once again are cheering for the destruction of civil society. (286)

Talk about your false empathy. The most extreme conservative authors delve into the liberal mentality only (as in the fiction thrillers) to make Democrats seem alien and horrifying, their views unworthy of serious contemplation.

The particular brand of religious faith evinced in virtually every conservative bestseller supports these black-and-white perspectives. Simply put, God not only exists, but also is Christian and a Republican. According to Savage, in *The Enemy Within*,

> You will come to see the right-wing supports God, country, family, the military, and has far higher moral standards than the Left. The Left operates specifically to undermine God, country, family, and the military . . . It is clear to me if God could vote, He would be a member of the vast right-wing conspiracy. (xi)
>
> By and large you will find that Republicans come from a stronger relationship to the Judeo-Christian doctrine of monotheism, or one god. (135)
>
> As I've studied the teachings in the Bible, I've come up with only one conclusion: God is a conservative. (137)

A common theme running through these books is the liberals' "remorseless campaign to de-Christianize the public life of the nation" (Buchanan, 215). Often tied into the authors' antiterrorist ambitions are campaigns against abortion, stem cell research, cloning, and sexuality, especially but not exclusively homosexuality. (In fact, Pat Buchanan—unlike his neo-conservative rivals—laments that the war against terrorism detracts from these far more important social issues.)

One of the more pointed analyses of these authors on the Right, by liberal Thomas Frank, concludes that such posturing is the central strategy of conservatives. In his *What's the Matter with Kansas? How Conservatives Won the Heart of America*, Frank argues that the conservative backlash uses—in fact nourishes—a cultural class war while denying that social class has an economic basis. The Right, he suggests, even enjoys the non-win culture issues such as prayer in the schools because they maintain the image that the conservatives are underdogs, the oppressed victims of the Left. These "backlash" authors channel readers' anger against a constructed "intellectual elite" to divert attention from the very conservative economic policies that have caused such damage to the readers' lives and brought about their anger. A "decadent" liberal culture is invented as the oppressor.

But whether they are being deliberately manipulative or not, authors such as Limbaugh (*See I Told You So,* 80–81) and Hannity (*Deliver Us from Evil,* 61; *Let Freedom Ring,* 137) state that liberals/Democrats are nihilistic and atheistic and that they thus reject absolute truth of any kind. Ann Coulter's infamous response to 9/11 got her fired from *National Review Online,* but it helped promote her book sales, and she repeats it whenever she can: "For reasons I cannot understand, I am often asked if I still think we should invade their [Muslim] countries, kill their leaders, and convert them to Christianity. The answer is: Now more than ever!" (*How to Talk to a Liberal (if You Must),* 37). She explains,

> The fundamental difference between liberals and conservatives is: Conservatives believe man was created in God's image; liberals believe they *are* God. All their other behavioral tics proceed from this one irreducible minimum. Liberals believe they can murder the unborn because they are gods. They try to forcibly create "equality" through affirmative action and wealth redistribution because they are gods. They can lie, with no higher power to constrain them, because they are gods. They adore pornography and the mechanization of sex because man is just an animal, and they are gods. They revere the U.N. and not the U.S. because they aren't Americans—they are gods. . . . The left's anti-

Americanism is intrinsic to their entire worldview. Liberals promote the rights of Islamic fanatics for the same reason they promote the rights of adulterers, pornographers, abortionists, criminals, and Communists. They instinctively root for anarchy and against civilization. The inevitable logic of the liberal position is to be for treason. (*Treason*, 292)

Coulter may be the most paranoid about the evil surrounding her—and her rhetoric is only slightly less inflated, if a good deal more highbrow, than Savage's (or Moore's, for that matter)—but her themes can be found in most of the conservative books.

The bestselling books from the Left examine religion differently. They analyze George Bush's fundamentalist religiosity in great detail, but no one claims that his faith is "wrong"—one-sided, myopic, and occasionally frightening in a Commander-in-Chief, yes, but not wrong per se. They also repeatedly point out, in response to the claim of "de-Christianizing," that Americans overwhelmingly believe in God (95 percent)—and a Christian God at that (over 80 percent)—and that many leading figures of the Right lead lives in stark contrast to their own stated moral mandates (multiple divorces, illegitimate children, deadbeat dads, drug and gambling addictions, shady financial dealings, lack of Christian compassion, and so on). These charges are ignored in the conservative works.

There is also a difference in tone between the books from the Left and those from the Right. The Right, convinced of its rightness, tends to punch first (with roundhouse hooks) and only rarely questions its position. Of all the conservative authors under consideration, only Bill O'Reilly admits that he "could be wrong" (*Who's Looking Out for You?* 6), though, to be sure, one gets the impression that he considers the chances of this to be small—small as Bill Clinton's moral IQ. The Left, on the other hand, fairly certain of its correctness—and absolutely certain that Bush is wrong—has primarily limited itself to counter-punching with nerdy jabs. Contrast the evangelistic titles of books from the Right with the schoolyard taunts from the Left:

Right	Left
Treason: Liberal Treachery from the Cold War to the War on Terrorism	*Bushwhacked: Life in George W. Bush's America*
The Enemy Within: Saving America from the Liberal Assault on Our Schools, Faith, and Military	*Stupid White Men . . . and Other Sorry Excuses for the State of the Nation!*
Deliver Us from Evil: Defeating Terrorism, Despotism, and Liberalism	*Rush Limbaugh Is a Big Fat Idiot and Other Observations* *Bushworld: Enter at Your Own Risk*
An End to Evil: How to Win the War on Terror	
A Matter of Character	*Lies and the Lying Liars Who Tell Them: A Fair and Balanced Look at the Right*
The Way Things Ought to Be	
Let Freedom Ring: Winning the War of Liberty over Liberalism	

The two sides have very different tactics, as Al Franken admits:

> No, turning the public arena into a wasteland of personal destruction takes an entire army of like-minded ideologues hell-bent on shredding the already tattered standards of decency that once permitted reasonable discourse on matters of import. The left, sadly, has no such army. Our attack dogs are a scrawny, underfed pack of mutts that spend half the time chasing their own tails and sniffing each other's butts. The right, by contrast, appears to have a well-oiled puppy mill for pit bulls, bred to kill and trained to go for the jugular. Or the balls. (*Lies and the Lying Liars Who Tell Them,* 133)

Some of the books from the Left are actually funny—such as some of Franken's satires and *America (The Book)*—but there is no equivalent from the Right. The conservative authors make snippy jokes, but mostly they are consumed by the epic seriousness of the battles they believe America faces. (Libertarian/conservative humorist P. J. O'Rourke, who would be an exception to this rule, has had four collections of essays make it into *USA TODAY*'s weekly top 150 for several weeks at a time, but not since 2001, and none have appeared on a *Publishers Weekly* annual list since 1991.) The books are filled with apocalyptic language: "If we fail to reform, the consequences will be incalculable." "Civilization is in the balance." "Taken all in all, it could be said that we have reached the crisis point." "Why this book now? Because the hour is getting late." Though one would expect such dire pronouncements to refer to terrorism, Iraq, or Al-Qaeda, only one does. All of them, however, are concerned with perceived evil of one sort or another and the impending demise of America as we know it.

The political nonfiction books, then, especially those from the Right, follow the pattern of the bestselling novels examined in the first part of this chapter. Good is defined broadly—everything *we* believe in—and evil is subsequently limited to raving terrorists and their liberal chums. False empathy techniques are employed to make the other side seem utterly destructive and insane. This is a comforting, containable presentation of evil: *they* are evildoers, and they are nuts.

Although many of the books from the Right rely on a fundamentalist Christian paradigm for their discussion, rarely is evil described as it is in traditional religious language—as something within human nature, which is a much more disturbing vision with a long Western pedigree that goes back through Augustine to the ancient Greeks. Instead, evil in these books is primarily external and cultural; not even does Michael Savage's *The Evil Within* refer to the obvious.

External evil of this ilk does not require the sensitivity or compassion that many religions—and Jesus himself—direct to those struggling with universal human weaknesses. Empathy, not just for "sinners" but also for those who disagree with one's definition of "sin," is completely absent from the political books. The authors make no attempt to examine issues from the other side or view life through another's eyes.

Left and Right alike display a lack of empathy, almost a pride in rejecting the other side without consideration. The two-party system has always engendered spirited and heated conflict, but esteemed representatives of the past often gave at least lip service to the folks across the aisle. Even Newt Gingrich, whom Bush-cheerleader Ronald Kessler blames for the nasty tone of politics in Washington (*A Matter of Character*, 114), claimed that he had some Democratic friends (*To Renew America*, 125) and that Franklin Delano Roosevelt was probably the "greatest president of the twentieth century" (36). He certainly felt that liberals were grossly misdirected and woefully inadequate and, as Bill Clinton observes, that "his *values* were better than ours" (*My Life*, 635)—but the point is that he did *not* feel the need a dozen years ago to write that all Democrats sided with Satan. The most any recent conservative author is willing to concede is that long-dead Bobby Kennedy is Bill O'Reilly's hero (*Who's Looking Out For You?* 69).

To think a reader could already long for the "civil" days of Gingrich and Clinton. Is there no hope for our idiot nation of hate-filled soul vampires?

YES, THERE IS

Luckily, bestselling books *are* written about politics, and even the war in Iraq, from a more objective point of view. Although Bob Woodward writes now as a well-heeled insider, his *Bush at War* and *Plan of Attack* let readers form their own opinions for the most part. However, his third book on Bush and the war in Iraq, *State of Denial* (#10 nonfiction in 2006), is more critical of Bush and his administration—is this because Woodward has more information now and has revised his opinions, or because the war has gone so badly that he wants to cover his heinie? One of the most illuminating studies in the bestselling list is *The Rise of the Vulcans* by James Mann, a book that recounts in fascinating detail the formative experiences and dominant philosophy of Bush's war cabinet. He remains relatively neutral, concluding that both sides in the debate about the war in Iraq were right and wrong in serious ways. Charles Lewis's *The Buying of the President 2004: Who's Really Bankrolling Bush and His Democratic Challengers—and What They Expect in Return* takes on the whole system of American elections, a "rigged game" that all candidates play, even if Bush has taken the greatest advantage of it.

All the President's Spin: George W. Bush, the Media, and the Truth comes to us from the founders of Spinsanity.com, a nonpartisan website devoted to debunking all varieties of political spin. The book offers detailed analyses of *how* the White House uses political doublespeak and public relations techniques to further its agenda: "Bush has gone well beyond the stereotypical 'spin' of emphasizing one side of an issue while downplaying another. Instead, he has built his sales campaigns around blatantly misleading factual claims and insinuations. However, because those claims usually rest on some slender foundation of truth, Bush and his aides have frequently avoided scrutiny of their tactics by the press" (Fritz, Keefer, and Nyhan, 238). Though this particular book is focused on George W., the website shreds the claims of political spinners from all sides, including John Kerry and Michael Moore. Unfortunately, the founders of the site closed up shop in January 2005, but their articles are still available at Spinsanity.com.

There are also partisan books that manage to focus on facts. Mostly. Molly Ivins and Lou Dubose present a devastating review of the White House policies, both domestic and foreign, in their *Bushwhacked: Life in George W. Bush's America*. They enlarge the picture by recounting the seedier side of Bush family politics in Texas and the failures of Governor Bush's policies there, the same kinds of policies now becoming law for the other forty-nine states. Kevin Phillips's *American Dynasty: Aristocracy, Fortune, and the Politics of Deceit in the House of Bush* is a masterly examination of the politics and personalities of America's "royal family." (Just a recommendation: go for *American Dynasty* over Kitty Kelley's *The Family: The Real Story of the Bush Dynasty*, a gossip-laden tome that attempts to cover the same material.) In *Losing America*, Democratic Senator Robert C. Byrd passionately defends the crucial role of Congress in American government, warning us about the dangerous and disturbing trend of presidents attempting to circumvent our legislative branch.

On the other side, Bill Sammon's *Misunderestimated: The President Battles Terrorism, John Kerry, and the Bush Haters* manages to criticize Democratic politics and the "leftist Press" without entirely demonizing them. And Bill O'Reilly—despite his egomaniacal blustering and incivility on his FOX News television program—does not always stick to party-line opinions in his books. Although he does hold conservative views on many topics, he also believes in global warming, and he makes good arguments for more fuel efficient cars, the monitoring of energy prices against collusion and gouging, the negotiation of discounted drug prices, and reasonable sex education in schools (*No Spin Zone*). He's against capital punishment and even admits that President Bush "is a child of privilege and brings a sense of entitlement to his job" and does not "get very upset about injustice in our society" (*Who's Looking Out for You?* 50).

Unfortunately, the sheer vociferousness of much of the Right can drown out arguments that are worthy of full consideration by thoughtful citizens on any side of the debate: the dangers of terrorism in general and of radical Islam in particular; the widespread display of sex and violence in the media; the corruption of public figures usually held sacrosanct by liberals (e.g., Jesse Jackson); the suppression of freedom of expression through political correctness; and the successes of tough American foreign policy (e.g., the Cold War) and some recent military intervention (e.g., Serbia-Croatia, Afghanistan).

EMPATHY NOW!

Out of all the bestsellers we reviewed, the most sobering book in the lot is not about environmental damage, or the collapse of American morals, or political corruption, or corporate control of just about everything, or missing WMDs, or even the threat of Islamists—but an account of the Bush Administration's indifference, indeed *hostility*, to differing opinions. In *The Price of Loyalty: George W. Bush, the White House, and the Education of Paul O'Neill*, Ron Suskind recounts the short tenure of budget hawk, corporate CEO, and long-time Republican Paul O'Neill as George W. Bush's first Secretary of the Treasury. O'Neill thought it irresponsible to build up a big federal debt through tax cuts without spending cuts— old-fashioned economic conservatism of the kind advocated by Peter G. Peterson in his bestselling *Running on Empty*. But "both preemptive war and deep tax cuts were proving to be ideologies that, as O'Neill often said, 'were impenetrable by facts'" (307).

> "The biggest difference between then [the Nixon adminis-
> tration, in which O'Neill worked] and now is that our group
> was mostly about evidence and analysis, and Karl, Dick,
> Karen, and the gang [of Bush advisors] seemed to be mostly
> about politics. It's a huge distinction." (169)
>
> [O'Neill says] "Loyalty and inquiry are inseparable to me,"
> and that may be where he and the President most fundamen-
> tally diverged. Bush demands a standard of loyalty—loyalty
> to an individual, no matter what—that O'Neill could never
> swallow. "That's a false kind of loyalty, loyalty to a person
> and whatever they say or do that's the opposite of real loy-
> alty, which is loyalty based on inquiry, and telling someone
> what you really think and feel—your best estimation of the
> truth instead of what they want to hear." (325–326)
>
> He felt, to the end, that it was his duty to ask hard ques-
> tions, even as he watched some in the administration construe
> that as a faintness of conviction or even disloyalty. (327)

O'Neill's faith in rational critique, self-examination, and "evidence and analysis" earned him a quick dismissal from an administration "impenetrable by facts." He wouldn't play along with an economic forum that was "just a lot of people reading from a script that says, 'I love the President.' Where, exactly, does that fit in the grand American ideal of free and honest inquiry?" (270). Where indeed.

Does it have to be this way in the wayward world of politics? As Doris Kearns Goodwin shows in her bestselling *Team of Rivals* (#15 fiction in 2005), Abraham Lincoln invited four of his political rivals— three of them, in fact, were fairly bitter opponents for the Republican nomination he had won—to form the heart of his cabinet. The result wasn't always pretty, but in the long run, Lincoln—and the country—benefited from having the best men in the position, regardless of their initial disagreements with (and lack of respect for) the President.

Today, however, dissent is rarely tolerated within the same political constituency, and agreement across party lines is almost nonexistent. Senator Byrd says that in Congress, "there is virtually no attempt to build consensus through the hard work of reaching across the aisle to find common ground. Real consultation does not exist" (*Losing America,* 21). And this seems to be how we Americans are treating each other as well. In how many of our communities is it assumed that everyone around us thinks exactly the same way? In how many of our communities is it acceptable to pass blanket judgments on the millions of constituents of the "other" political party?

The denial of the seriousness—or, in some cases, the very existence—of threats like Islamic terrorism or global warming is only possible in a vacuum. When we are so divided, so afraid, so unable to trust our leaders and media, we retreat to circles of the like-minded and hope for the best. We *want* to believe that we and our friends think the right things and that the other side is horribly wrong about absolutely everything. So it's no surprise that inflammatory political books are successful.

But in a complicated and dangerous world, we need action based on evidence and analysis. For that, we have to listen, even when we hear things we do not like. We need to see things from different perspectives. Empathy is not just a morally good thing in the abstract; it has practical consequences—it is a way of avoiding and even defeating evil. We can't dismiss the evil acts of terrorists, the fact that there are thousands who want to destroy us. But understanding the way they think would actually be helpful in reducing the danger. The neo-cons may be right that failed Muslim cultures hate us for who we are, for our very success. But Michael Scheuer may also be correct that they hate us as well for what we do—for our arrogance, our policies, our wars. To understand this we must understand them. It's a matter of self-preservation.

Listening is not the same as acquiescing. Hearing all sides before making up one's mind is not waffling. Changing one's opinion in light of new evidence is not weakness. Seeing things from another's perspective is not disloyalty, much less treason.

Empathy is not evil!

And lack of empathy is. We see in *Reading Lolita in Tehran* the misery enacted by a rigid and blind regime violently opposed to other perspectives. Why would we tolerate such a thing in our democracy? Nafisi explains of her favorite literature: "It is not accidental that the most unsympathetic characters . . . are those who are incapable of genuine dialogue with others. They rant. They lecture. They scold. This incapacity for true dialogue implies an incapacity for tolerance, self-reflection and empathy" (268–269). This describes all too eerily some of our most popular political commentators.

Unfortunately, many of these books allow (indeed, encourage) readers to submit to their frustration and fear—emotions all of us have these days—and so tune their internal radios to a single blaring voice that will exonerate their party, their policy, and their values and blast somebody else to smithereens.

The world can be a big, complicated, and scary place, especially since 9/11. And at times, everyone gets that nagging feeling that we are stuck in a world of spinners, where undistorted truth is harder to find than Ann Coulter's maternal instinct. Readers have turned, in both fiction and nonfiction, to tales of good and evil that reduce or even eliminate the need to disentangle conflicting perspectives. In fact, most of these books ignore or attempt to eradicate conflicting perspectives entirely. In formula fiction, such comforting escapism is understandable, even if extremely unlikely to lead to the irony and complexity of great literature. But there is something quite unsettling about the lack of reasoned argument, or any genuine effort to understand opposing points of view, or just plain tolerance of any difference, in the world of contemporary political analysis.

The year 2005 was quieter but no less divisive than the election year, with the two bestselling political books still representing the irascible edges of both the Right and the Left. The first section of Al Franken's *The Truth (with Jokes)* is even entitled "The Triumph of Evil," describing how the Bush team used "smears," "fears," and "queers" to win the second election. Frankly, Franken is less funny and more self-serving in this book. His revealing account of election-day jubilation—he and his staff anticipated a Kerry victory (why *do* American liberals so often seem to live in a fog of illusion?)—may go a long way toward explaining his bitter change of tone.

In *100 People Who Are Screwing Up America (and Al Franken Is #37)*, on the other hand, Bernard Goldberg makes a disingenuous attempt to appear fair and nonpartisan by including a handful (seven) of non-liberals in his list. All the usual suspects are rounded up here: Hollywood celebrities, wacky university professors, liberal columnists and politicians, feminists, rappers, activist judges, and tort lawyers. Every single human associated with the *New York Times* makes Goldberg's hall of shame. Or maybe it just seems that way. Typical of his bias (he's an expert on bias) is his discussion of "TV Schlockmeisters—News Division": "By now we all know about bias in the news and how destructive it has been to the credibility of network news divisions" (20). He berates Dan Rather, Dan Rather's producer, the president of CBS, the president of ABC news, and the president of NBC news. But nowhere does he mention FOX (on which he frequently appears), the only television news network with an explicitly (conservative) political agenda.

2006 was the year Iraq officially became a quagmire, producing retrospective books with bashful titles such as *The Greatest Story Ever Sold, Hubris,* and *Fiasco.* Conservatives, put off their international game by the mess in the Middle East, were still fighting the culture wars with another bestseller by Bill O'Reilly (*Culture Warrior*, #5), and a book by Ann Coulter (*Godless*, #15) that begins with the claim that "Liberalism is a comprehensive belief system denying the Christian belief in man's immortal soul" and then somehow manages to plummet downhill from there. With Republicans on the run after the midterm elections, we can expect renewed conservative attacks on Congress and liberal values as we head into the next presidential election. Hillary bashers, get ready for some exhilarating reading!

Yikes. Perhaps it *would* be better to give up and go out for tacos. Or maybe we can turn to the wisdom of another bestseller and ask ourselves that timeless question: what would Morrie do? We're pretty sure what Morrie would say, at least: We have a duty to try harder than we have been, a duty to think for ourselves, a duty not to listen to the loudest voices but the most reasoned ones. If we love what America stands for, and believe in a moral global community, we have a responsibility not to dismiss each other out of hand.

"Ignore the preachers of partisanship, Mitch," we can hear him say, twinkle in eye. "Let's send them off to *Jerry Springer* where they belong."

And while they're using their chairs to beat each other silly, we can use ours to sit and read some well-reasoned words from a different political perspective, trying a little harder—even when it makes us uncomfortable—to reach across that aisle.

HOPEFULLY EVER AFTER: LOVE, ROMANCE, AND RELATIONSHIPS

"Normal, healthy women yearn to be in love, married, and raising children with the man of their dreams."
The Proper Care & Feeding of Husbands by Dr. Laura Schlessinger, xxii

"But it has a happy ending?"
"Oh, yes," she said fervently. "It *has* to."
Romancing Mister Bridgerton by Julia Quinn, 370

We love to read about love. And sex. The most popular search term on Abebooks.com—"the world's largest online market-place for books"—is sex. Book titles containing the word "love" made it onto *USA TODAY*'s weekly lists of the 150 bestselling books more than 240 times in the last sixteen years. *The Starr Report* even climbed to the top of the weekly chart in 1998 when Monica Lewinsky's dress slipped out of the oval office and into public view. Such bestselling efforts as *What to Expect When You're Expecting*—which had labored in *USA TODAY*'s top 150 for 673 weeks up to the end of 2006 (the third edition alone was #6 and #11 in trade paperbacks in 2002 and

2003, respectively)—would have been stillborn without love, or at least sex. The Kama Sutra still sells well. John Gray's *Men Are from Mars, Women Are from Venus* was the ninth bestselling book of the 1993–2003 decade—among *all* books. In fact, without Harry Potter's magic, Gray's "practical guide" to relationships would have outsold all but three other books. His website claims that the Mars and Venus books have sold over thirty million copies, which is almost enough for one book for every person in California.

But that's just the nonfictional tip of the volcano. Few works of fiction can avoid the complications of romance, and we are frequently disappointed when they do. Even gawky Harry Potter—much to the dismay of several ten-year-olds we know—couldn't avoid the entanglements of a femme fatale in his epic struggle against evil. Dan Brown was not the first, although he certainly has been the most successful, to exchange a mellow, prudish Christ for a hot and sexy Jesus.

And according to industry statistics from the Romance Writers of America, romance fiction is the bestselling genre in the United States. Glance at these numbers from 2004: Romance fiction made up over half (54.9 percent) of all popular paperback fiction sold in North America—and almost 40 percent of *all* popular fiction sold! Almost sixty-five million Americans read romance novels—up from forty-one million in just the past seven years.

What accounts for so much interest in relationships and the amorous arts? Are we a nation in emotional crisis? Are Americans erotically challenged? Judging from the books we read, three things are clear: we are not pleased with our relationships, we feel that we deserve to be, and the "we" here refers almost exclusively to women. Although men *may* be just as dissatisfied (we can't tell), we find that it is women who turn to books, both nonfiction and fiction, for answers and solace.

Here we explore the nature of the answers they are seeking—or at least receiving—by investigating some of the most popular books about love, sex, and relationships published in recent years. It bears repeating, however, that we make no claims of being comprehensive. We haven't included *Dating for Dummies* or pondered the metaphysical implications found in such reflections as *If Buddha Dated* (although we *have* wondered, if one hand is clapping, what is the other hand doing?). We're not going to discuss *How to Get Laid Today! The System,* even though one Amazon reviewer insists that after a single reading he gained "a complete understanding of what I am to do when dealing with women." The truth be told, books explicitly about sex—the whats, hows, dos, and don'ts—weren't as popular in the 1990s and early part of the twenty-first century as they had been in the previous decades. They disappeared completely off the lists after *How to Satisfy a Woman Every Time* and Madonna's *Sex* in 1992 (#3 and #10, respectively, in hardcover nonfiction). Perhaps the craving for a sensuous man (and woman), the protean G-spot, and the hour-long orgasm have been rendered obsolete by the increasing availability of all things sexual, especially on the Internet. (At last count—by those who count such things—there may be as many as 1.6 million pornographic websites, which generate over two billion—with a "b"—dollars. Holy webcam, Batman!)

And by no means have we read all of the popular romance novels. Considering that just three months of *USA TODAY* bestseller lists can yield sixty distinct romance authors, attempting to keep up would be a Sisyphean task. Instead, we highlight in this chapter only a handful of the bestselling authors in selected romance "subgenres." We also, by necessity, do not discuss the romantic elements in other types of popular fiction (which would include just about every book on the list). Instead, we concentrate on those works thematically focused on love and relationships—the romance novels, of course, but also a few literary bestsellers.

Space Hoppin' and Trash Talkin'

> A woman would do well to understand that an honest, faithful husband who goes on a three-week hunting trip is not telling her he doesn't love her. He just wants to kill something. Nothing more complicated than that.
>
> —quoted in The *Care & Feeding of Husbands* by Dr. Laura Schlessinger, 171

We begin our study by looking at several of the bestselling nonfiction handbooks on relationships. What do we think is wrong with our love lives? What do we believe we can do to fix things? What is a good relationship? What do we want? And more particularly, who *is* this person in my house, and why does he or she make everything so difficult?

These are knotty, age-old questions. But luckily, various relationship gurus—usually celebrity PhDs or talk-show therapists (or both)—have made bestselling efforts to answer them. We review some of the most prominent of the recent past, focusing on *Men Are from Mars, Women Are from Venus* by John Gray, *The Proper Care & Feeding of Husbands* by Dr. Laura (Laura Schlessinger), and *Relationship Rescue* by Dr. Phil (Phillip McGraw).

No one in the past sixteen years has been more popular in addressing Americans' relationship woes than John Gray, creator of the Mars and Venus franchise. The ninth bestselling book from 1993 to 2003 was his *Men Are from Mars, Women Are from Venus: A Practical Guide for Improving Communication and Getting What You Want in Your Relationships*. Originally published in 1992, it was in the *Publishers Weekly* top-fifteen nonfiction list for five straight years (1993–1997) and has spawned the requisite (if impressively comprehensive) brood of companions for all the stages of relationship pathologies: *Mars and Venus on a Date* kicks things off, followed by *Mars and Venus in the*

Bedroom, which may or may not come before either *Mars and Venus in Love* or *Mars and Venus in the Workplace.* In any case, with enough reading we will eventually make it to *Mars and Venus Together Forever.* Or, should age and calories creep up on us and threaten our interplanetary union, we can turn to *The Mars and Venus Diet and Exercise Solution.* And if all these books fail, well, there's still *Mars and Venus Starting Over: A Practical Guide for Finding Love Again After a Painful Breakup, Divorce, or the Loss of a Loved One.* It's one-stop shopping for the emotionally bewildered. You can meet, have sex, get married, raise kids, and get fat and happy and then slim and divorced all under one roof! And now you can even play the CD-ROM home-game version, while Venus serves her Mars a Super Food Shake for Men fresh from the dietary-supplement division of the franchise.

Gray's popular thesis is quite simple—men and women are so different in every way that they might as well be different species:

> *Men Are from Mars, Women Are from Venus* is a manual for loving relationships in the 1990s. It reveals how men and women differ in all areas of their lives. Not only do men and women communicate differently but they think, feel, perceive, react, respond, love, need, and appreciate differently. They almost seem to be from different planets, speaking different languages and needing different nourishment. (5)

Rule number one, then, is quite clear: never (and this means never ever) assume for a minute that your heterosexual partner is at all like you. (Partners from the same planet don't seem to exist in Gray's galaxy. Perhaps *Mars and Mars at the Mall* or *Venuses in Vests* will someday join their more conventional bestselling pals—although the idea that same-sex couples, or even same-sex friends or relatives, could have communication problems would sort of destroy Gray's entire thesis.) The key to a successful relationship is to realize these differences, accept them, and learn to negotiate around them. The book is filled with lists of these differences as well as ways we should and absolutely should not—but probably do—respond to the behavior of the opposite sex.

More on these responses in a moment. But first it is important to note the comforting metaphorical hook on which Gray's scheme is hung. Imagine, he suggests, that creatures from one culture (let's say they're from Mars) meet an entirely different species (who, for argument's sake, turn out to be from Venus). And they like each other for their, er, differences:

> Their differences especially attracted the Martians. Where the Martians were hard, the Venusians were soft. Where the Martians were angular, the Venusians were round. Where the Martians were cool, the Venusians were warm. In a magical and perfect way their differences seemed to complement each other. (44)

This magical joining of opposites would not happen easily, though. The species would quite naturally behave completely differently and would need to learn to communicate. As they mastered translation, both linguistic and behavioral, they would have to keep in mind the significant differences between the races. Difference would be maintained, even celebrated: we'd have two creatures living together in harmony, mighty popsicle-men with their cookie-dough gal-pals.

But what would happen if, after many generations, the two species forgot that they were fundamentally different and began to believe that there was a genuine common ground, some sort of universal (we won't say "human," given that no one in this scenario is from Earth) basis for a relationship? Why, it would be chaos! And a familiar chaos, too—one that resembles the state of relationships at the turn of this millennium. The solution, then, is to get back to our differences, to understand them and learn to live with them through better communication. What we need—and what Gray has set out to provide—are the two essentials for compatible living: (1) a guide to those differences and (2) a codebook that translates the meaning of what one gender does, and especially says, into the language of the other gender, so that both can interpret the unfamiliar words and behaviors being displayed and respond in a manner that best leads to "getting what they want" in the relationship.

Gray's program is based on a broad, familiar, immutable portrait of men and women and what they want. Martians (men) are problem solvers whose goal-oriented characters drive them on a constant search for proof of their competence and autonomy. Venusians (women) have relationship-oriented natures that make them want to talk in loving cooperation and to give advice at all times. A Venusian is "not immediately concerned with finding solutions to her problems but rather seeks relief by expressing herself and being understood. By randomly talking about her problems, she becomes less upset" (36). That's right—by talking *randomly*.

Martians retreat (into their "caves") to work things out for themselves; Venusians need to share. Martians are motivated and "empowered when they feel needed," Venusians when they "feel cherished" (43). Men are like rubber bands, pulling away from intimacy and then getting close again, until they finally get so old and brittle they snap in half and must be thrown away in disgust. (Okay, we made up that last part.) Women are like waves, their self-esteem and thus their ability to give love rising and falling (into the "well") in a cycle that averages out to twenty-eight days, a number that Gray assures us is coincidental (121). Unlike women, "[men] don't read magazines like *Psychology Today, Self,* or *People*. They are more concerned with outdoor activities, like hunting, fishing, and racing cars" (16). You know, sometimes they just want to kill something.

Both species, however, are insecure and miserable without the approval or validation of the other. To get that all-important boost, women must stop giving any unsolicited advice or criticism whatsoever. They are never to try to alter or "fix" their favorite Martian: "The secret of empowering a man is never to try to change him or improve him" (145). "The four magic words to support a man are 'It's not your fault'" (88). Women are to let men go into their caves and come out when they wish. In the meantime, women can kill time with a variety of suggested distractions, such as shopping, listening to self-improvement tapes, or seeing a therapist (77).

Further, men need approval—all the time: "To approve of a man is to see the good reasons behind what he does. Even when he is irresponsible or lazy or disrespectful, if she loves him, a woman can find and recognize the goodness within him" (166). In other words, stand by your man. Sit by him too. Can't you see the goodness? Oh, sorry, that's just barbecue sauce.

What's with the Hugs?

For a long time there has been an epidemic of hugs in the self-help world. We thought it might have passed. But even Dr. Phil, whose "get real" world of *Life Strategies* and *Relationship Rescue* claims to take a revolutionary stance against current "pop-psyche nonsense," insists that "the hug is an unspeakably effective tool for healing" (*Relationship Rescue,* 222). One of the first excerpts in *Chicken Soup for the Soul* tells the story of the "hugging judge" who takes out his "Hugger Kit" and offers people a red embroidered heart sticker in exchange for a hug (12). (And to think that Americans' confidence in the judicial system is waning.) One of the *Chicken Soup* authors brags that they "always teach people to hug each other in [their] workshops and seminars" (16). Sign us up!

Men, for their part, must learn to listen and stop offering solutions. Women don't want them: "The last thing a woman needs when she is on her way down [the wave toward the well] is someone telling her why she shouldn't be down" (115). Instead, Martians should respond to their Venusians with poignant expressions such as "Humph, sounds like you had a hard day"; "Hmmn"; "Oh, no"; and "You are such a loving person. Come here, let me give you a hug" (23). Indeed, sympathetic grunts and hugs are a nostrum for Venusians in Gray's solar system.

Gray's initial advice sounds easy enough. Martians and Venusians are so dramatically different, however, that they can never tell just what the other is feeling or trying to say. We mistakenly believe we speak the same language, but in perhaps the most entertaining chapter ("Speaking Different Languages"), Gray provides a glossary (a "Venusian/Martian Phrase Dictionary") for interspecies translation.

The approach taken here to differences between male and female speech is not the subtle sociolinguistic kind of a Robin Lakoff or a Deborah Tannen (whose comparatively scholarly book on gendered conversation was #10 in hardcover nonfiction in 1991). Gray is not interested in exploring the relationship between power and language; he just wants us to get along. For example, when a Venusian says, "Everyone ignores me," a Martian might take this as an implied criticism, or instead casually reply, "I'm sure some people notice you." (We personally don't know anyone who would say that without intentional sarcasm, but this kind of bitterness does not exist in Gray's universe. In fact, we don't know anyone who speaks as lithologically as the leaden folks in Gray's examples, either before or after translation. His couples all sound as if they learned to speak by watching *Iron Chef*.)

Such a response—an effort to assuage her pain—would be very wrong, of course. A Venusian does not want counterevidence, much less a debate. She wants validation for her feelings:

"Everyone ignores me" translated into Martian means "Today, I am feeling ignored and unacknowledged. I feel as though nobody sees me. Of course I'm sure some people see me, but they don't seem to care about me. I suppose I am also disappointed that you have been so busy lately. I really do appreciate how hard you are working and sometimes I start to feel like I am not important to you. I am afraid your work is more important than me." (63)

Whoa! No wonder we need a Venusian glossary. What poor Martian could have seen that translation coming? But it turns out that after a bit of study, Venusian is not so hard. In fact, virtually every statement a woman makes can be reduced to a single sentiment: "I know you love me, but I'm feeling insecure: would you give me a hug and tell me how special I am to you?" Well, okay, maybe she also wants him to take out the trash. But implied in just about *every* Venusian comment in this book is a request for a hug and an affirmation of love.

Though communication is everything for Gray, he is not so naïve as to deny that there are times when talking just isn't beneficial. But he is true to his theme even then, for when speaking doesn't do the trick, there's always the "Love Letter." This is no ordinary love letter, to be sure, but a scripted articulation (lots of sample letters are provided as models) of frustrations. This epistle is not merely for venting, but for sharing and evoking an appropriate and salutary response. Indeed, part of the exercise is to write that response yourself! (Little can be left to chance in the tricky galaxy of love.) The Love Letter involves a carefully integrated expression of your feelings of anger, sadness, fear, regret, and love (each must have its own paragraph), along with a Response Letter expressing what you want to hear from your partner. Gray recommends but does not *insist* that you share your Love Letter and Response Letter with your partner (apparently, sometimes communication can be so valuable that sharing with one-self is healing enough).

One of the most distinctive things about Gray's approach is that the goal of a relationship is to learn to coexist in some kind of zoological harmony, like animals on the African savannah accepting their places in the food chain. Nary a word can be discovered here about finding or rekindling some sort of passionate intensity. The assumption, apparently shared by millions of readers, is that couples would be foolish to expect genuine emotional connection. And it's not hard to see why, when men and women are assumed to be so categorically different. There is simply nothing intense in the entire book; even the arguments between spouses feel staged. (Unsurprisingly, Gray specifically forbids couples to argue in any fashion, 150–151.) Another self-help book noted this peculiarity in its title (while at the same time trying to cash in on the branding and the magic number): *The Seven Steps to Passionate Love: Why Men Are Not from Mars and Women Are Not from Venus.*

A recent bestseller by Laura Schlessinger, *The Proper Care & Feeding of Husbands* (#13 hardcover nonfiction in 2004) is all for passion too. Schlessinger, the author of numerous other bestsellers (including #97 for 1993–2003, *Ten Stupid Things Women Do to Mess Up Their Lives*), brings many of the same premises about men and women, as well as the same simplicity of explication, to her examination of failing marriages. But Schlessinger rejects half of Gray's thesis: it's not about Martians and Venusians. It's about Venusians. Lousy marriages are almost always the woman's fault—so often, in fact, that she promises us there will never be a need for *The Proper Care & Feeding of Wives.* Women need to change the way they treat their husbands, pronto. Conduct counts.

For Gray, whose approach to relationships derives in great part from trends in the social sciences and marketing, the problem is not the behavior itself, but our interpretation of it. *Men Are from Mars, Women Are from*

Venus is, as the subtitle promises, a guide for "improving communication." Martians and Venusians learn "how relationships could work better by creating or changing a few simple phrases" (84). Behavior is not "bad" or "wrong," just different. Human character is not the problem; words are: people don't kill marriages; alien languages do. (We could find only one occasion—on page 196—when any form of what Gray considers natural, gender-specific behavior is chastised, with the less-than-stern phrase "not really fair.") Men are not really insensitive dolts; women are not actually manipulative nags. We just don't understand each other.

To Schlessinger, however, behavior is everything. The responsibility for dead marriages can be squarely placed on the shoulders of nagging, frumpy, emasculating wives:

> Most of the women who complain that they are not getting what they want from their husbands should stop and look at how disrespectful and disdainful they are of them. (xvi)
>
> The main source of husbands' bad attitudes, negative responses, and disappointing behaviors is their wives' attitude toward them and *their* feelings. Plain and simple. (68)
>
> But how can husbands *feel* respected, appreciated, or loved when they are the constant brunt of their wives' negativity about everything? (73)

The solution, then, is just as straightforward. If women want good relationships, then they had better start acting right:

> Remember, men are simple creatures and very dependent upon their wives for acceptance, approval, and affection. When those 3 A's are restored, all is well in their world. (30)
>
> And your basic male is a decent creature with simple desires: to be his wife's hero, to be his wife's dream lover, to be the

protector and provider for his family, to be respected, admired, and appreciated. Men live to make their women happy. (64)

It's worth repeating that men yearn for, first, their mothers' acceptance, approval, and appreciation, and then their wives', and when they get those three A's, they'll do just about anything to please their wives. (174)

The problems with communication are a symptom, not a cause, in Schlessinger's analysis of marital problems. True, men are not as forthcoming with their feelings as women, who "desire to talk endlessly about 'what happened'" (66–67). But so what? Too many women, she thinks, seem to have bought into something like Gray's visions: they expect their husbands "to show interest, agree, and remain uncritical and unchallenging" (94). Men *do* want to solve problems, but according to Schlessinger, they must be allowed to solve them. Alone. Women have been turning their husbands into mere listening boards—"girlfriends or shrinks"—leaving men "cuddly teddy bears" rather than "white knights" (155).

Yet as different as their tones and recommendations may be, both books appeal to a surprisingly old-fashioned view of how men and women should relate. Despite a title that resonates a certain new-age hipness, Gray's approach differs only slightly from Schlessinger's overtly conservative agenda. His unstated but obvious assumption is that there is natural (perhaps evolutionary?) behavior to be expected from men and women. It is eternal—culture's only role has been to mess up the naturally correct dynamics. The modern world has forgotten that men are the hunters and women the gatherers, and both have tried to patch over their completely alien natures with disastrous results. Gray doesn't point any fingers—time and history are the culprits—but Schlessinger does not hesitate to give one to the villain in her scenario, the "ugly part of the feminist movement" (20) that has led to the "denigration of female and male roles in families, as well as the loss of family functioning as a result of divorce, day care, dual careers, and the glorification of shacking up and unwed motherhood by choice" (3). To Schlessinger, working women are a symptom of the success of a feminist agenda, a part of a larger attack on traditional values that has led to the current marital crisis:

> Why did notions like assuaging "male ego" and using "feminine wiles" rocket into disrepute? How is it that so many women are angry with men in general yet expect to have a happy life married to one of them? There are a number of reasons for this, and I believe they all revolve around the assault upon, and virtual collapse of, the values of religious morality, modesty, fidelity, chastity, respect for life, and a commitment to family and child rearing. With a religious foundation, both women and men appreciate that they become more complete when bonded to the opposite sex in holy matrimony. (52)

Nothing could be further from Gray's nurturing, nonjudgmental tone, his Navajo White sense of style. But beneath the surface, both Gray and Schlessinger see a disastrous devolution in the definition of the sexes. The modern world does not understand or appreciate, much less support, the distinctly different "temperaments, needs, attitudes, physiology, or psychology" of men and women; we live in a false "unisex world" (Schlessinger, 27). Women and men have unique, instinctive urges. Gray has entire lists of our differences, but they boil down to Schlessinger's insistence on the familiar clash between the bonding, nesting, nurturing female and the protecting, providing, conquering male.

Schlessinger and Gray even use the same metaphor to describe the way a man approaches the world and his relationship with the woman he loves:

A man needs to feel strong and needed as a protector for women—basically, to conquer the beast and rescue the fair maiden. . . . The man should be the major breadwinner in the family. Every man needs a battle or war to win to prove to himself that he is strong and capable of conquering any and all dragons that life throws his way. Taking care of his family by working and providing are his battles. (Schlessinger, 76–77)

Gray tells a parable about a knight in shining armor who saves his princess from a series of nasty dragons (138–140). He slays the first dragon on his own, but during each successive battle, his princess offers helpful advice on how to kill the beast. Although this assistance is essential for his survival, the knight grows increasingly confused, depressed, and dissatisfied with both his critter-slaying and his lover. What's the point if he can't do it himself? Finally, he goes back to his original (pre-princess) method of dispatching dragons and abandons his princess for a new town and bride, "after making sure his new partner knew nothing" about dragon-fighting (140).

It's a simple tale with a simple moral for all wannabe princesses: "Remembering that within every man is a knight in shining armor is a powerful metaphor to help you remember a man's primary needs. Although a man may appreciate caring and assistance sometimes, too much of it will lessen his confidence or turn him off" (140). The caring wife is in a bit of a bind: she must not criticize, attempt to improve, or give life-saving advice to her partner. Better to have a dead knight than a demoralized one.

Even Dr. Phil (Phillip McGraw), whose bestselling *Relationship Rescue* (#7 nonfiction in 2000) unhesitatingly rejects the "love letter" approach of "psycho-babbling" therapists, bases his "seven-step strategy for reconnecting with your partner" on the impossibility of true compatibility with an inherently alien spouse, stating, "We could talk forever about the differences between men and women" (263). The number one myth swallowed by struggling couples is that they should be more alike: "It's a crock" (48). In Dr. Phil's world, God designed men to be strong and logical, women to be irrational and nurturing. That is the "natural order." In God's master plan, differences simply need to be "managed":

> I am embarrassed to confess to you how many years I spent being frustrated with my wife, judging and resisting her for doing exactly what God designed her to do. God didn't design us to be the same; he designed us to be different. . . God gave men less of those qualities [e.g., intuition, sensitivity] and more of certain other qualities such as logic and physical strength, because he determined that those characteristics would lend themselves well to certain jobs that he contemplated for the males in society . . . She [McGraw's wife] does not have to be as linear and logical in her thinking as I am. (261–263)

(A side note: There seems to be a redefinition of "logic" going around in these books. We've been assured by both Gray and McGraw that men are rational and women are not, yet the examples provided have nothing to do with the reasoning abilities of either gender, but their differing values and priorities. That's not to say that women can't be illogical. It's just that men who would rather be lost for seven hours than ask for directions are probably not being logical either. Anyone who bases decisions on emotions—including, yes, the desire to appear powerful or manly—is by definition irrational. We find it interesting that the concept of "logic" is so linked to the idea of masculinity that the authors don't even recognize that their own impulses are emotional processes, as divorced from reason as the supposed female obsession with trash collection and hugging.)

Dr. Phil even shares Gray's spelunking by admitting to his own "caveman mentality" (296), although he has the modern sensitivity to drag his wife inside his bunker along with him. As he tells her, "you were attracted to me because, among other things, I made you feel safe and secure, I protected you and protected our cave" (262). Given such premises, it is not surprising that the best hope he can offer men and women of any true meeting of the minds is expressed with double negatives: "Please understand: I'm not telling you that two people of the opposite sex should not try to be compatible" (50).

Clearly these authors are reacting to something, responding to a cultural movement that rejects gender distinctions, or one that encourages each gender to incorporate the characteristics of the other. Gray doesn't specify his adversaries, and McGraw rather blandly accuses most marriage counselors, but Schlessinger doesn't hesitate: "that part of the feminist movement that dismisses marriage, child rearing, and home-making as insignificant and insulting to women" leads directly to the evils of "promiscuity, shacking up, abortions, illegitimacy, rush-hour traffic, and office politics" (169). Women in Schlessinger's Manichaean world face devilish choices: Marriage or promiscuity? Child rearing or abortion? Homemaking or rush-hour traffic?

Dr. Laura's hysteria is amusing—and puzzling. (Even conservative author Bill O'Reilly challenged her insistence that mothers not work—O'Reilly relies on the talented women who run his "No Spin Zone.") Perhaps she is reacting to the silly extremes of some academic feminism and the social sciences that insist that all gender is "constructed" for the convenience of those (males) in power, that a drunken, one-night fling between consenting co-eds is literally a crime, and that sexual intercourse even between married partners is tantamount to rape. But such views sway such a tiny share of the American population as to be insignificant. Alternative, more liberal (i.e., post-1960s) philosophies with a less rigid view of gender or marital dynamics did not make it into bestselling lists in recent years. Even less serious love-related bestsellers were conservative, such as the water-cooler darling *The Rules: Time-Tested Secrets for Capturing the Heart of Mr. Right.* There is an overt longing here for a time when men were men and women were women, and we all knew who was what. How much better were things in, say, 1876, when T. L. Haines and L.W. Yaggy could write in *The Royal Path of Life*—without fear of contradiction from feminazis (heck, those days were so good that there weren't *any* kind of Nazis then!)—the following?

> Man is bold—woman is beautiful. Man is courageous— woman is timid. Man labors in the field—woman at home. Man talks to persuade; woman to please. Man has a daring heart; woman a tender loving one. Man has power; woman has mercy. Man has strength; woman love. While man combats with the enemy, struggles with the world, Woman is waiting to prepare his repast and sweeten his existence. (14)

There's that rational white knight again, with the little princess cookin' up some dragon steaks in the castle.

Could this reactionary angst be a response to nothing more than women working outside the home? If so, the remarkable success of these books could reveal an American reading public decidedly unhappy with the shifts in roles of men and women over the past half-century. No doubt, there is a great crossover between Schlessinger's radio audience (which airs on 300 stations to an estimated twelve million listeners) and her book buyers. But Gray did not have such a large built-in audience when his book became popular, so his readership was attracted by the themes of his advice. The message that men and women must get back to their "traditional" roles is clearly resonating with enough Americans to produce excellent book sales.

On the other hand, the bestsellers could reveal a married public so indeterminately discontent that they are willing, in their search for a quick relationship fix, to read the advice of those who are unhappy with the post-1960s cultural shifts. Perhaps these books, so diligently trying to rescue relationships from modernity, are the final resting place of the fading "Men's Movement," the last residue of Robert Bly's bestselling and grim *Iron John* (#1 hardcover fiction in 1991), the death throes of the Promise Keepers' failing promise.

Personally, we cannot figure out why, if men and women are so different, they would even want to marry in the first place—or do much of anything together, for that matter. "To have children, you yahoos!" we hear you shout. But these books are not about parenting, or becoming better moms and dads; they claim to be advice to couples on how to get closer. Yet the ideal relationships depicted in these books are like business partnerships, with each person performing certain (distinct) duties that contribute to the smooth functioning of a household. John Gray says there is love, and Dr. Laura says there is passion, but whence do they spring? Learning to avoid frivolous arguments and admiring someone's differences are excellent bits of advice to war-torn spouses, but do Americans really believe that marital love is ideally limited to the appreciation of the useful tasks one's partner can accomplish?

Indeed, these books presume most conversations, arguments, and troubles between modern couples still involve getting the man to perform basic household chores. Why don't they ever fight about money or sex or the in-laws or how to raise their children or the toilet seat like real couples do? Gray assumes men don't do much around the house. Time and again, the examples in his book are based on a woman asking questions like these: Would you pick up the kids? Would you bring in the groceries? Would you clean up the backyard? Would you bring in the mail? Would you take us out to eat tonight?

Do wives in America really have to ask their husbands to take the family out to dinner?

And, of course, there is the most daunting, oft-requested task of all: Would you empty the trash? (If they had just read *Don't Sweat the Small Stuff,* their problems would have been solved. Lesson 40, titled "When in doubt about whose turn it is to take out the trash, go ahead and take it out," informs us that "making things like garbage less relevant in your life will undoubtedly free up more time and energy for truly important things" (104)—like hugging.)

Schlessinger, on the other hand, agrees with Henry Higgins that men (excepting the odd sociopath here and there) are "on the whole, a marvelous sex":

> These men are involved in family activities and outings, and work around the house on the weekends and evenings when needed. They cook, do dishes, fix the cars, repair the house, mow the lawn, trim the hedges, go to kids' sporting events and school functions, drive kids to and from their activities and school, stop off at the market on the way home, even "baby-sit" the kids when the wife wants to go off to shop, eat lunch out with her mother or girlfriends, or go to aerobics. (175)

Dr. Phil doesn't glorify either sex; his "Get Real" branding insists from beginning to end that his reader accept responsibility and accountability for what might be wrong with the relationship. He does, however, agree with Gray and Schlessinger about the dangers of complaining—though he's gender-neutral on the issue. To promote a partner's self-esteem, both husband *and* wife must resist "even justified criticisms" (125–127). So convinced is he that God chooses a mate for each of us—as part of His "overall plan for our lives"—that Dr. Phil does "not believe that you can reject and criticize your mate and at the same time accept God and his will for your life. By rejecting and criticizing your mate, you are basically saying, 'God, I know better than you'" (289–290). The concept that someone may have married her loser high school sweetheart before actually finding her divinely sanctioned husband does not seem to be a possibility.

Although these authors are avowedly, if not consistently, secular and therapeutic, they swim in the same cultural waters as the biblical flood of Christian books on divinely approved spousal behavior (what one Amazon reviewer has dubbed the "Stepford Wives for God" genre), such as *Liberated through Submission; The Excellent Wife (A Biblical Perspective); Finding the Hero in Your Husband: Surrendering the Way God Intended; Me? Obey Him? The Obedient Wife and God's Way of Happiness and Blessing in the Home;* and *Hearing the Master's Voice.* (We are reminded, without any intended blasphemy, of the parodic book *The Rules for Dogs: The Secret to Getting Free Treats for Life.*)

So everyone seems to be on the same wavelength. But how do we know that such arrangements will work?

As therapists, the authors do not need to prove any of their premises. These are not works of scholarship, but words of advice from people who make a living giving advice. The proof is in the pudding, but the pudding is the marriages improved by the authors. We don't know that the advice works, but the authors must convince a reader it does. So all of them rely heavily on anecdotes from their own experiences, surrounding readers with ecstatic testimony from the saved. In fact, so many miracles happen in these books that an unwary reader can be buried in the pile of discarded crutches: "Mein Führer, I can walk!"

Approximately a third of Schlessinger's short book is composed of personal stories from her radio talk-show listeners. Many stories are from traumatized men who responded to her request to reveal what they wanted from their marriages. Some are from unhappy wives;

some are from formerly unhappy wives who now (often with the help of God and/or Scripture and/or Dr. Schlessinger) have seen the light. In other words, Schlessinger espouses a view on the air that attracts a particular sort of individual (i.e., either "victim" or "survivor") who then tells her what is wrong with his or her marriage.

Gray is a seminar guy. His anecdotes—much less frequent and a good deal more stilted than Schlessinger's—are derived mainly from his seminars, an experience he promises "will be a cherished memory that you will never forget" (287). There are frequent references to these cherished events, as well as casual allusions to must-be-there moments like his lecture on the "secrets of great sex" (82), which we assume formed the basis for his subsequent *Mars and Venus in the Bedroom.* His wife, too, has taught him much about Venusians, and the anecdotes he tells about her certainly suggest that she is from a different planet. Somehow, though, he seems to be aware that his credibility needs bolstering. Statistics come to the rescue, statistics gathered in perhaps not the most scientifically objective of environments: "At least 90 percent of the more than 25,000 individuals questioned [in his seminars] have enthusiastically recognized themselves in these descriptions" (4).

And if this were not enough to convince the wary reader, there's always defensive blustering: "The truth of these principles is self-evident and can be validated by your own experience as well as by common sense" (5). As well as by book sales, one might add. With thirty million copies sold, someone or something (besides Gray's self-esteem) is being validated.

But what? Why are these the books Americans have turned to over the past decade for advice on relationships? They may be physically dissimilar brothers, but the DNA nevertheless proves their connections: a preference for celebrity authorities; simple analyses of problems; quick and relatively easy, comfortable fixes; and an appeal to our deepest preconceptions (and fears) about the roles of men and women. The multicolored messiness of real-life partnering is filtered through nature's (or God's) chromosomal prism to prove that only the ends of the spectrum actually exist: red versus blue; Mars versus Venus; male versus female. The differences between genders are exaggerated and caricatured to the point where surrender is the only reasonable response. Through this dualistic legerdemain, the complexities of a struggling relationship are reduced to uncomplicated problems of communication or behavior that are capable of correction within days with the proper therapeutic adjustment. If the few hours it takes to read his book don't cure the marriage, Gray notes that a weekend of intensive work should do the trick: "I have witnessed thousands of couples transform their relationships—some literally overnight. They come on Saturday of my weekend seminar and by dinnertime on Sunday they are in love again" (285). One of the more recent manifestations of Gray's franchise—the "Mars, Venus and Beyond" program—combines diet, exercise, and advice to bring about what the (numerically iconoclastic) subtitle promises will be a "9 Day Relationship Makeover."

Schlessinger's recipe for marital salvation is equally facile: "Give him direct communication, respect, appreciation, food, and good lovin', and he'll do just about anything you wish—foolish or not" (xvii). After trying just one of the hints in her book for five days, miracles occur: "*The Proper Care & Feeding of Husbands* has salvaged and revitalized innumerable strained, stagnant, boring, disappointing, annoying, frustrating, and even seemingly dead marriages" (xi). This is a truly remarkable claim, especially coming from the first hardback edition.

Though *Relationship Rescue* possesses many of the same characteristics, refreshingly—and self-consciously—Dr. Phil promises his shipwrecked readers no weekend lifeboat. He takes great pains to remind us of the great pains his program will evoke, drilling into us at every turn how "tough" the work will be, telling us that we will have to take "substantial risks" and that it is going to "be hard" and make us at times "feel uncomfortable." It's a demanding regimen: the reader will have to take tests, conduct personality profiles, fill out "partner awareness" quizzes, keep a journal, memorize formulas, and participate in a two-week "reconnection" program that requires half an hour each day of concentrated effort.

Perhaps most challenging of all, to salvage a sinking marriage, one may have to read an entire book—a particularly ambitious requirement for men. Even though his recovery program is gender-neutral, Dr. Phil assumes his book will be bought by wives and then thrust upon their husbands. At the end of *Relationship Rescue,* he jots a quick note "To My Men Readers," which begins with his confession, "I'm assuming that this letter is the first thing you're reading in this book" (298). John Gray also slyly reveals his audience early on: "[Men] are interested in the news, weather, and sports and couldn't care less about romance novels and self-help books" (16). And Dr. Laura, of course, is explicit about her intended audience. (And we think we know why: *Ten Stupid Things Men Do to Mess Up Their Lives* was on the *USA TODAY* list for sixteen weeks. The woman's version was there for 162.)

Not surprisingly, then, one of the more recent bestsellers in the genre, *He's Just Not That Into You: The No-Excuses Truth to Understanding Guys* (#7 hardcover nonfiction in 2004), is explicitly directed at women readers. Indeed, rarely has a book so blatantly sucked up to its readership. This funny guide, written partially by an editor (Liz Tuccillo) and mostly by a consultant (Greg Behrendt) on the wonderful HBO series *Sex and the City,* is the ultimate example of one paragraph of genuine insight milked for 165 additional pages. The premise is simple and basically valuable: if a guy consistently gives a girl excuses for not calling, writing, having sex, moving in, getting married (or not divorcing his current wife), going out, sobering up, or being nice, he's simply just not all that interested in the girl. Women need to stop accepting these excuses and waiting for their guys to change. Drop them and move on. Immediately.

Behrendt, a one-time jerkish bad boy himself but now a happily married family guy, writes with the monolithic conviction of the converted. *Every* excuse *any* guy gives to a girl is a lie—either deliberate or an attempt to avoid being honest and hurting her feelings—and each should be interpreted as a sign to find another guy at once. Tuccillo, on the other hand, ends each chapter with a section titled "Why This One Is Hard," a reality check on Behrendt's cloyingly Augustinian certainty. Guys are creeps, Behrendt insists, at least until they meet the right woman. Then they aren't. It's a Christmas miracle! But if you're not the right woman, he's simply going to make excuses. That doesn't mean the female reader, Behrendt assures us, has anything at all wrong with her. In fact, the reader is never the problem in this mess called dating, except when she lets the guy get away with his excuses: "You know you deserve to have a great relationship" (6); "You, the super-fox reading this book, are worth asking out" (17); "I know you're hot" (47); "He *should* miss you. You're deeply missable" (95); "You're far too busy and popular for that" (110); "You *are* better than these relationships" (137); "You are an excellent, foxy human being worthy of love" (145). Aren't we all.

If *The Rules* is an old-fashioned guide to finding and hooking the right man, *He's Just Not That Into You* is an old-fashioned guide to dumping the wrong one. Here once again we come across "primordial impulses that drive all of human nature"—that is, guys must be the pursuers. Geez, enough with the white knights! "Men, for the most part, like to pursue women. We like not knowing if we can catch you. We feel rewarded when we do. Especially when the chase is a long one" (16–17). A woman shouldn't call a man. It's *his* job—along with taking out the trash.

So although the premises are completely antithetical to those of Dr. Laura—it's the guy's problem, always, always, always—the biological determinism and resulting responsibilities are still the same: finding the right mate and keeping the relationship together, as well as ending things cleanly, are the *woman's* jobs. All of the bestselling books in this genre in the past sixteen years were ultimately written for a female readership. Indeed, it's not completely clear that men can read. More than one romance-novel heroine is surprised to see her "quintessentially masculine" lover with a book in his hand (*Season Beyond a Kiss,* 99; *Suddenly You,* 86). How do the therapeutic visions of love and gender compare to those offered up by popular romance novels? It is to this "Tempestuous, Tumultuous, Turbulent, Torrid, and Terribly Profitable World of Paperback Passion"—as a *New York* magazine article by Alice K. Turner once called it—that we now turn.

Romance in my Pants

"You have to be a true romantic person to fully appreciate her books."
Amazon.com reviewer of *The Wedding* by Danielle Steel

Fiction, of course, is different from nonfiction, and surely people don't read it for the same reasons: relationship manuals dispense advice, and novels dispense, well, other things. Even so, both offer visions of happy relationships, and almost sixty-five *million* people (78 percent of them women) had read at least one romance novel in the year 2004. According to the website of romance writer Janet Dailey, there are over 325 million copies of her books in print, which, by some accounts, makes her the third bestselling author of all time. At any given moment, ten to fifteen of the books on the *USA TODAY* weekly list are romances. So we set out to see just how the fictional fancies compare with the real-life "romances" described by our popular therapists and talk-show hosts.

According to the Romance Writers of America (the "professional association for 9,500 published and aspiring romance writers"), "two basic elements comprise every romance novel: a central love story and an emotionally satisfying and optimistic ending." *Any* book that fits those two criteria is, by their definition, a romance novel. Pamela Regis, a feminist scholar and the author of *The Natural History of the Romance,* claims that all romance novels contain eight particular narrative elements, including a "point of ritual death." (Some readers, however, would prefer a "point of genuine death," such as the disgruntled Amazon.com reviewer who hoped a Danielle Steel heroine would "crash and die" during her furious 85 mph race down the Pacific Coast Highway.) The goal of Regis's study is not to complicate the basic definition, but instead to prove that the romance novel's conventions and predictable rosiness make it not dismissible trash, as many have suggested, but instead a venerable art form practiced by such greats as Jane Austen.

But however specific one wants to be about the conventions, the two main criteria stand: a romance is a love story with a happy ending. From there, anything goes, though titles usually fall into one of several well-established categories. To illustrate the differences, the flavor of each type, we now dip into a few bestsellers from the "romantic suspense," "contemporary," "Regency," and "historical" subgenres. (We do not address the noteworthy but less beloved "paranormal" and "time-travel" categories.)

The most popular of these subgenres is "romantic suspense," home of the mind-blowingly successful Nora Roberts (aka J.D. Robb), author of well over 150 *USA TODAY* bestsellers since her first big hit in 1991. That's, if you're counting, an average of over ten full-length books a year, one every five or six weeks. Her website boldly proclaims dozens of heart-rending statistics, including the number of her books in print (280 million as of January 25, 2005) and the number of weeks her books have spent on the *New York Times* list since 1991 (632). In 2001 she was the second bestselling author by *USA TODAY* accounting, beaten only by J. K. Rowling; in 2005, says *Publishers Weekly,* she wrote ten of the top thirty-seven bestselling mass-market fiction titles.

The year 2006 was even better: the top four mass-market fiction sellers were all by Roberts; she had fourteen separate titles that sold more than a half-million copies each. Over the last two decades, an average of twenty-three Nora Roberts books were sold every minute!

Given this output, it's also extraordinary that she is recognized as one of the most gifted of today's romance authors, with a knack for storytelling and characterization that isn't diminished at all by her insane pace. She's so good that even fellow heavyweights can get jealous: in 1997 Janet Dailey admitted to plagiarizing ten of Roberts's novels (Regis, 161). Roberts has published in every romance subgenre, as well as other fictional genres, but most prolifically in the category of romantic suspense.

Birthright, the #13 mass-market paperback in 2004, introduces us to ex-spouses Callie Dunbrook and Jacob Graystone, fiery lovers edgily reunited on an excavation site where she reigns as head archaeologist and he as master of anthropology. They make each other as hot under the collar as they do below the waist; when they're not swearing and screaming, they're writhing and plunging. "Sugar, it's always like that with you two," remarks a friend. "Sparks just fly off the pair of you and burn innocent bystanders" (184).

The main plot is not actually a romantic one; Callie learns she was adopted—in fact stolen from her birth parents—and she sets out to "dig" for the truth (archaeology metaphors, regrettably, abound). Her discoveries lead to explosions and murder. But all throughout the journey, she's wrestling with Jake, sometimes literally, trying to figure out how she feels, what to do, what went wrong. It's a classic love-to-hate-you story; we know they love each other, but will their overwhelming passion make harmony—and therefore lasting commitment—impossible? (We'll give you a hint: No.)

Another bestselling romantic suspense writer is Linda Howard, author or coauthor of forty-five bestsellers, including *Mr. Perfect,* which the *New York Post* generously called a "frightening and funny look at the search for an ideal mate." The novel introduces us to four female friends who, during a girly gab session, invent a list of the top characteristics of the perfect man. The list—which at the bottom includes the requirement of a ten-inch member that can dish out "thirty minutes of thrusting time" (54)—becomes the buzz of the town and soon the talk of the nation (one excited coworker explicitly compares it to *The Rules*—high praise indeed!), earning its authors invitations from *People* magazine and *Good Morning, America.*

No, really. But the exposure turns deadly when someone starts knocking off the authors one by one. Heroine Jaine must get Sam, who "kissed the way no man should kiss and still be allowed to run free" (203)—whatever that means—on the case. Well, he *is* a cop. He's also, ahem, "hung" (85). Before she gets her head bashed in with a hammer, Jaine's coauthor Marci posits, "I think every woman daydreams about a man with, shall we say, certain generous parts, don't you?" (110). And we thought they only wanted hugs!

Janet Evanovich takes yet another approach to romantic suspense—a lighthearted, character-driven approach not typical of this genre. As different as her style is, it's working: Evanovich's novels have exploded in popularity in the past few years, with six books selling a combined six million copies in 2005 alone. In 2006 she had five different books (including #7 in fiction) sell more than 850,000 copies each! She owes her greatest success to her "One for the Money" series, currently numbering thirteen titles, which are not *exactly* thrillers and not *exactly* romances but mostly amusing stories about the mixed-up adventures of heroine Stephanie Plum.

Stephanie is an accident-prone bounty hunter ("not the world's best," she confesses in *Eleven on Top*) living in a crappy apartment in New Jersey and torn between two steamy-hot guys. She stumbles around, solving crimes mostly by accident. Her hair is big. Her cars are always getting blown up. And since she stars in a series, her happy ending has yet to come.

The real difference—and the best thing—about Evanovich novels is that they don't take themselves too seriously. In a note to readers in *Love Overboard*, Evanovich describes her books as "red-hot screwball comedies"—a fitting description that makes them almost entirely different from every other romance novel on the shelf. Only in Evanovich will you find a golden retriever that eats (and later defecates) underwear, a man who answer questions with only the word "Babe," and an amorous woman with a tingling "doodah" (*Love Overboard*, 158).

You will certainly never find those things in the pages of Danielle Steel. Ironically, hers is the name perhaps most widely associated with romance, yet she is not actually a member of the Romance Writers of America (RWA). We wonder if there was some falling-out years back, maybe a snubbing or a catfight over the copyright of certain breathy verbs. But whatever the reason, Steel is palpably absent from the RWA web pages, though her books (which fall into the "contemporary" subgenre) have appeared on every *Publishers Weekly* list—usually in both hardcover and paperback—for the entire duration of this study.

The Wedding, #11 hardcover fiction in 2000, follows Allegra Steinberg, a "long and lean and beautiful" entertainment lawyer who is "totally unaware of her looks" (12). Everyone around her is equally stunning: her mother has "Allegra's long, lean looks, and a model's body" and has only needed minimal plastic surgery (16). Her father, at sixty, is "still the handsome man he had always been" (16). Her seventeen-year-old sister (5'9" and 112 pounds) is a model. Her boyfriend boasts "long, tall, blond splendor" (12). Her best friend (coincidentally a movie star) has the "face and body of a Greek god, but he also happened to be intelligent" (27). (We love the casual phrasing—he "happens" to be intelligent like someone "happens" to be born with a third nipple.)

But it's not all rosy. Allegra, though she loves her job, works too hard babysitting her spoiled celebrity clients. Her boyfriend is distant and won't commit; in fact he hasn't even divorced his wife after years of separation (but Allegra knows there's nothing going on; Joanie is "dependent and whiny" and, most importantly, "overweight," 46). Allegra worries that she's destined to pick "men who couldn't give and eventually ran away" (156).

Then, on a business trip, she meets Jeff Hamilton, who is "long and lean"—anyone starting to feel like we're talking about show dogs here?— "with dark hair, and the aristocratic look of a true New Yorker" (91). (Steel clearly has not spent much time on the streets and subways of the Big Apple, where true New Yorkers brilliantly conceal their aristocratic looks.) Of course he is a successful writer, both commercial and literary. They instantly connect. After long talks and ice-skating, they share kisses that make her feel "like a kid again, and at the same time, very much a woman" (119), but Allegra is determined to remain faithful to her lame boyfriend.

Even so, things fall apart in about two seconds, and Jeff and Allegra instantly settle into life, regular life, in love. The rest of the novel covers the interminable details leading up to their fairy tale wedding.

It's worth noting that these four books, all set in modern day, are staggeringly different novels. With all their death and thrills and mystery, *Birthright* and *Mr. Perfect* are close in subject matter, of course, but in terms of writing style, characters, and preoccupations, the books have little in common. Hands down, Nora Roberts and Janet Evanovich are the most able storytellers; the plots are engaging, the characters multidimensional, the independent clauses not separated by commas. (You know, the little things.) And Evanovich brings a goofiness to the genre that's truly refreshing.

But those are contemporary romance novels—let's step into the past. Almost as popular are "historical" and "Regency" romances, both of which regularly launch titles to the bestseller lists. "Historical" describes any novel set before the world wars, whereas "Regency" spec-ifies those set in England in the early 1800s. And one can take the names somewhat literally: as Janice A. Radway notes in *Reading the Romance,* readers and publishers expect the novels' backdrops to be rig-orously researched and historically accurate, even if the relationships described therein are less realistic (109).

In these subgenres too, we find dissonant sets of styles and assump-tions. Some novels are light and quirky, particularly the Regencies, which are concerned with fortuitous matches and balls and the sea-sonal release of debutantes into the stream of London society. The charming *Romancing Mister Bridgerton* by Julia Quinn (a Harvard graduate, and it shows) tells the tale of twenty-eight-year-old spin-ster Penelope, who has been in love with Colin Bridgerton since 1812, "two days before her sixteenth birthday." Unfortunately, "he cer-tainly didn't fall in love with her in 1812 (and not in 1813, 1814, 1815, or—oh, blast, not in all the years 1816–1822, either, and cer-tainly not in 1823, when he was out of the country the whole time, anyway)" (1). But 1824 is Penelope's year, and her Odysseus finally returns and falls for the shy, perceptive woman who has loved him for so long.

Other novels are more sweeping and visceral. Kathleen E. Woodiwiss begins her "historical" *A Season Beyond a Kiss* with a thirty-one-page sex scene, voraciously nitpicking heroine Raelynn's inward struggle and eventual loss of virginity. The sex-crammed novel is romance at its most hysterical, stuffed with horseback riding, ball-gowns, and shopping sprees, as well as marauding brigands (with *accents*), several manly rescues, and prose too pretentious to be swallowed without a chaser: "From the edge of the bed where he stood tall and naked, Jeff slowly perused the curving form now illumined by the whimsical radi-ance of the solar orb" (94). These two are so insatiable that *only* after a vicious attack by the aforementioned brigands (with *accents*) does Jeff not stir from sleep when Raelynn slides "a hand downward over his taut, flat belly" and takes "possession of the torpid fullness" (398).

Although it's impossible not to chuckle at the more purplish language, the themes we find repeated in these works are often no laughing matter. Though there are exceptions in the books we have reviewed here (especially the Evanovich novels), let alone the ones we haven't, a few commonalities are worth exploring as we analyze the vision of love and relationships put forth by these books—and attempt to determine what romance readers gain from them.

LOVE WILL SAVE THE DAY, DAMN YOU

Depending on the company one keeps, being labeled a "romantic" can be a compliment or an accusation. But the label exists, separating those with a propensity toward love and relationships, or even just emotional decision-making, from those drawn toward other avocations, such as hunting, fishing, and racing cars.

Not so in the romance world. These authors delight in snaring confirmed bachelors and spinsters (this wretched word inundates the historical and Regency romances, which are unfortunately all too historical to replace it with the gentler "singletons" of *Bridget Jones's Diary* fame) and making them grovel at the altar of love.

Of course, such scenarios often do happen in real life—a wounded soul swears never to love again and then finds itself sashaying around in twitterpated ecstasy, spewing renewed hope in cafes and making everyone sick. It happens; people are resilient. But these novels really relish that sort of thing. Typically at the opening of a romance novel, at least one partner has sworn not to marry, not to love, or not to marry for love.

After three failed engagements, Jaine has given up on men (*Mr. Perfect*). Olivia vows as a child not to marry (*The Least Likely Bride*). Twenty-five-year-old spinster Freyja, scarred by rejection, plans never to love again, and "the last thing [her Joshua] wanted was to be seriously in love with anyone" (*Slightly Scandalous,* 266). Single mom Joanna insists that "never again would she look to a man for happiness," and her happiness-providing man Tanner is at first equally averse to making the inevitable commitment (*Darling Daughters,* 13). Tristan is busily searching for a "sweet-tempered, biddable, gentle female who would cause him not a moment's angst" instead of a woman for whom he feels genuine passion (*The Lady Chosen,* 60). Amanda, struggling to cling to her conviction that only practical marriages work, gets scolded by the man who will change her mind: "But someday, peaches, your romantic side will triumph over your practical nature. And I hope I'm there when it happens" (*Suddenly You,* 163).

Oh yes, we're always there when it happens—to "peaches" and every other hypocoristically enhanced heroine—and it always happens fast. Days after declaring "I want the kind of marriage where neither person is blinded by passion," and actually getting engaged to someone she doesn't love, Sophie changes her mind (without even an internal explanation) and pursues the man she wants (*Midnight Pleasures,* 48). Leonora won't marry Tristan, convinced that he will lose interest in her, but after a few days (and four sexual episodes), she admits, "He'd been right; the attraction between them wouldn't fade. . . . It hadn't. It had grown" (*The Lady Chosen,* 279). Maybe it's just us, but it seems that one might need more than a couple good orgasms to reverse a life philosophy.

The majority of these authors clearly do not take a "romance for romantics" viewpoint; they're not writing about people hunting for the right partners, or—all too common in *real* life—those stuck with the wrong ones. They're writing about people who have sworn off love entirely, people who have pursued, and even succeeded in, *unromantic* (though not necessarily asexual) lives.

From one angle, the "someone out there for everyone" approach is kind of comforting and sweet. But from another angle, this urge to assimilate everyone seems a bit desperate. Why do disinterested or independent people need to be converted? Why does *everyone* need to be leveled by passion? In a society crammed with love stories and people who crave them, there should be absolutely no need to lasso the few who opt out of the whole mess. It's as though they're afraid the mere existence of happy single people threatens the whole love-enterprise, like those who fret about homosexuality being contagious. (This brings up an interesting side note: there is no RWA category for gay romantic fiction. Why not? Think of the spectacular cover art!)

Love, though, often regarded as the ambassador of goodness itself, represents a generally warm and hopeful force in a scary world. Love softens people (well, except perhaps for the Earl of Trentham, who becomes all the rougher and more possessive the deeper love burrows into him in *The Lady Chosen*). Perhaps in a superficial but sincere way, the idea of love taking hold of bachelors and spinsters (usually in their twenties) is appealing because it suggests that goodness is always out there, going about its snoopy work, neutralizing evil and making flowers grow. It invades the lives of even the hopeless and resigned. It makes people smile. It brings things to a not-so-torpid fullness.

In fact romantic love in these books possesses none of the ambiguity and causes none of the moral lapses that it does in tragic works and, well, life. None of the characters really regrets falling in love—fair enough, though, since in these books only everlasting bliss ever comes of it. In this universe, passion doesn't drive people to philander or kill or contract ugly diseases or pine in disillusionment for the solitude of the fjords. Love is *only* good and absolutely safe; the road might be stony at first, inspiring haughtiness and words like "insufferable," but once you're there, you're happy forever with the spouse of your dreams who will crave you always and never, ever hurt you.

Given the ravages wreaked by heartbreak in the real world, this is no surprising fantasy. But the lack of danger weakens the entire concept. Loving someone wholly, intimately, and passionately is the greatest emotional risk a person can take. There's no safety net, no guarantee. That combination of intensity and fragility gives love its power, the offering of self despite inherent and unavoidable risk. To pluck out the danger is to pluck out the greatness—to pluck out the enormity of what we gamble when we love and what we achieve when we're loved in return.

Granted, the characters don't realize how safe they are. But their convictions about their relationships—"This one intense passion would last her lifetime" (*The Least Likely Bride*, 183); "He had never experienced, nor would he ever experience again, a desire as profound as that which he consistently felt for Sophie York" (*Midnight Pleasures*, 148)— are, we think, not meant to be ironic indicators of eventual turmoil, boredom, or devastation. We really are supposed to believe that their love for each other will protect them from disintegration and challenge. No one in these novels need fear the contraction of rubber bands or the unsettling undulation of the wave; everyone simply basks in the whimsical radiance of the solar orb.

In fact, "vulnerability" in these books is mostly a physical concept, a word used to describe a woman's trembling helplessness before a powerful, aggressive, sexually experienced male. We are constantly reminded how big and imposing these men are, how easily they could break our little ladies:

> The hard texture of his skin, muscles that wouldn't give, coarse hair that tickled on his chest, the very expanse of him that made her feel so small and feminine. (*The Heir*, 204)

> It was not a handshake, it was a possession. The difference

in their height was so extreme that she was forced to incline her head at an uncomfortable angle to look up into his face. Despite her sturdy and substantial figure, he made her feel almost doll-like. (*Suddenly You,* 116)

In the deepening darkness, he was literally a god, powerful and intent as, braced above her, he looked down on her. Then he bent his head and took her mouth again, and his sheer vitality—the fact he was all hard muscle and bone, and hot, heated blood—captured her.

The crinkly roughness of his haired skin chafed, abraded, reminded her how soft her own skin was, how sensitive. Reminded her how vulnerable and defenseless she was against his strength. (*The Lady Chosen,* 191)

Clearly this audience finds it erotic for women to be weaker partners, even to be afraid of their lovers:

He brought her up close against him, allowing her to feel *the enemy* against her. "Don't be afraid. We were made for each other."

She trembled, fully conscious of the manly blade that would rend her virgin's flesh, but Jeff gave her trepidations little time to solidify into a full-fledged fear. (*Season Beyond a Kiss,* 27)

The staggering popularity of the "loss of virginity" scene is evidence enough of the audience's delight in watching a scared, naïve woman be led, taught, and taken by a dominating man. Never is the man a virgin or a novice. "He seemed a very bold and accomplished lover," Raelynn decides without any frame of reference whatsoever (*Season Beyond a Kiss,* 148). Such scenarios are right in line with the advice offered by *The Rules:* "In a relationship, the man must take charge . . . We are not making this up—biologically, he's the aggressor" (9).

Female timidity, however, doesn't always extend to mental pursuits. Many of these books do depict intellectual equality between the sexes. In *Birthright,* Jake insists that, though he was immediately attracted to Callie, he was "nearly as aroused by [her] mind" (234), and the two do work together as equal partners. In *Mr. Perfect,* Jaine is "exhilarated by their conflicts" and the fact that Sam possesses "the same verbal agility and speed" (170–171), though the book provides little evidence of her brain's rumored "lightning-quick workings." In *The Least Likely Bride,* Olivia proves her intelligence by beating Anthony at chess (141); Sophie, in *Midnight Pleasures,* happily discovers that her husband is not threatened by her knowledge of seven languages. It is clear that audiences want their heroines educated and smart.

However, we still get the feeling that, in many instances, the man's respect for the woman's mental gifts is less crucial than his desire to possess her both physically and legally. As Jack muses in *Suddenly You,* "Aside from [his] considerable regard for her intelligence, he couldn't help thinking of [Amanda] as a tidy little bonbon" (143). It's as if slapping a book in the heroine's hand or a "doctor" at the front of her name makes the novel palatable to the modern reader, even though the man still holds all the power, power he uses to possess:

> "You cannot go around grabbing my hand, seizing me as if I in some way belonged to you—"
> "You do."
> She looked up. Blinked. "I beg your pardon?"
> Tristan looked into her eyes; he wasn't averse to explaining. "You. Belong. To me." It felt good to state it, reinforcing the reality. (*The Lady Chosen,* 237)

And though she resists then, she eventually marries him and agrees "to be [his] wife, to act in all ways as [his] wife, and obey [him] in all things [reasonable]" (317).

Indeed, in many of these books, the word "possessive" is used over and over and over with obvious pleasure. In this universe, being claimed as property is not a warning sign of abuse, but a mark of status. It's also, apparently, an aphrodisiac: "[Amanda] climaxed at once, overcome with the searing delight of his possession" (*Suddenly You,* 327). (Possession is, after all, nine-tenths of the orgasm.)

In this regard, the romance genre takes sort of reasonable, healthy emotions and makes them extreme enough to be disturbing. Sex *is* an act of physical and emotional vulnerability. There *is* power in recognizing the weakness that comes with trusting another person intimately—power in relinquishing power. And wanting to feel desirable, special, to the person you love is nothing strange.

But fear, branding, and one-sided surrender? The fantasy here is not partnership. The fantasy is *being weak.* It's having a protector who is strong and primitive enough to claim you as a possession and defend you from the scary world, yet who is also so enraptured by you that he will continually take you "far beyond the galaxy into another universe entirely" (*Season Beyond a Kiss,* 403). Ah, the white knight. Clearly this medieval image of love is *not* simply being inflicted on us by conservative relationship gurus: these are fantasies written and read by women themselves, many of whom must genuinely desire to be sheltered by a man, to be under the control of someone who will take care of everything—to be a fundamentally weaker partner in a relationship.

DAZZLING HEIGHTS OF RAPTUROUS JOY

But it's not all possession and plunder. It's also about sky-high pleasure— and really, it could be argued that sex is the only reason to read a romance novel in the first place. Like flipping to the girlie-magazine centerfold, skimming for sex in a romance gets you right to the point. Each sexual encounter is a new juicy moment, the author's chance to shine—and to flex her euphemistic muscles as she spawns ever grander, sillier descriptions of body parts ("the dark veils shrouding the secret places of her womanhood"), techniques ("drawing a pale limb up over his hip, he slowly teased her with the heat of his desires"), and sensations ("it was as if she had been caught in a vortex of whirling flames") (all courtesy of Woodiwiss's *A Season Beyond a Kiss,* 29 and 26).

But for all these worthy efforts, sex in romance novels remains remarkably regimented. First come the electric kisses. Then the nipple-lapping and manual exploration. An agony of wriggling and panting. And finally the coital capers: all bliss and throbbing, synchronized climaxes leaping up from their loins like dolphins at Sea World. Even virgins experience orgasm upon first meeting with the "fiery blade," their initial shock of pain instantly "massaged away" (more Woodiwiss, 97 and 31).

We know, it's not supposed to be realistic. But there's something suspicious about the combination of over-the-top language and under-the-top routine. For one, we find it strange that oral sex makes little more than a cameo appearance in these otherwise slurpy odes to carnal indulgence. Certainly fellatio, still a tender topic in some circles, would have to stay reserved for the most brazen of heroines, but would it really be so shocking if Mr. Wonderful went downtown? Teenagers these days give head more often than they give directions, but out of the fifty sex scenes we reviewed, only seven included oral sex (and three of those were in the same book—the characters tried it after reading a scandalous publication penned by a prostitute). If even this widespread practice is such a stranger to the romantic page, one can only imagine how Raelynn might react should Jeffrey confess a hankering for light bondage or ask to don her pantaloons.

So although on the surface explicit sex seems a daring, potentially subversive element of the romance novel, underlying the seeming variety and candor are mostly just tameness and timidity: these are slight variations on basic acts and predictable patterns. Not that they don't sound fun and all. They're just not all that naughty.

At the same time, the fact that women might fantasize about the glory of sexual intercourse is not particularly surprising either. Social lore elevates the act above all others; many Americans, as we learned in the Clinton era, consider it the only "real sex." Yet of all the sexual acts, its track record for female satisfaction is the least exemplary. It's not surprising that readers who have achieved less than rapturous results might dream about having climax after stellar climax while perched upon this "aching shaft of flesh" (*The Least Likely Bride*, 210), especially if they believe that intercourse is supposed to be the most intimate, pleasurable act of all, the *only* act of completion. Indeed, one of the few lucky ladies to receive oral attention still feels "incomplete" afterward, even though "her senses shattered. The world disappeared into shards of bright light, into a pulsing radiance that surrounded her, sank into her, through her" (*The Lady Chosen*, 326). Talk about difficult to please! Doesn't she know it's a miracle he even takes out the garbage?

And let's not forget the most obvious consequence of intercourse, ecstatic or otherwise. The concept of birth control is a troubling little brainteaser for these authors. Even those authors who embrace the raunch of explicit sex tend to stumble when it comes to the unsavory world of foams, latex, and calendars. Birth control, it seems, just plain isn't romantic.

Some of the historical books, more than we expected, do take an honest approach. A few incorporate surprise pregnancies into their plotlines, sometimes resulting from spotty but earnest attempts at the rhythm method.

It's in the contemporary works that we get a variety of strange solutions—the notoriously unsexy condom not being one of them. In *Birthright*,

Nora Roberts elects to ignore the whole matter. Both couples in the novel have unprotected sex without discussion (and no omitted discussion is implied), which is strange given the general realism of the characters in other aspects. The issue is simply nonexistent. Many other authors share this see-no-evil, hear-no-evil tactic.

But the strangest approach we found comes in Linda Howard's *Mr. Perfect,* a contemporary novel that aims to present its heroine as a savvy modern woman. As soon as Jaine starts lusting for Sam, she has a heart-to-heart with herself: "Okay. What she was dealing with here was a major case of the hots. The fact was there, she had to face it, which meant she had to be a sane, intelligent adult about this and get on birth control pills as fast as possible" (100).

But these pills aren't a backup method. Jaine is so sane and intelligent, so modern and practical, that she never thinks to protect herself against sexually transmitted diseases. She's willing to risk infection, shell out for a prescription, and tweak her body chemistry for a *possible* encounter with a man whom she's known for a week and has been describing as a drunken sleazebag for most of that time. In fact a great deal is made about the ingesting of these pills, the arrival of Jaine's period, and the likely coordinates of her slinky egg. Though Sam queries her later on her own venereal status—not particularly seriously—she never thinks to ask after his. The focus on preventing pregnancy is almost neurotic, which makes the disregard of modern sexual risks all the stranger: why make such a big deal about safe sex that isn't safe at all?

In short, the handling of birth control is up for grabs in romance novels. One gets the feeling that the topic is just too catastrophically unromantic to enable these authors to reach any sort of consensus on how it ought to be discussed. We imagine hysterical voices rising from a conference room at RWA-HQ, fists pounding in impotent rage, inconsolable authors beating their foreheads on the table and wailing, "Not *spermicide!* No! *No!*"

But perhaps our favorite bit of sexual silliness is the incarnation of the flames of passion. Now certainly fire and its derivatives have long been associated with lust, so the metaphor is far from original. What is a bit more original is that the metaphor has been extracted . . . in favor of actual fire. In *A Season Beyond a Kiss*, Raelynn discovers that "indeed, the vibrant heat [Jeffrey] now displayed infused her whole being with warmth" (27–28). Penelope notices (as anyone might) that "there was something else at her entrance, something hard and hot, and very, very demanding" (*Romancing Mister Bridgerton*, 288). "[Leonora] was slick, wet, so hot she scalded [Tristan]" (*The Lady Chosen*, 244). Perhaps Tristan should try an oven mitt. These people's genitals could heat a cabin in the Rockies.

THE NEED FOR SPEED

Okay, flames and rapture and yada yada yada, but when it comes right down to it, Dr. Laura was right: what everybody in these books wants is marriage (or, in rare cases, a nonmarital but lifelong commitment). No one even questions, let alone challenges, this seemingly universal aspiration. Roberts's Callie might be tough, rational, and potty-mouthed, but in her heart of hearts, she wants it "right": "You want me all the way back . . . you get down on one knee, and you ask" (498). Jake protests, scowls, and huffs—and does it. Then he gushes:

> "We'll . . . have a real wedding. And we're buying a house."
> "Are we?"
> . . .
> "I don't care where, we can stick a pin in a map. But I want a home this time, Callie. I want kids." (501)

They failed the first time because they were a little too wild, a little too cavalier, a little too transitory; they didn't anchor their passion to these widely accepted marks of permanency. If they want their love to work, they'll have to settle down like everybody else.

Although conventional wisdom might advise that overhasty marriages are the domain of the drunk and pregnant, in the romance world they're the surest sign of true love. In these books, it usually takes a matter of days or weeks for two lethargic strangers or snarling enemies to become breathy, pledge-ready companions. Though this sort of behavior might be expected in the "historical" books—when sex was in fashion and bastards weren't—it's also weirdly common in the contemporary novels.

In *Mr. Perfect,* for example, Jaine rationalizes,

> They had been lovers for almost a week, and in another few weeks they would be married. She couldn't believe she was making such an important move so hastily, but it felt right. . . . She hadn't rushed into anything with her other three fiancés, and look how well those engagements had turned out. This time she was just going to do it. To hell with caution; she was going to marry Sam Donovan. (385)

Better sign a prenup, Jaine. And then there's Danielle Steel's Allegra:

> It was incredible. She had known [Jeff] for a little over two months, and yet it felt completely right to both of them. She had had other relationships for years, and they had hemmed and hawed, and kept her at arm's length, and avoided any real intimacy. And here she was with Jeff, and it was as natural as could be. It was amazing. "I love you so much," she said, with her arms around him and kissing him. She had never been this happy. . . . Jeff wanted to be with her for

the rest of her life. It was what she had always wanted. It was a dream come true, and it was all so easy. It wasn't "work," and it didn't have to be "ironed out," and they didn't have to "try" or "give it some thought." She didn't need therapy to figure out if she wanted him, and he didn't need ten years or two or four to figure out if he loved her. They loved each other, and it was right, and they were getting married. (219)

Interestingly, a couple's ability to get along—so vital in the self-help books—has almost nothing to do with the success of a relationship in the romance novels. Most couples in these books fight, sometimes viciously, but such ire is presented as just another facet of passion, or as frustration born of misunderstanding. The books sort of suggest that the screaming matches will disappear once both partners commit to the relationship, though the secret to this transformation is not provided. Getting along just isn't presented as an important issue.

It's the exact opposite of John Gray's Mars–Venus doctrine. Communication is irrelevant here; successful love depends solely on finding the right person. "You'd be surprised how fast things happen when the right man comes along," Allegra's mother beams (192). Fast and easy: no work at all.

And in that sense the two concepts are identical: whether we believe that true intimacy is impossible because men and women are too different to achieve it, or that intimacy is as simple as meeting the right pair of eyes over a punchbowl, we don't have to worry too much. It *is* fast, and it *is* easy. Just learn to humor the alien sharing your bedroom, or go about your business until your "predestined" (Steel, 108) mate comes along. Even Dr. Phil says so. What could be easier?

Okay—even though the distended, noncommittal brand of modern relationship can be demoralizing, surely there's a middle ground to be explored, a passionate yet rational relationship that's proven over time as it gradually grows in depth and intensity. But clearly readers want instant results, instant "forevers"; they want passion to be a sign of eternity, all the kinks worked out during the first heady week of courtship when people still care enough to try.

Frankly, it's just plain strange that people are thought to be this lazy. The way these books avoid it, you'd think that working on a relationship for more than a few minutes was some sort of grim, vomity chore.

This aversion to effort is especially curious when viewed in the light of the underlying fear that has to spawn all these ideas. In a time of rampant divorce, adultery, and ennui, it's no surprise to find books that reaffirm the importance and possibility of lasting love. The number one trait of imaginary Mr. Perfect is "faithfulness," and even the few couples that choose not to marry in a traditional sense still remain "in thrall . . . each to the other" and "oblivious of all but the connection that bound them, the certainty of their union, sealed within their own circle of enchantment" (*The Least Likely Bride*, 320). *This. . . will. . . last,* you can almost hear the authors insisting through gritted teeth.

Lifetime aspirations and J-Lo odds. It's troubling that—instead of depicting passionate relationships marked by depth, intimacy, and time—these novels celebrate a quick and often superficial path to romantic bliss. Far from being the antidote to divorce, adultery, and ennui, these false expectations may be one cause of them.

CAN'T START A FIRE WITHOUT A SPARK

There's a man out there who writes bestselling romances.

We'll let that sink in for a moment before telling you . . . there are actually *two* men out there who write bestselling romances.

You won't find these men rubbing elbows (or anything else) with RWA socialites, and you won't find their books plastered with heaving bosoms or Indian braves—and that's because some of their stories fail to meet one crucial criterion of the genre. That's right, folks—they don't all have an optimistic ending.

But we still say they're romances. What else might you call a book written for women that's entirely about soul mates, eternal love, and rolling, multiple orgasms? Hmm?

Indeed, the subject matter is not any different from the books we've already examined in this chapter. But the type of man who swells these pages, and the type of relationship he creates, is significantly different from the romance fare that has carried us away so far. We will see that this style of romance complements the more traditional version, offering women a whole spectrum of fantasy from which to choose.

The sensitive gents responsible for this alternate universe are Nicholas Sparks, author of several huge bestsellers, including *The Notebook* and *Message in a Bottle* (he's sold an estimated fifty million copies of his novels worldwide), and Robert James Waller, author of 1992's #1 hardcover fiction title, *The Bridges of Madison County*. Sparks is the hokier and more genre-oriented of the two, but Waller's novel—even though it was not published as a romance—shares several characteristics of the Sparks style. Let's take a closer look at the male contribution to this very female genre.

Vadge Badge

Most significantly, the men in these novels are not the rough and possessive brutes of romance lore. They are deeply loving and thoughtful, sensitive yet masculine, and loyal to the end of their days. They crave passion, intimacy, and mutual sexual satisfaction as much as the women they worship. When they lose their loves (and some of them do), they go about their now-pale lives in perpetual grieving endurance. Noah, the hero of Sparks's *Notebook*, even recites poetry constantly like some sort of awful parody of himself.

Both authors show us that these men are different, more natural, more timeless, than the mere modern mortal. All of them appreciate nature, working with their bodies and hands: Noah repairs houses and "hunt[s] dawn from the bow of a canoe" (136); Garrett (*Message in a Bottle*) lives on the beach, restores ships, and scuba dives; Robert (*Bridges of Madison County*) is a nature photographer frustrated with the growing commercialism of his profession. They are presented as What Man Was Supposed to Be, though the contemporary world is squeezing them out:

> This was a worker's world, not a poet's, and people would have a hard time understanding Noah. America was in full swing now, all the papers said so, and people were rushing forward . . . toward long hours and profits, neglecting the things that brought beauty to the world. (*The Notebook*, 135–136)

> "There's a certain breed of man that's obsolete," he had said. "Or very nearly so. The world is getting organized, way too organized for me and some others. . . .
>
> "Not all men are the same. Some will do okay in the world that's coming. Some, maybe just a few of us, will not. You can see it in the computers and robots and what they portend. In older worlds, there were things we could do, were designed to do, that nobody or no machine could do. We run fast, are strong and quick, aggressive and tough. We were given courage. We can throw spears long distances and fight in hand-to-hand combat.
>
> "Eventually, computers and robots will run things. Humans will manage those machines, but that doesn't require courage or strength, or any characteristics like those. In fact,

men are outliving their usefulness." (*The Bridges of Madison County,* 100–101)

These disappearing cowboys are contrasted with other, less alluring men that the female protagonists have known, loved, or married. In *The Notebook,* Allie's fiancé is a nice person, a gentlemen, but he works too much and doesn't know how to talk or listen; "there's always going to be something missing in our relationship," she says, meaning passion (82). Theresa, the heroine of *Message in a Bottle,* is still chafing from her ex-husband's infidelity and manipulative charm. Francesca's Madison County husband is some loser hillbilly threatened by change, eroticism, and subtlety.

These women need love, and they need to get laid. Luckily their heroes offer the full package (size undisclosed). Each man falls in love, and not just because of the woman's beauty, but because she has "traits like intelligence, confidence, strength of spirit, passion, traits that inspired others to greatness" (*The Notebook,* 59). They have awesome sex, which is less explicit than that in the other romance novels, but which always delivers "long sequences" of orgasms (all three books use this exact phrase)—even poor Francesca, who "had ceased having orgasms years ago" (107). These relationships are characterized by profound conversation, cuddling, dancing, joint bubble baths, and "whispering to each other until the early morning hours" (*Message in a Bottle,* 222).

Then what? Sometimes happiness, sometimes tragedy. In *The Notebook,* Allie leaves her fiancé and spends forty-nine happy years married to her sexy poet. But Francesca chooses differently. Married with children, she can't bear to humiliate her husband by leaving him, so she kisses her love (and orgasms!) goodbye. Only after Francesca's death do her children learn of her passionate affair and lifelong love.

These books don't insist that all relationships work out. They invite the reader to invest instead in the romance of engulfing passion—

regardless of its earthly outcome—and then they show that it endures. Readers' hearts are ultimately supposed to swell because once-in-a-lifetime love exists, not because it begets marriages. And because that passion provides such sustenance for its heroines, transforming lackluster life into a shimmering and rapturous thing, the heroines are even forgiven the marital indiscretions that men in the same books would be demonized for considering.

But of course these books are female fantasies; double standards aren't the point. They are so "by the book," in fact, that we were actually relieved to come across them—because they represent the far more obvious fantasy than the RWA-style romance novels do: hot and tender stranger appears out of nowhere to save woman from humdrum life, sweeping her up in intimate relationship and eternal love. Why bother imagining yourself a virgin in a hoop skirt when you've got this easy-bake fantasy right here?

Seriously, though, it's all part of the "realism" that the heroines aren't virgins; they are mature women, sometimes with children, who get a second chance at love. Further, it's important that this "realistic" brand of fantasy honor various female choices—showing that it's possible for a woman to have that passionate second chance, that sustaining eternal connection, without necessarily threatening her husband and family.

Really, it's the feel-good fantasy of the year.

ALTERNATIVE PERSPECTIVES

Before we move on to our conclusions about America's recent romance-related reading, we feel obligated to take a peek at a few works of literary fiction. Though these too deal primarily with love and relationships, they diverge from the genre-based fare in some important ways that might help to expand our vision of romance novels and even "romance" itself.

The most traditional love story of these is Arthur Golden's *Memoirs of a Geisha,* which was the #2 trade paperback in 1999. The book is narrated by Sayuri, whose father—a poor, aging fisherman—commits her to the life of a geisha upon the death of his wife. Full of fascinating details of geisha (and Japanese) culture, *Memoirs* follows Sayuri's difficult childhood and eventual rise to prominence in Kyoto in the 1930s and '40s, tracing her triumphant attempt to work within the confines of her profession to be with the man she loves. Readers of historical romances especially should enjoy the cultural particulars of *Memoirs,* as well as its happy—but not entirely traditional—ending.

Tracy Chevalier paints yet a different picture of romance in *Girl with a Pearl Earring* (#7 trade paperback in 2001), a fictionalized account of the relationship between sixteenth-century Dutch painter Johannes Vermeer and sixteen-year-old Griet, a maid hired to clean his studio who eventually becomes his assistant and the subject of one of his intriguing portraits. The movie previews make this out to be a rather racy number, full of adultery and obsession, but the book is actually much more subtle than that: it tells the story of Griet's unlikely entrance into the world of art and explores the power of creative communion.

What makes the novel most believable, and different, is its narration. Griet tells her own story in a voice as practical, understated, and humble as a girl of her station would naturally have. She certainly enjoys the company of Vermeer, wants to assist him in his work, and wants him to care for her. But simple statements are the extent of her passion: "I did not like to think of him in that way, with his wife and children. I preferred to think of him alone in his studio. Or not alone, but with only me" (77). She doesn't talk about burning loins, whirling ecstasies, or ravaging heartbreak; she doesn't even talk about love. She and Vermeer never do anything, in fact, that would violate garden-variety marriage vows. She prepares his paints. He teaches her about art. She has a knack for it and helps him perfect his paintings.

Their calm relationship is actually quite refreshing and, we would argue, not unromantic. Griet and Vermeer are never a couple; he's already married, and her destiny lies in humbler pastures. But they share something profound and lasting, a connection they will never have with their spouses. This is a romance on another level, a book that celebrates the power of artistic accord and shows how creative callings can ignite and unite the most unlikely hearts.

But the best romantic work of this time period is one that truly explores the depth and intensity, joy and sorrow, of lifetime love. It is Audrey Niffenegger's *The Time Traveler's Wife,* a beautiful book that crystallizes the passion, longing, and commitment of true love better than any novel we have ever read.

Ironically, it is perhaps the only book in our study that incorporates elements of science fiction—a genre not usually associated with the most romantic of stories (or readers!). Henry DeTamble is indeed a time traveler, though he has no time machine or souped-up DeLorean at his disposal. His wanderings are, in fact, completely out of his control, though they tend to occur at times of stress, often planting him around people or places of emotional importance. At age thirty-six, for example, Henry travels back in time twenty-two years, where he meets his future wife, Clare, then six years old. Clare's young life, in fact, is shaped by these meetings—152 of them—with the man who will one day be her husband, though she won't meet him in real time until she is twenty years old.

The intricate chronology of this book is one of its great charms, but we're here to talk about romance and relationships. And no book we've reviewed here does it better than *The Time Traveler's Wife.* Gone are the huffy fights and euphemistic sex scenes of traditional romance novels ("I now have an erection that is probably tall enough to ride some of the scarier rides at Great America without a parent," Henry describes instead, 17). Gone is the implication that only courtship counts. Gone is any trace of a "Mars and Venus" mentality. This is a book about two lives inextricably woven together—soul mates and their shared destiny, which is at once sad, funny, and joyous. Despite the book's fantastical premise, its rendering of real love rings profoundly true. And although we know that not everyone will believe love is really like this, we find it hard to believe that anyone wouldn't want to.

Me Love You Long Time

So what do we gain from all this (besides the aching desire to be referred to as tidy little bonbons)? What are women to take from the nonfiction advice books and the romantic fiction written for them? Why do they make these particular books bestsellers?

Sociologist Wendy Simonds interviewed women readers of self-help books for her 1992 book *Women and Self-Help Culture.* Now a bit out-of-date (she examined self-help books on the *New York Times Book Review* bestseller list between 1963 and 1991 and interviewed readers), her conclusions can still form a starting point for our own sweeping generalizations (or, as the sociologists say, "sociocultural analysis"). Although "searching for answers," women readers did not necessarily expect the books to fulfill their promises. They looked primarily for "validation of how they already felt, for inspiration, for comfort, for explanation of situations they could not understand," to "gain control over their lives," to feel good and bolster their self-confidence. For one, it was good to know that other women felt some of the same frustration and confusion. And sometimes the anecdotes of bad marriages and screwed-up partners actually made readers feel better about themselves, like watching incestuous couples rip off their shirts on daytime talk shows. "Look at that," viewers mutter. "Bubba and I may have troubles, but at least we wear shoes, our kids have only ten fingers, we haven't tried to run over each other with the minivan, we all go out for barbecue on Saturdays, and our satellite dish gets 140 stations. We're doing all right."

Romances, for their part, have a long and noble history in the West. The earliest extant novel, *Chaereas and Callirhoe,* was a romance, penned by a Greek named Chariton sometime around the dawn of the common era. And modern romances have appealed to women in America for over 250 years. Samuel Richardson's *Pamela,* perhaps the first "modern" bestseller, was published in the United States by the enterprising Benjamin Franklin himself in 1744. The 1850s gave birth to the initial round of native chick lit, with such blockbusters as Fanny Fern's *Fern Leaves from Fanny's Portfolio,* Susan Warner's *The Wide, Wide World,* and Maria Susanna Cummins's *The Lamplighter* outselling Hawthorne and Melville by the hundreds of thousands. *The Lamplighter* sold 40,000 copies in just eight weeks, and *The Wide, Wide World* had sold more than half a million copies by the end of the century. Swallow that, Moby Dick. The success of female writers of romance irritated Hawthorne to such a degree that he griped in a letter, "America is now wholly given over to a d——d mob of scribbling women, and I should have no chance of success while the public taste is occupied with their trash . . .What is the mystery of these innumerable editions of the 'Lamplighter,' and other books neither better nor worse?"

What *is* the mystery of the success of the romance novel? The nineteenth-century versions are not about female brain surgeons finding true love and great sex on the hood of a Land Cruiser. But romance novels, then and now, have always been about female aspirations, the ideals and hopes of mostly housebound women. Pamela Regis insists, "The genre is not about women's bondage, as the literary critics would have it. The romance novel is, to the contrary, about women's freedom. The genre is popular because it conveys the pain, uplift, and joy that freedom brings" (xiii).

Janice A. Radway, in *Reading the Romance,* takes it a bit deeper. The readers interviewed in her study maintain that romance novels are "chronicles of female triumph" (54) and gratefully discuss the profound pleasure they receive from reading them. However, they also acknowledge their ongoing marital and familial frustrations, openly comparing their romance-reading to addictions such as alcoholism and pill-popping—but as a positive alternative, a healthier way to escape their discontent. Radway summarizes,

> In the end, what counts most is the reader's sense that for a short time she has become other and been elsewhere. She must close that book reassured that men and marriage really do mean good things for women. She must also turn back to her daily round of duties, emotionally reconstituted and replenished, feeling confident of her worth and convinced of her ability and power to deal with the problems she knows she must confront. (184)

Although we don't mean to suggest that all romance readers are miserable (indeed, even Radway's subjects wouldn't have described themselves thus)—or that all the miserable ones necessarily use these books to cope—reading romances is certainly more than an idle pastime for the more than six million people who gobble up more than twenty titles yearly. *Over a million* of those readers consume an astounding 51–100-plus books a year! These numbers suggest that a great many people are intensely reliant on the emotional effects of reading these books. (As a reader put it, the need for a pick-me-up can be so great that "sometimes even a bad book is better than nothing," Radway, 50.) Whatever critics and lit geeks might think about the quality of the books or the nature of the relationships portrayed in them, romance novels must be taken seriously for the therapeutic role they perform.

And they must be taken particularly seriously because—if it's true that they are coping mechanisms—their excessive and growing consumption presents a sobering picture of the emotional state of women in America. The reading may provide temporary relief and genuine joy, but it doesn't actually *solve problems*, first and foremost because escaping from difficulty will never revolutionize an unhappy marriage. More troubling, many of these books, especially the traditional romance novels, airbrush and glorify the old-fashioned marital standards that make women unhappy enough to read romances in the first place! Think about it: although many single and/or employed women also read romances, it's not Dr. Laura's abortion-happy career girl who has the time to read multiple books a week. Indeed, Radway's findings suggest that the types of men and relationships featured in traditional romance novels are not necessarily women's fantasies, but (excepting, in most cases, the ten-inchers) their *realities;* women read to renew their hopes that marriages to the hyper-masculine can be emotionally fulfilling. And if that doesn't work, there's always a message in a bottle or a bridge in Madison County to nourish the hope that a different guy, a poetic and emotional soul mate, could be out there.

Whatever our talk-show therapists might say, a lot of women don't seem to be happy, or fulfilled, living role-driven lives with alien spouses. Those who read romance novels—either the traditional type or the Sparks type—seem to be craving passion, connection, and emotional sustenance and not getting enough of them from their relationships. And so they can escape into novels to convince themselves for a few hours that sensitive cowboy-strangers might materialize and cherish them—or that a husband's aloof mien is actually a sign of a powerful love that might be coaxed out at any time. They can also turn to self-help guides to convince themselves that distance is God's desire or nature's plan, that their experiences are shared by 90 percent of the population. In their opposite ways, both approaches provide momentary comfort. But they don't take away the ache. Like the water-weight gleefully shed in the first few weeks of the latest diet, these instantaneous marriage-saving "results" and romantic fantasies are mere illusions of progress. These books provide relief, yes. But they are not solving problems. If they were, millions upon millions of women would not still be reading them.

Of course, illusion has its purpose. Readers may be saddled with spouses who want different things, who have drifted away emotionally, or who can't or won't or *shouldn't* change (sorry, Dr. Phil, but some couples just don't belong together). For readers not willing to accept that certain partnerships will never fulfill their needs—those not willing to leave their relationships—reading hopeful tomes about transformed marriages or multiple orgasms might be the best way to remain upbeat in the face of perpetual dissatisfaction.

But it's awfully sad, no way around it, when a book provides more sustenance than a mate.

And it's sadder still to learn that we love to read about love because we have so little of it.

SOUL TRAIN: RELIGION AND SPIRITUALITY

"Man is a Religious Animal. He is the only Religious Animal.
He is the only animal that has the True Religion—several of them."
Mark Twain

"You see, everybody needs a God who looks like them."
The Secret Life of Bees, Sue Monk Kidd

As a young woman, Betty J. Eadie died and went to heaven. She
met Jesus, learned the secrets of the universe, and finally—it not
being "her time"—returned to her earthly shell. Twenty years later, she
recorded her experiences in a book called *Embraced by the Light*, which
quickly became a bestseller: #4 in 1993, #7 in 1994, and #44 in the
list of the top one hundred for the years 1993–2003. According to
Eadie's website, the book has sold six million copies and has been
translated into twenty-seven languages.

A blend of Mormon, straight-up Christian, and New Age philosophies, Eadie's book explains how everything works—prayers, angels,
the tunnel of light, and the meaning of life. Eadie's magical mystery
tour takes her to a Council of Elders, to a pulsing control center where
angels answer prayers, and even to other worlds ("earths like our own
but more glorious, and always filled with loving, intelligent people,"

88). In the end she returns to her body assured that life has meaning and that she herself has a special mission that she must accomplish before returning to heaven for good.

That might sound suspiciously awesome, but Eadie tries hard to expunge all doubt. The book kicks off with an endorsement by Melvin Morse, MD, who assures readers of the book's scientific legitimacy: "near-death experiences are absolutely real and not hallucinations of the mind" (viii). Perhaps you will be persuaded . . . or maybe you will feel there is something undeniably *Wizard of Oz*-ish here: our near-dead Dorothy wakes from a dream that just happened to incorporate the elements and beliefs of her real life. ("And you were there . . . and you . . . and you!")

Don Piper follows Eadie's lead in his recent hit *90 Minutes in Heaven* (#9 nonfiction in 2006), a book we were pretty excited to read until we learned the title was meant to be taken literally. On the scene of a horrific car accident, the dead and mangled Piper is prayed back to life by a Baptist preacher who "had no doubt that the Holy Spirit was prompting him to act" (42). After this miraculous yet unwanted resurrection, Piper spends the rest of his book pouting, healing, converting people to Christianity, illustrating the boundless power of prayer, and finally learning why God elected to rip him from the very wellspring of joy and fling him into a life of helplessness and excruciating pain back on Earth. Though Piper's account of heaven is different, and far shorter, than Eadie's, his heaven crystallizes his existing beliefs and expectations just as neatly: angels, music, loved ones, pearlescent gates, and gold-bricked streets greet the newly, temporarily departed Christian.

But *Embraced by the Light* and *90 Minutes in Heaven* are really just extreme examples of a fact that holds true for all bestselling religious writing: it's about trust. Because the premises cannot be proven, readers must place their faith in the sincerity of the author. Even when a writer is simply interpreting the Bible, readers must have a sort of blind confidence in that person's training, perceptiveness, and motives, not to mention the divine inspiration of the text. Some exegetes may have more credentials than others, but it's all sort of a strange game—who, really, can be credentialed enough to have the last word on the unknowable? Ultimately, accepting spiritual guidance from such a book must be a matter of trust. No other category of reading is so dependent on the guru factor. (Even the self-help guides, which share many characteristics with these books, often have a measurable bottom line: after trying out the recommended regimen, are you in fact healthier, wealthier, or at least thinner?) So the question becomes, in whom have American readers been putting their faith, and why?

In this chapter we discuss the didactic religious and spiritual titles that have ripped up recent bestselling charts. Only two religious categories have scaled the highest peak in this time period: (conservative) Christian and (miscellaneous) New Age. Each is well and warily aware of the other; in some cases they are even openly combative. Yet the ultimate purpose of each is virtually identical: these books are here to tell us how it is—these guys and gals *know*—and to make us feel good about it.

If nothing else, these authors are sure of themselves. One of the central ironies in this most unironic of genres is the absolute certainty with which such immensely uncertain issues are posited. The Christians' dogmatic swagger feels plenty familiar—and sure, their beliefs are backed up by their Bible and traditions (as open to interpretation and disparate as they may be)—but such conviction is a bit more startling when it comes from folks like Gary Zukav, author of *The Seat of the Soul,* who seems completely unabashed about his lack of supporting evidence. Zukav never reveals any source of his knowledge, but simply teaches us about "multisensory humans" and the collective "dolphin soul" with all the confidence and zeal of any man with a pamphlet.

We'll get back to Zukav later. What's notable is that these authors claim they know how the universe is constructed, and thus they have a unique insight into how we should live. Naturally they feel an obligation to share their secrets. The result is inspiration with divine oomph, a sort of Self-Help with Angels—offering insights into God, peeks into the afterlife, and lots of day-to-day nudging and hectoring.

Despite the obvious theological differences, all the books we review in this chapter share three fundamental conclusions:

1. Everything in life has meaning; there are no accidents.
2. Love is the answer.
3. What other gurus say is almost always wrong.

Obviously these books are popular because they are comforting: there's a plan, there's a system, there's a god, and there's an afterlife. But we need to look at these particular bestsellers in detail to discover what answers and qualities have tickled readers' fancy the most.

Moreover, the set of bestsellers in this chapter is probably the least familiar to a general American reading audience. Few but the most fundamentalist of Christians (and book reviewers), for example, are going to make it through *The Purpose Driven Life* without itching to burn down a church. Readers entranced by the chilled-out creator in *Conversations with God* are unlikely to wade through the 5,000 pages of apocalyptic punishment in the *Left Behind* series. And many readers of mainstream bestsellers—the thrillers, the romances, even the *Tuesdays with Morrie* types—are likely to have missed all spiritual books entirely. But it is exactly in the thrust and parry of Christianity versus New Age that these bestsellers reveal the spiritual angst of contemporary society. So we must take a close look at the tensions between the titles, exploring their competing visions of life's purpose and the heavenly infrastructure, to catch a glimpse of America's religious soul. In some cases, these books *respond* to other religious beliefs almost as much as they promote their own—which says quite a bit about spirituality in the United States and the experiences and self-perceptions of the American religious.

(A moment of confession is perhaps in order, given that so much of this chapter deals with issues that readers find deeply personal. We have read these books as curious and determined—if easily exasperated—outsiders. We come at this from neither a Christian nor a New Age perspective. Indeed, we subscribe to no particular spiritual vision and would undoubtedly be consigned to the lowest level of post-mortal existence by most religions, organized or otherwise. If at times we appear a bit, well, impatient with an author's fuzziness or an argument's gelatinous foundation, it's nothing personal; it's business.)

Let's Meet Our Guests

We'll start with an overview of the Christian and New Age perspectives before looking in detail at two overtly competitive representatives. First to the Christian vision, which in these bestsellers is quite uniform—Protestant and evangelical. Here's the skinny: human beings are lost and in need of salvation, which they can achieve only by receiving Jesus Christ as Lord and Savior and by surrendering their lives to His will.

According to our bestselling authors, however, there's more to this intriguing offer. In addition to spending eternity in heaven with God/Jesus, believers also enjoy untold benefits on Earth. But sometimes they need a little guidance to help them collect on God's promise. And that's where authors such as Bruce Wilkinson and Rick Warren come in.

WIN ONE FOR THE GIMPER!

Bruce Wilkinson, a developer of ministry materials and leader in the early days of the Promise Keepers movement, is the author of *The Prayer of Jabez: Breaking Through to the Blessed Life,* which ranked #11 in 2000 and #1 in 2001 and has sold over nine million copies since its publication. Written for the restless Christian, *Jabez* encourages the reader to become a "gimper"—"someone who always does a little more than what's required or expected"—for God (9–10). The book has a simple premise: ask God to bless you, to "enlarge your territory" and give you more influence over the world, and He will. The name comes from a passage in Chronicles 1:

> And Jabez called on the God of Israel saying,
> "Oh, that You would bless me indeed,
> and enlarge my territory,
> that Your hand would be with me,
> and that You would keep me from evil,
> that I may not cause pain!"
> So God granted him what he requested.
> 1 Chronicles 4:10 (New King James Version)

Wilkinson encourages the reader to repeat this prayer daily, claiming that it is "not the self-centered act it might appear, but a supremely spiritual one and exactly the kind of request our Father longs to hear" (19). According to Wilkinson, God is simply waiting for His believers to ask for more: "Your business is the territory God has entrusted to you. He wants you to accept it as a significant opportunity to touch individual lives, the business community, and the larger world for His glory. Asking him to enlarge that opportunity brings Him only delight" (31–32). Of course, this same idea also applies to other pursuits outside the business world.

All this plenty, however, does not come without some serious spiritual commitment. Asking for more than a normal person can handle requires the Christian to depend fully on God. But that's also what God wants, "because for the Christian, dependence is just another word for power. . . . As God's chosen, blessed sons and daughters, we are expected to attempt something large enough that failure is guaranteed . . . unless God steps in" (60–61, 47).

The Prayer of Jabez is a tiny book with giant print and a simple message. It's written for the reader who believes, as Wilkinson does, that God will delay plane flights so that bestselling authors can make their speaking engagements (79). But a reader who wants a more comprehensive overview of Christian opportunity can turn to *The Purpose Driven Life: What on Earth Am I Here For?* by pastor Rick Warren. It's a sequel of sorts to his *Purpose Driven Church,* which is essentially a seminary textbook that was named one of the "100 Christian Books That Changed the 20th Century." *The Purpose Driven Life,* however, is for individuals, and it caught the layman eye in 2003, rose to #1 in 2004, and then returned to the charts for another bestselling stint in 2005 after a woman named Ashley Smith maneuvered her way out of a kidnapping by reading passages of the book to her captor. Warren's book was still the 11th bestselling nonfiction title in 2006.

According to Warren, *The Purpose Driven Life* is "more than a book; it is a guide to a *40-day spiritual journey* that will enable you to discover the answer to life's most important question: What on earth am I here for?" (9, emphasis original). This spiritual guide is written in a "devotional" format—that is, it's composed of forty short chapters designed to be read over forty days (no skipping ahead!). That's a long time, but heck, it's a tough question. Once it's all over, "you will know God's purpose for your life and will understand the big picture—how all the pieces of your life fit together. Having this perspective will reduce your stress, simplify your decisions, increase your satisfaction, and, most important, prepare you for eternity" (9).

Warren organizes the book into five sections, based on his five overall purposes of the human life:

1. We were planned for God's pleasure, so your first purpose is to offer real worship.
2. We were formed for God's family, so your second purpose is to

enjoy real fellowship.

3. We were created to become like Christ, so your third purpose is to learn real discipleship.

4. We were shaped for serving God, so your fourth purpose is to practice real ministry.

5. We were made for a mission, so your fifth purpose is to live out real evangelism.

Within each section, then, he expands on these topics in chapters such as "Becoming Best Friends with God" and "Growing through Temptation," explaining how we can better serve God and our fellow man through kindness, service, and conversion. Not to spoil the forty-day surprise, but basically, living a purpose-driven life boils down to this: refocus your life on God and use the abilities and passions that He has given you to further His kingdom.

This book owes its real success, we think, not to this fairly standard sketch of Christian responsibilities, but to its format and distribution. Even though *The Purpose Driven Life* does not assume a Christian audience, and it goes to the trouble of explaining why one must foster a relationship with Jesus to avoid damnation, the book was designed as part of Warren's church curriculum and has thrived within the church setting. In fact, Warren's ardent emphasis on church involvement, to which he devotes almost a quarter of his book, is the only thing that really sets *The Purpose Driven Life* apart from the other Christian bestsellers of this time period. He passionately makes his case:

> The person who says, "I don't need the church," is either arrogant or ignorant. The church is so significant that Jesus died on the cross for it. . . . Satan loves detached believers, unplugged from the life of the Body, isolated from God's family, and

unaccountable to spiritual leaders, because he knows they are defenseless and powerless against his tactics. (132, 136)

It is no surprise then that the churches eat it up. Warren has even developed a nationwide "40 Days of Purpose" campaign focused around the book: for a nominal fee, church leaders can receive sermons for their weekly worship services and group study materials, including videos of the author himself, that complement the lessons being gobbled up by the congregation during the forty-day journey.

Has *The Purpose Driven Life* made a real difference for the churches that have embraced it? The website claims so. Though Warren himself notes on day 29, "The *last* thing many believers need today is to go to another Bible study. . . . What they need are *serving* experiences in which they can exercise their spiritual muscles" (231), this book provides voluminous opportunities for small-group busywork. (Indeed, there are now enough *Purpose Driven Life* study-guide and devotional spin-offs to keep one occupied for years.) Warren does spend twelve chapters discussing the importance of service and evangelism, but ultimately, the whole program is church-focused; it's entirely possible for congregations to shut themselves into classrooms and *talk* about service for weeks without doing a thing. In this regard, the program reminds us of a talky version of the self-help books we reviewed in chapter 1: here, the reading *and* talking about being better Christians can stand in for action.

GOD HELPS THOSE WHO HELP THEMSELVES

For those readers who'd rather not bare their skeletons in front of the whole study group, there are, of course, Christian self-help books. God is the only real difference between these titles and their secular counterparts; in style and advice and perky positivity, they are identical.

Joyce Meyer, the author of more than sixty inspirational and devotional books, is the Nora Roberts of this genre. In 2005 alone she had six bestsellers; although none of these made the annual chart for that year, the combined sales of all her books would have put her high in the top ten. Her three bestsellers in 2006 sold over a million copies total. Whether you are *Overcoming Emotional Battles* or finding the *Power of Being Positive,* God's might is Meyer's answer. Her analysis of our current "epic of insecurity," *Approval Addiction: Overcoming the Need to Please Everyone,* combines folksy, pop-psych advice (e.g., "love yourself," "establish boundaries") with a basic Christian call to belief: "We can be secure through Jesus Christ." It's a tough world out there—Satan himself has at times tried to steal her confidence (32). What marks Meyer's approach is her use of examples from the Bible as case studies. Mary Magdalene, for example, "could have succumbed to approval addiction," but she wisely stuck it out with Jesus. And Saul? Well, let's just say that things might have turned out differently if he hadn't been such a "people-pleaser."

Like Joyce Meyer, Joel Osteen knows that God wants us to "think positive" and stop comparing ourselves to others. In *Your Best Life Now: 7 Steps to Living at Your Full Potential* (#2 nonfiction in 2005), Osteen appropriates the secular self-help seven-step program, presenting the most enthusiastic and omnipresent deity we have seen this side of jolly Bacchus. God helps us get front-row parking spots (and if not, well, He probably knows we need the exercise); God lets us slip in front of cars in traffic; God heals cancer; God uses the slowness of a wife's dressing to teach patience; and God cares what outfit we wear to the grocery store: no cruddy workout gear ("If God has ever spoken to me, he spoke to me right there!" Osteen recalls, describing how he hurried home to change clothes, 285).

At times Osteen's unflagging metaphysical cheeriness may strike the unconverted as a bit shallow—perhaps it would be easier to take him seriously if he stopped referring to his (mortal) father as "Daddy." But there's a message here that goes beyond his seven rather platitudinous steps toward fulfillment: "Understand, you are not a cosmic accident, wandering randomly and aimlessly through life. God has a specific purpose for your life" (62). And that purpose is always good: God wants us to be happy, excited, wise, and even financially comfortable. He'll make it all happen, even overcoming our limitations of education and ability, as long as we trust His timetable and plan.

ENERGY BLENDS

Now that we have a basic grip on contemporary bestselling Christian nonfiction, it's time to turn to the non-Christian spiritual blockbusters, a group of disparate titles usually shoved on a shelf labeled "New Age." Although "New Age" is a fairly broad and vague (and comparatively recent) category, with no single text to link its offshoots, the New Age movement itself could be described as an attempt to view God, spirituality, and the meaning of life in new, less restrictive, more empowering ways than those traditionally afforded by organized religion. Underlying this general objective are a few common ideas.

First, many of our bestselling New Age writers believe that we create our circumstances on Earth, either because our souls choose these circumstances before birth or because we create them in our lives. Many mention the existence of energies, frequencies, and vibrations, sometimes for the purpose of extending scientific and quasi-scientific principles into the spiritual realm. Some are more critical of mainstream religion than others, but these books almost always make a point of honoring "masters" such as Jesus and Buddha. And always there is an appeal for seekers to take control and responsibility for their choices and personal growth.

Still, the bestselling authors of this genre share no master text (such as the Bible), nor any traditional framework (such as Protestantism), so their visions diverge much more than those of the Christian writers. Consequently, we describe the main points and execution of each

New Age title in this chapter in a bit more detail. Once finished with our survey, we'll be appropriately equipped to study the clash between these viewpoints and those of conservative Christianity.

BE TRUE TO YOUR SCHOOL

If you're looking to plunge into the New Age pool, you might as well start with the plainspoken and dauntless *Seat of the Soul* by Gary Zukav, which never made it to an annual chart, but still ranked #55 in the one hundred bestsellers from 1993 to 2003. Zukav, as with all our New Agers, paints a pretty picture of a benign universe and then explains how to get the most out of it. From other authors of religious and spiritual tomes we learn that such visions of existence come from secret manuscripts, from initiated masters, or even directly from the mouth of God. Zukav, however, doesn't bother to tell us how he knows what he knows. He just, apparently, knows. It seems that our immortal souls choose physical incarnations on Earth to aid our spiritual evolution; Earth is a "school" where—aided by spiritual guides and teachers—we learn to master "authentic power":

> Our deeper understanding leads us to another kind of power,
> a power that loves life in every form that it appears, a power
> that does not judge what it encounters, a power that perceives
> meaningfulness and purpose in the smallest details upon the
> Earth. This is authentic power. (26)

To shift from seeking "external" power to "authentic" power, we must develop from "five-sensory" into "multisensory" humans—recognizing the compassion and guidance of the universe in our lives; valuing intuition, emotions, and intentions; and acknowledging the reality of karma and the interconnectedness of everything. That evolution is our entire purpose here. Eventually, it's going to happen to every human being.

However, we can dink around for millennia if we feel like it. We can also get caught up in the chains of karma, which "governs the balancing of energy within our system of morality and within those of our neighbors. It serves humanity as an impersonal and Universal teacher of responsibility" (41). Unfortunately, this doesn't always happen within a single lifetime. So if you do beastly things, you may have to pay for it in your next life.

The Indigo Girls: Down with Gary

If you're curious about reincarnation, but don't have time for a long book about collective dolphin souls, we'd recommend you take a listen to the Indigo Girls' hit song "Galileo" instead. In a mere three minutes, the Girls cover several of Gary Zukav's points, griping about their cruddy karma and ascribing their groundless fears to events that happened in previous lives.

However, Zukav does not necessarily second the Girls' assertion that Galileo's is a soul that "got it right." In fact, he omits (and therefore totally disses) Galileo in the opening of his book, choosing William James, Carl Jung, Benjamin Lee Whorf, Niels Bohr, and Albert Einstein as his favorite mystical geniuses.

Zukav claims that, because of karma's steady rule over the universe, nothing in this world is unfair or deserving of judgment. We do not know what karmic circumstances require the suffering we see around us or "what is being healed through each interaction" (43). Therefore, we should react with compassion, and not with anger or condemnation: "Non-judgmental justice relieves you of the self-appointed job of judge and jury because you know that everything is being seen— nothing escapes the law of karma—and this brings forth understanding and compassion" (45). (Interestingly, Joel Osteen's concept of divine justice provides a similar justification for suppressing impulses of personal vengeance—that's God's job.) It also means that we'd better make responsible choices if we want to keep our souls evolving and our good karma purring along.

Though the entire cosmic vision of *The Seat of the Soul* conflicts with the textbook Christian viewpoint, Zukav does not take a combative stance. He seems to be primarily interested not in challenging Christians or snagging religion-hoppers, but in reaching the wandering masses whose lives feel inexplicably "splintered." He uses karma and spiritual evolution to justify his views, but ultimately he wants to convince readers to live responsibility and "reverently," taking care with their thoughts and actions and devoting their time to more than scrambling for money and power. All in all, it's pretty harmless stuff, and it reminds us a lot of the more spiritual end of the self-help selections.

WHAT A COINKIDINK

In *The Celestine Prophecy,* James Redfield attempts to convey some of the same ideas. But instead of just writing them down, he does something really odd: he tries to turn spirituality into an adventure story, a sort of Moses-and-the-Ten-Commandments meets *The Da Vinci Code.*

The premise of *The Celestine Prophecy* is this: there's a document called the "Manuscript," somehow written in Aramaic by the Mayans around 600 BC, that "predicts a massive transformation in human society" and provides nine "Insights" to help people get a clue (4). The book's first-person narrator is informed about the Manuscript's existence by an old acquaintance and then begins a wild journey through Peru to find the Insights one by one and protect the Manuscript, which is being captured and destroyed by the Peruvian government. (Let's skip worrying about the plot—Mayans in Peru, scribbling Aramaic? Let it go.)

The heart of this new spiritual way of life is the coincidence. Says Redfield in the book's introduction, "We notice those chance events that occur at just the right moment, and bring forth just the right individuals, to suddenly send our lives in a new and important direction." This is, indeed, the First Insight. Such coincidences are not coincidences at all, but the magical workings of the universe. When enough people start to understand that this "mysterious movement is real and that it means something, that something else is going on beneath everyday life," the other Insights will be revealed, and we will all learn "what mysterious process underlies human life on this planet" (7–8).

The other Insights proceed from this one. Guided by the coincidences, our narrator dodges various undesirables and meets others who are seeking the Manuscript. His experiences help him to find and then comprehend each Insight in turn. Ultimately he learns that the goal of human existence is to reach a high enough vibration to become invisible, "crossing the barrier between this life and the other world from which we came and to which we go after death" (241).

We'll be honest with you. Although *The Celestine Prophecy* was immensely popular—it was #3 in 1994 and #6 in 1995, plus #18 of the top one hundred list from 1993–2003—it's not all that good an adventure story, and it's not a very convincing spiritual system. The fictionalization is an interesting idea and fills up a heck of a lot more space than a list of nine Insights would, but this is really bare-bones fiction—the story is a forced delivery mechanism for the ideas, not a full and compelling work on its own. (Compare to Ayn Rand, who may be strident but who still writes full, fleshy fiction.) The point, it would seem, is to give the reader the experience of learning the Insights one by one ("You have to discover them in the course of your own life," 36), but even that doesn't really happen because the reader isn't actually experiencing any of it.

Ironically, this really could be the stuff of fiction—the concepts of guiding coincidences and manipulable energy fields could be part of a wonderful fantasy world. As a cogent basis for spirituality, though, it fails pretty much from the get-go. Even if you accept that you haven't given coincidences their fair due, the system would seem to fall apart upon reaching the Third Insight, which is "to see an energy field hovering about everything" (44). No really, try to see it! This energy is "the basic stuff of the universe . . . a pure energy that is malleable to human intention and expectation" (42). The rest of the Insights teach how to work with that energy, absorbing strength from it (instead of stealing energy from other people) and using its visible guidance to make the right choices—which road to take, when to speak up in a conversation, and presumably how to find the best parking spaces. We doubt that millions of readers have spotted the energy field, even though Redfield seems to be quite serious about it and claims to believe in the ideas put forth in *The Celestine Prophecy.* The end of the book encourages readers to subscribe to Redfield's *Celestine Journal,* "which chronicles his present experiences and reflections on the spiritual renaissance occurring on our planet." He also offers audiotape analyses of individual sun and moon signs, which will help you "understand your particular control issues and discover your most inspired, spiritual mission."

But unlike *The Seat of the Soul, The Celestine Prophecy* is not trying merely to scoop up the lost and shiftless. It is actually attempting to "clarify many religions," including Christianity (239). But clarification doesn't come easily. Those trying to suppress and destroy the Manuscript are actually church authorities and their flunkies. Says Cardinal Sebastian, the head honcho,

> "This Manuscript is a curse. It would undermine our basic structure of spiritual authority. It would entice people to think they are in control of their spiritual destiny. It would undermine the discipline needed to bring everyone on the

planet into the church, and people would be caught wanting when the rapture comes." (237)

Those supporting the Manuscript, however, believe that it explains just how Jesus was able to walk on water and then transcend death:

> "The Manuscript says that sometime in history one individual would grasp the exact way of connecting with God's source of energy and direction and would thus become a lasting example that this connection is possible. . . . Didn't Jesus, himself, say that what he did, we could do also, and more? We've never really taken that idea seriously, not until now. We're only now grasping what Jesus was talking about, where he was leading us. The Manuscript clarifies what he meant! How to do it!" (239, 236)

In sum, the Manuscript is meant to unite: "The truth is a synthesis of the scientific and religious world views. The truth is that evolution is the way God created, and is still creating" (236). The Insights also validate the philosophies of both East and West: "They show us that the West is correct in maintaining that life is about progress, about evolving toward something higher. Yet the East is also correct in emphasizing that we must let go of control with the ego. We can't progress by using logic alone" (142). The book even unites one's parents—each of us can determine our mission in life by analyzing the beliefs and purpose of each parent and "reconcil[ing] these two positions by pursuing a higher synthesis" (149).

TOLTEC TREK

Another vision offered up by our friends in the southern Americas is *The Four Agreements* by Don Miguel Ruiz. Unlike the other authors in this group, Ruiz claims to have credentials: a Toltec *nagual* (master), Ruiz "has been guided to share with us the powerful teachings of the Toltec," who were "scientists and artists who formed a society to explore and conserve the spiritual knowledge and practices of the ancient ones" thousands of years ago in southern Mexico (xiii). These teachings have been passed down in secret for generations, though "ancient prophecies foretold the coming of an age when it would be necessary to return the wisdom to the people" (xiv). That age, apparently, has come. *The Four Agreements* was the #14 trade paperback in 2001, and it ranked #30 out of all books between 1993 and 2003.

Ruiz's lessons are largely practical. As the book's introduction states, the Toltec knowledge "is most accurately described as a way of life, distinguished by the ready accessibility of happiness and love" (xiv). It is not a religion, per se, but "does embrace spirit" (xiv), which is close enough for us.

So, what's an "agreement"? Ruiz begins his book by explaining that we inherit our values and beliefs from the larger world (see, Morrie is everywhere!). We absorb what we are taught and go along with it because we soon learn that we will be rewarded if we do and punished if we don't. We didn't choose these beliefs, but we "agreed" to them all, and "eventually we become someone that we are not. We become a copy of Mamma's beliefs, Daddy's beliefs, society's beliefs and religion's beliefs" (8). "Ninety-five percent of the beliefs we have stored in our minds are nothing but lies, and we suffer because we believe all those lies" (13).

Ruiz provides the way out. As difficult as it is, we must make four new agreements with ourselves. Ruiz warns, "You need a very strong will in order to adopt the Four Agreements—but if you can begin to live your life with these agreements, the transformation in your life will be amazing" (23). These Agreements are as follows:

1. Be impeccable with your word.
2. Don't take anything personally.
3. Don't make assumptions.
4. Always do your best.

The way of the Agreements requires a thick skin and a certain non-chalance. We are not to be hurt by the words of others, knowing that they are seeing the world through their own eyes. We are not to feel bad if others accuse us of hurting them—for they are choosing to be hurt. We are not to stay in relationships with those who want to change us: "Real love is accepting other people the way they are without trying to change them. . . . If others feel they have to change you, that means they really don't love you just the way you are. . . . Find someone else" (70–71). So much for most marriages.

Barring a few loopy comments, Ruiz's way does make a real if mostly unattainable sense. It's true that people don't always think for themselves or communicate with clarity and integrity. Still, it's hard to imagine anyone but a heavy meditator pulling off some of this stuff. Try telling Mom, for example, not to take it personally that you don't want to spend the holidays with her. "I'm not hurting you, Mom; you're hurting yourself!"

Let us know how it turns out.

Like the other New Age authors, Ruiz believes that human choice is the key to happiness—or misery: "Who stops us from being free? We blame the government, we blame the weather, we blame our parents, we blame religion, we blame God. Who really stops us from being free? We stop ourselves" (94). Ultimately, he encourages readers to create their own joy. To Ruiz, heaven is a reality that we can choose now, not a reward for the saved: "We can reach heaven while we are alive; we don't have to wait until we die. God is always present and the kingdom of heaven is everywhere, but first we need to have the eyes and ears to see and hear that truth" (104). Still, Ruiz does not seem to care one way or the other about traditional religion. He criticizes its propensity to force beliefs on people, but also says, "You don't need to worship idols of the Virgin Mary, the Christ, or the Buddha. You can if you want to" (87).

Taken as whole, it's not surprising that these bestselling religious books, both Christian and New Age, strike a resonant chord with readers. Each presents a picture of a primarily benevolent universe that, with the help of a Teacher, holds the possibility of happiness for us all. Given the nature of the world as understood by these authors, humanity's familiar tensions, uncertainties, and tragedies melt away. Or if not that, at least inveterate, irresolvable neuroses are swapped for a new batch of neuroses. The modern materialistic, status-conscious, individualistic, mortal, existential world gives way to a spiritual, egalitarian community of eternal souls enveloped in meaning. Because none of these visions has any evidence to support it, the bestselling authors are those who can persuade readers to give their particular interpretation of the universe a chance. There's a natural competition, then, even if some of the specific insights overlap: do we adopt one prayer, four agreements, five purposes, seven steps, nine insights, ten commandments, or the multi-senses? We have no doubt—and the Amazon.com reviews make it clear—that just as in the case of romance novels, many of these books have been bought by serial spiritual self-helpers. The issues and conclusions are often complementary. But when you get right down to it, the New Agers disagree with each other, the Christians have different understandings about scripture, and the two camps really cannot live on the same side of the spiritual lake. So far in our review, there has been little direct conflict: the Christians try for the most part to ignore their naughty neighbors; the New Agers sometimes clear a little room near the campfire for Jesus. But all that is about to change.

Let the Battle Begin

Now that you've gotten a flavor of the Christian and New Age world-views, it's time to take a deeper look at two additional bestsellers that bring this potential ideological conflict into the limelight: the *Left Behind* series and *Conversations with God.* Here we find authors who take real exception with the other point of view and who allow us to dig deep enough to find out exactly what bugs them so much. We'll begin with the *Left Behind* series, a fundamentalist Christian tale of the Rapture in twelve parts (plus prequels and a sequel), written by Tim LaHaye and Jerry Jenkins. Brace yourself—all hell is about to break loose.

STUCK IN THE MIDDLE WITH YOU

Ah, Revelation. Undoubtedly the freakiest book of the Bible, it's a fantastical, disturbing vision of the Apocalypse (that is, the end of the world) written by someone named John—some say the Apostle John. It's the last book of the Bible and has been around since the late first century. But 1,900 years later—that is, in the early 1990s—biblical scholar Tim LaHaye and author Jerry K. Jenkins felt it was time for Revelation to do something more than creep out impressionable middle school students. They began to write the *Left Behind* series, a fictionalized account of the end times based on their "Premillennial" interpretation of Revelation.

The first book came out in 1995, but wasn't an immediate bestseller. It wasn't until 1998 that *Left Behind* hit the charts, but it went on to cause a craze, eventually snagging the #61 spot on the list of the one hundred bestsellers from 1993 to 2003. Each of the subsequent eleven books was also a top seller, and the new series sequel, *Kingdom Come,* will surely be too. Today, the series has sold some sixty-five million copies (seventy-five million if you count the children's versions!). *Publishers Weekly* hailed it as "the most successful Christian-fiction series ever," and *Time* claimed that the authors "are doing for Christian fiction what John Grisham did for courtroom thrillers."

The twelve books of the main series comprise nearly 5,000 pages of end-time mayhem, and yes, we have read every one. The story begins with—and ultimately focuses on—Rayford Steele, a generally upstanding commercial pilot in his forties. Rayford is professionally successful, married, and the father of two, known for his temperance and honesty. Nonetheless, he is discontent:

> Rayford used to look forward to getting home to his wife. Irene was attractive and vivacious enough, even at forty. But lately he had found himself repelled by her obsession with religion. It was all she could talk about.
>
> God was OK with Rayford Steele. Rayford even enjoyed church occasionally. But since Irene had hooked up with a smaller congregation and was into weekly Bible studies and church every Sunday, Rayford had become uncomfortable. Hers was not a church where people gave you the benefit of the doubt, assumed the best about you, and let you be. People there had actually asked him, to his face, what God was doing in his life. (1–2)

Rayford Steele may like God well enough, but God doesn't return the compliment. In midair, just as Rayford is contemplating making a move on a bimboish flight attendant, God whisks away all the dedicated Christians from the face of the earth. Fortunately for his passengers, Rayford is not among the chosen, but he lands the plane and returns to a world in chaos—where millions of people, including *all* babies and children, have vanished, leaving their clothes and trinkets behind.

Though theories abound, Rayford knows instantly what has happened: "The Rapture had taken place. . . . Irene had been right. He, and most of his passengers, had been left behind" (48, 19). He returns home to find his wife and young son gone, discarded pajamas in their beds, and waits in agony for news of his older daughter, a Stanford undergrad named Chloe.

In the meantime, Rayford seeks out Irene's former church, where he meets a pastor named Bruce Barnes, left behind because of his shoddy faith. Repentant Bruce has figured out what he did wrong, and he helps Rayford (along with many other seekers) to come to Christ the right way. Rayford is reunited with his daughter Chloe, who takes more time but also becomes a believer.

Through Bruce, the new converts learn that they must now attempt to live through the Tribulation, a seven-year period of great suffering when all the undesirables have one last chance to accept God and thus get themselves out of the discard pile. Though they will have to suffer through the Tribulation and its two dozen plagues (the Egyptians had it good by comparison) and likely will be martyred by the followers of the Antichrist, in the end they will live with Jesus during his thousand-year reign of peace on Earth. So—along with a sprightly young journalist named Cameron "Buck" Williams—Bruce, Rayford, and Chloe form the Tribulation Force, vowing to fight the Antichrist and bring as many people to Jesus as they can in the time they have left.

The eleven subsequent books describe this epic war between good and evil, but (lucky for you) we do not have the space here to go into all the details. More interesting at any rate are the religious and social views and assumptions espoused therein. Though the books endorse the same conservative Christian theology of *The Prayer of Jabez* and *The Purpose Driven Life,* the fiction medium and sheer length of the series enable us to delve more deeply into the authors' beliefs, intentions, and pet peeves. The series also shares some characteristics of the "good and evil" books we discussed previously, shedding additional light on the experiences and values of American readers.

VIRGINS OR WHORES

True Christians, you will recall, are those who put their faith in Jesus as Lord and Savior, asking Him for salvation and forgiveness. In the *Left Behind* series, only those who met that description were Raptured (excepting children). The devout of other religions, lukewarm attendees of Christian congregations, and the nonreligious good did not achieve the divine endorsement. Faith trumps morality every time.

The narrowness of this definition and its consequences pose some interesting challenges for the authors. Clearly the Raptured Christians were right, and everybody else wrong—but LaHaye and Jenkins can't create nasty, unsympathetic characters, or they'd have no hope of keeping readers interested for nearly 5,000 postapocalyptic pages (did we mention that we read them all?). Their solution is essentially to create likeable characters that simply made mistakes in faith, but become devout believers after the Rapture.

This is fair enough, and the authors genuinely seem to realize that there are countless reasons why basically good people missed Christianity. Rayford and Chloe were too driven and intellectual for religion (a theme we will discuss in further detail later on). Buck went to church as a child, but "it was the lack of any connection between his family's church attendance and their daily lives that made him quit going to church altogether the day it became his choice" (109). Loretta, a member of Bruce's church, "was considered a pillar in this church. I was active in everythin', a church woman. I just never really knew the Lord" (28–29). Some were "better than most religious people we knew," but agnostic (*Assassins,* 34). Some had atheist parents and had been in church only for weddings and funerals (*Left Behind,* 281). Some just "didn't think about religion" (*The Remnant,* 202) or even "had never heard of Jesus" (*Glorious Appearing,* 325). Despite these mistakes and missed opportunities, most of these characters are kind and good people who can and do convert, becoming believers as vibrant as any that had lived before the Rapture.

However, as sympathetic as they can be to nonbelievers, the authors undercut their generosity on a number of occasions, ultimately implying that Christians are essentially kind and selfless and nonbelievers the opposite. After all, "Everyone . . . who's gone is either a child or a very nice person" (*Left Behind,* 62), whereas "lost people" have "a lot of pride" (*Tribulation Force,* 409). When thinking about his former life as a nonbeliever, Ree Woo says, "I worshiped me, you know what I mean?" and his friend replies, "Of course. Didn't we all?" (*The Remnant,* 261). Though the authors can grasp that people-with-potential can miss the one true faith, they seem to believe that goodness, even basic decent behavior, comes in most cases only with Christianity.

The authors are also uneasy about secular thinking and modern social mores, to the extent that they make Buck—a thirty-year-old, world-famous, globe-trotting journalist—a virgin, presumably so that he can be "pure" when he marries Chloe in the second book. Chloe is a virgin herself—more common for a twenty-year-old, perhaps—but she is also a mature, formerly nonreligious college student; and frankly, we would expect a less gung-ho response to his confession than this one: "That's something to be proud of these days" (*Tribulation Force,* 200).

Basically, the most significant left-behind characters in the novels have followed Christian practices, some of them fairly stringent, without actually having been Christian. Buck and Chloe are virgins until marriage; Rayford almost never touches alcohol and never commits the adultery he desires so greatly. The authors allow a few minor characters to stumble, especially Hattie the flight attendant, who becomes illegitimately pregnant with the Antichrist's baby. (It would have been so much better if they had been married.) Hattie considers *all* her options, prompting voluminous and creative antiabortion argument. But the authors don't let even poor Hattie go that far, and the problem is solved with a handy miscarriage.

This careful characterization reveals two things: that LaHaye and Jenkins accept that non-Christians, or at least non-fully-believing Christians, can be very clean-living folks (if perhaps not as nice and selfless as dedicated believers) and simultaneously that the authors can't or won't invest deeply in protagonists who have done things they consider immoral. Though they insist that God forgives all who ask and that "the Bible says that all have sinned, that there is none right-eous, no not one" (*Left Behind,* 204), the authors don't soil their hands with the mud of real life. This ambivalence toward nonbelievers, an uneasy balance of empathy and disdain, runs throughout the series.

PEOPLE OF OTHER FAITHS

Of course, though, there are many other categories besides Christian and nonbeliever, some of which are extensively explored in the series and others almost wholly ignored.

Most are dismissed, often in ways that reveal a certain fear and igno-rance of the belief systems in question. George, a military man who gets captured by the bad guys, tries to employ transcendental medita-tion to endure his captivity, with the authors hastily adding, "Even back then, even before becoming a believer in Christ, he didn't want any-thing to do with any religious aspects of meditation" (*Desecration,* 373–374). (Here again we see the pervasive need to keep the protag-onists "pure," even before conversion.) Fortunately for his soul, the attempt at meditation fails anyway.

Neither Buddhism nor Hinduism is mentioned by name. The one Muslim in the series eventually converts to Christianity.

But the Jews the authors like. Two Jewish protagonists are central to the story, and the Jewish masses are involved throughout the entire series, sometimes receiving exotic divine privileges (God's chosen people and all). Buck assures them, "When Jewish people such as yourselves come

to see that Jesus is your long-sought Messiah . . . you are not converting from one religion to another, no matter what anyone tells you.
You have found your Messiah, that is all" (*Armageddon,* 331).

The Catholics don't fare quite so well. (Even in our hypersensitive
age, Catholics appear to be fair game for demonization of every flavor, whether in *Left Behind, The Celestine Prophecy,* or *The Da Vinci
Code.*) Although the old Pope was Raptured because he was essentially
a Protestant-in-disguise, the new Pope is a "real" Catholic and a lousy
Christian and represents All That Is Wrong With Society Today. More
than just the pontiff, this guy also heads up the one-world religion
established by the Antichrist (though to the Pope's credit, he takes the
job without knowing the sneaky devil's secret identity). In this role,
he departs farther and farther from the tenets of Christianity:

> "I don't care to be too specific, at the risk of offending those
> few who still like to refer to themselves as Catholics, but the
> idea of a literal virgin birth should be seen as an incredible
> leap of logic. The idea that the Holy Roman Catholic Church
> was the only true church was almost as damaging as the
> evangelical Protestant view that Jesus was the only way to
> God." (*Nicolae,* 360)

As the series continues, the new leader absorbs all the religions of the
world to absurd excess, dressing in a ridiculously decorated costume and
encouraging his congregation to "seek our multilayered plural godhead
in your own fashion" (*Apollyon,* 55)—that godhead being "the universal father and mother and animal deities who lovingly guide us in our
path to true spirituality" (*Apollyon,* 54). Boo-yah! There's a big snap to
New Age and pre-Christian religious ideas. But the Catholics aren't the
only ones moving in a flaky direction: with few exceptions, all other
religions crumble into one after the Rapture. In one of our favorite

passages, a biblical scholar muses, "It may be that many of these belief systems eagerly gave up their claims of exclusivity because they never made sense" (*Soul Harvest*, 327). That the Christians refuse to join the one-world religion, maintaining their exclusive stance, is critical: if there's anything the authors hate, it's toleration of all religions as equally valid. Such tolerance is what the Antichrist preaches; it can only lead to damnation for the suckers that fall for it.

SITTING ON A THRONE OF LIES

So what's all this about an Antichrist?

Let us explain briefly: his name is Nicolae Carpathia, a thirty-three-year-old "businessman/politician" who "[took Romania] by storm with his popular, persuasive speaking" and became president "with the seeming unanimous consensus of the people and . . . government" (*Left Behind*, 113–134). Nicolae goes on to charm the world with his pacifist convictions, stellar memory, and toothy smile. He gets elected to a seat in the United Nations and then takes over the whole thing. Eventually, of course, he rules the world, gradually transforming from sweet-talker to horn-sprouter.

Now, don't be confused. The Antichrist is not Satan. He's human—albeit with special powers—and at first he does not know he's the Antichrist. Later, when he seems to have raised his right-hand man from the dead, he begins to think he may be God. Midway through the series, he is assassinated and resurrected—and only *then* is he "indwelt" with Satan. We do learn at some point that he's been worshipping Lucifer for years.

But what's actually interesting about Nicolae is that he is perhaps the only character in the series whose beliefs and knowledge are a mystery for a good long while. The whole plot is spelled out long in advance, and all the other important characters are forthcoming about their beliefs, so the series provides very few opportunities for curiosity and guesswork. (Spoiling the ending—or the middle, for that matter—does not seem to be a concern for these guys; God is faithful in telling the characters what will happen, and the authors provide readers with the same service.) Nicolae's confusion about his own identity is an intriguing aspect of his character as we watch him rise to power. But then he gets really nasty and satanic and predictable and just isn't fun anymore.

Anyway, what's significant about the authors' representation of evil is how, of course, they define their good. God is supposed to be not only good but also absolutely right in calling down this Tribulation thing. He not only allowed it; He orchestrated it! He also allowed the Antichrist to terrorize the world, and in the future, He will allow Satan to return to earth after God's thousand-year reign of peace.

It is God who sends demonic locusts to terrorize nonbelievers for five months—in addition to two dozen other horrible plagues.

It is God who hardens some nonbelievers' hearts so that they can't change their minds even when they see the error of their ways.

It is God who slaughters thousands of unbelievers upon returning, until the river of blood runs "several miles wide and now some five feet deep" (*Glorious Appearing*, 258).

Justifying this kind of suffering is a tricky task. Theodicy has always been the flat tire on the vehicle of monotheistic religions, and no one has looked harder for spares than the Christians. Like abuse victims or the cowed spouses of alcoholics, they are an endless font of excuses. LaHaye and Jenkins pull out the most familiar. Mainly, it's the What Else Could He Do? Defense, but there's also the We Don't Understand God's Eternal Plan Argument and the Heck, We Deserved It Anyway Theory. Here are a couple of choice examples:

[Character Tsion Ben-Judah says] "God is not willing that any should perish but that all should come to repentance. That is the reason for this entire season of trial and travail.

. . . In his love and mercy he has tried everything to get our attention. All of us remaining on earth to this day were delinquent in responding to his loving call. Now, using every arrow in his quiver, as it were, he makes himself clearer than ever with each judgment." (*Apollyon,* 156–157)

"This is the price we pay," [Amanda] said, "for ignoring the warnings when we had the chance." (*Tribulation Force,* 432)

Did this many people have to suffer to make some eternal point? He took comfort in that this was not God's desired result. Rayford believed God was true to his word, that he had given people enough chances that he could now justify allowing this to get their attention. (*Soul Harvest,* 108–109)

And then there is the money quote, from the character Tsion Ben-Judah: "How it must pain him to have to resort to such measures to reach those he loves!" (*Apollyon,* 330)

The locusts, the bloodbaths, hurt *God* more than they hurt us. It's an intervention. It's *the* intervention.

Okay, now one does have to accept the context: this is the world the characters are living in, the Rapture *has* happened, and their only choices are to believe in Christ or go to Hell. So it makes sense to make the best of it, to believe that the Guy in Charge is right (succumbing to a kind of spiritual Stockholm Syndrome?). But *honestly*—does an omnipotent God need to "resort" to anything? Couldn't He convince the characters using wonderful miracles instead of heinous ones? But that's not what Revelation says, so instead the authors have to try to convince their characters and readers that all this misery springs from divine mercy.

It's a tough pill to swallow, and to their credit, the authors know it and show it. All the characters, compassionate people, return to the same issue again and again: how can our loving God do this?

> Rayford knew the prophecy—that people would reject God enough times that God would harden their hearts and they wouldn't be able to choose him even if they wanted to. But knowing it didn't mean Rayford understood it. And it certainly didn't mean he had to like it. He couldn't make it compute with the God he knew, the loving and merciful one who seemed to look for ways to welcome everyone into heaven, not keep them out. (*Armageddon*, 17–18)

Leah, a bitchier character, takes a tougher stance:

> Were people insane? No, she decided, they were self-possessed, narcissistic, vain, proud. In a word, *evil*. They saw the acts of God and turned their backs on Him, choosing the pleasures of sin over eternity with Christ.
>
> God had, in the meantime, hardened many hearts. And when these unbelievers changed their minds—or tried to—they were not even capable of repenting and turning to God. That had seemed unfair to Leah at first, but as the years rolled by and the judgments piled up, she began to see the logic of it. God knew that eventually sinners would grow weary of their own poverty, but His patience had a limit. There came a time when enough was enough. People had had way more than enough information to make a reasonable choice, and the sad fact was they had made the wrong one, time and time again. (*Glorious Appearing*, 178–179)

The obvious response, it would seem to us, would be to accept that God is in control but to question his goodness—"Man, I'm glad I'm going to heaven, but why does God have to be such a nasty prick sometimes?" This response, however, does not surface in the series. Instead, the characters try desperately to convince themselves that God does everything for the greater good, blaming their limited understanding when the evidence seems absent or contradictory (a quest that the authors, as well as their Christian readers, undoubtedly must face in their own lives).

Although we think it's clear that God is far crueler than the Antichrist in these books (no earthly horror dished out by the Antichrist could compare to the *eternity* of suffering that God allows), we'll be generous and say that, at the very least, both supernatural figures display cruelty. So what exactly is the difference? What makes God "good" when He seems to display no more empathy than a psycho in a horror novel, no more empathy than the Antichrist himself?

Well, He does save the souls of many people, welcoming them to His paradise, and He does provide spiritual protection and comfort to living believers. But there's a more interesting distinction: God tells the truth. Whereas Satan and the Antichrist are deceivers, pretending to be humble and peace-loving only to unleash a reign of terror, God never claims to be anything other than He is or to do anything other than He does. God is, as the characters often remind us, *faithful.*

As you'll recall from our "good and evil" chapter, honesty and constancy are pivotal values for many of our conservative and religious political authors, much more important to them than empathy. If God is the leader of your universe, and His ways are your definition of good, would you not look for earthly leaders whose values resembled those of your divine one? Perhaps this vision of God—rigid, dualistic, unchanging—determines not only the religious beliefs and practices of conservative Christians, but also the politics, the social perspectives, the very vision of the world's underlying construction. From this image of Creator we create a world to match. Or have we here once again, as is so often noted elsewhere, formed the Creator in our own image?

LOSING MY RELIGION

We'll pause here and scoot over to the New Age side for a moment, reviewing what is probably the most controversial New Age title of the past sixteen years: *Conversations with God: An Uncommon Dialogue,* a three-part series by Neale Donald Walsch. The books are just that: dialogues between Walsch and God, questions and answers about every topic a searching person might ask of a creator. The first book was the #8 hardcover nonfiction bestseller in 1997 and ranked #83 for the years 1993–2003.

Walsch claims in the book's introduction, "This book was not written *by* me, it happened *to* me." He goes on to explain how, on one particularly frustrating and despairing night, he began to write God an angry letter:

> To my surprise, as I scribbled out the last of my bitter, unanswerable questions and prepared to toss my pen aside, my hand remained poised over the paper, as if held there by some invisible force. Abruptly, the pen began *moving on its own.* I had no idea what I was about to write, but an idea seemed to be coming, so I decided to flow with it.
>
> . . .
>
> Before I knew it, I had begun a conversation . . . and I was not writing so much as *taking dictation.* (1–2)

Walsch continued to play God's secretary over a period of three years. He assures readers, "When I became confused, or lost the feeling that the words were coming from somewhere else, I put the pen

down and walked away from the dialogue until I again felt inspired . . .
to return to the yellow pad and start transcribing again" (2). Whew!
Glad to hear that—we would hate to think the authenticity of the project had been compromised.

God—C.W. God, as we will call him here—has much to say in these
books, and he's not afraid to say it. He starts off with a bang: the Bible
and people of religion are not authoritative sources on the nature of God
and the universe. Your own experience is. If your experience of something
conflicts with the teachings of others, discard the words and believe the
experience. (Sex is one glaring example—C.W. God says, "Of course sex
is 'okay.' Again, if I didn't want you to play certain games, I wouldn't have
given you the toys" (205).) He soon dishes out additional shake-ups:

> If you believe that God is some omnipotent being who hears
> all prayers, says "yes" to some, "no" to others, and "maybe,
> but not now" to the rest, you are mistaken. By what rule of
> thumb would God decide?
>
> If you believe that God is the *creator and decider of all things*
> in your life, you are mistaken.
>
> God is the *observer,* not the creator. And God stands
> ready to assist you in living your life, but not in the way
> you might expect.
>
> *It is not God's function to create, or uncreate, the circumstances
> or conditions of your life.* God created *you,* in the image and
> likeness of God. *You* have created the rest, through the power
> God has given you. God created the process of life and life
> itself as you know it. Yet God gave you free choice, to do
> with life itself as you know it.
>
> In this sense, *your will for you is God's will for you.*
>
> You are living your life the way you are living your life,
> and *I have no preference in the matter.*

This is the grand illusion in which you have engaged: that
God *cares* one way or the other what you do. (13)

Okay, here's the summary. All of us are little bits of God, chopped
off so that we can *experience* things. We are not here to learn or evolve
(unless we want to). We have free will. There is no right and wrong,
but "by your decisions you paint a portrait of Who You Are" (154),
so if you *want* to be good, you should stop being such a darn hyp-
ocrite and just *do* it.

Though C.W. God uses semicolons in an unorthodox and potentially ungodly manner, he does a good job of pointing out all the ways
we are stupid, and many of these fly directly in the face of traditional
religion. We are stupid about sex, stupid about money, stupid about
health, stupid about world issues, and mostly stupid about God. We
are fearful, judgmental, and thoughtless, inventing a God who is as
vindictive and needy as we are:

> You have projected the role of "parent" onto God, and have
> thus come up with a God Who judges and rewards or pun-
> ishes, based on how good He feels about what you've been
> up to. But this is a simplistic view of God, based on your
> mythology. It has nothing to do with Who I Am.
>
> Having thus created an entire thought system about God
> based on human experience rather than spiritual truths, you
> then create an entire reality around love. It is a fear-based
> reality, rooted in the idea of a fearful, vengeful God. Its
> Sponsoring Thought is wrong, but to deny that thought
> would be to disrupt your whole theology. And though the
> new theology which would replace it would *truly* be your sal-
> vation, you cannot accept it, *because the idea of a God Who
> is not to be feared, Who will not judge, and Who has no cause*

to punish is simply too magnificent to be embraced within even
your grandest notion of Who and What God is. (17–18)

You can see why fundamentalist Christians might have some trouble with this. The description does sound pretty great, but Rick Warren warns in *The Purpose Driven Life,* "People often say, 'I like to think of God as . . . ,' and then they share their idea of the kind of God they would like to worship. But we cannot just create our own comfortable or politically correct image of God and worship it. That is idolatry" (101).

C. W. God shoots back,

> Most of you . . . spend the bulk of your adult life searching for the "right" way to worship, to obey, and to serve God. *The irony of all this is that I do not want your worship, I do not need your obedience, and it is not necessary for you to serve Me.*
>
> If you choose to believe in a God who somehow *needs* something—and has such hurt feelings if He doesn't get it that He punishes those from whom He expected to receive it—then you choose to believe in a God much smaller than I. You truly *are* children of a Lesser God. (64–65)

Believe it or not, the purpose of *Conversations with God* is not to bash Christianity (at least not primarily), but C.W. God simply doesn't hesitate to point out its flaws. The concept of damnation is a particular sore spot:

> There are those who say that I have given you free will, yet these same people claim that if you do not obey Me, I will send you to hell. What kind of free will is that? Does this

not make a mockery of God—to say nothing of any sort of true relationship between us? (39)

You are saying that I, God, made inherently imperfect beings, then have demanded of them to be perfect, or face damnation. You are saying then that, somewhere several thousand years into the world's experience, I relented, saying that from then on you didn't necessarily *have* to be good, you simply had to feel bad when you were not being good, and accept as your savior the One Being who could *always* be perfect, thus satisfying My hunger for perfection. You are saying that My Son—who you call the One Perfect One—has saved you from your own imperfection—the imperfection *I gave you.*

In other words, God's Son has saved you from *what His Father did.*

This is how you—many of you—say I've set it up.

Now *who is mocking whom?* (136–137)

As is customary in these types of books, C.W. God considers Jesus a master, even claiming that he did literally resurrect himself (196), but he is no more holy, has no more special relationship to God, and has no more inherent power than any of us. As for damnation, C.W. God assures us that even Hitler went to heaven, asserting, "When you understand this, you will understand God" (61).

This is exactly the kind of thing that gets conservative Christians all riled up. You'll recall how in the *Left Behind* series, the new Pope becomes head of a "one-world" religion called Enigma Babylon that incorporates the beliefs and symbols of all the remaining religions on Earth. To adherents of that new religion, the Christians are big party-poopers for not joining up, but Tsion Ben-Judah (a converted Jew and biblical scholar) insists,

Those who pride themselves on tolerance and call us exclu-
sivists, judgmental, unloving, and shrill are illogical to the
point of absurdity. . . . When everything is tolerated, nothing is limited.

There are those who ask, why not cooperate? Why not be
loving and accepting? Loving we are. Accepting we cannot
be. It is as if Enigma Babylon is an organization of "one-and-
only true" religions. It may be that many of these belief systems eagerly gave up their claims of exclusivity because they
never made sense.

Belief in Christ, however, is unique and, yes, exclusive on
the face of it. Those who pride themselves on "accepting"
Jesus Christ as a great man, perhaps a god, a great teacher,
or one of the prophets, expose themselves as fools. (*Soul
Harvest*, 327–338)

The particularly critical sentence here is "when everything is tolerated, nothing is limited." Fundamentalist Christians are terrified of a
world without divinely imposed law because they don't believe that ethical behavior can exist without it. With seeming innocence, LaHaye
and Jenkins describe how Hattie (a longtime holdout against
Christianity) "was the only unbeliever [in their safe house] and under-
standably selfish. She spent most of her time on herself" (*The Assassins*,
14). Rayford "had to remind himself that she was not a believer. She
would not be thinking about the good of anyone but herself. Why
should she?" (*Nicolae*, 295–296).

Why should she? The existence of ethical non-Christians (whether
New Agers, Jews, Buddhists, Muslims, or atheists) should be apparent to anyone venturing outside his congregation for even half an
hour. Yet Rick Warren echoes this sentiment in *The Purpose Driven
Life:* "If your time on earth were all there is to your life, I would suggest

you start living it up immediately. You could forget being good and ethical, and you wouldn't have to worry about any consequences of your actions. You could indulge yourself in total self-centeredness because your actions would have no long-term repercussions" (38). But because there is a God, and potential hellfire, we have to behave well.

Frankly, it's a mystery how this primitive argument could be taken so completely for granted. But we have a theory, thanks to some interesting narrative tactics in the *Left Behind* series. Here it goes: the Christian concept of morality is nearly identical to the concepts of most others—golden rule, no stealing, no lying, and so on. *However,* this basic ethical foundation is layered with "hot buttons" that, to fundamentalists, immediately signal depravity.

Here's how it works in the *Left Behind* books. Topics such as homosexuality, abortion, and fortune-telling are used as "triggers" that paint an instantaneous ethical portrait of the person, organization, or place being described. For example, the only gay character in the book starts out nasty and turns out to be untrustworthy. "There's a lot of cloning and fetal tissue research going on" at an Antichrist-run abortion facility—making it sound even more sinister. The presence of gay couples in a bar shows that Israel is polluted. And in another of our favorite quotes, "Real violence, actual tortures and murders, is proudly advertised as available twenty-four hours a day on some channels. Sorcery, black magic, clairvoyance, fortune-telling, witchcraft, séances, and spell casting are offered as simple alternatives to anything normal, let alone positive" (*Soul Harvest,* 326). The juxtaposition of these two sentences—the assurance that psychics inevitably go hand-in-hand with murderers, and should be taken as seriously—is bemusing at best, but it is meant to be eminently sincere. The lack of description as to why these things are bad shows exactly what's going on: readers don't need convincing. None of these details is essential to any plot device; they are simply there to switch on the negative reactions of readers and trigger a moral judgment.

We suspect it works that way in real life, too. So when nonbeliev-ers or liberal Christians admit to being pro-choice, watching *Queer Eye,* or having their tarot cards read, they might as well confess to seri-ous crimes. The fundamentalists hear "no morals." They hear "fallen," "worldly," "lost." Instead of acknowledging different premises, or ques-tioning whether all those issues are even moral ones, conservative Christians conclude that nonbelievers are unconcerned about ethics and that liberal Christians are falling prey to those darn worldly val-ues. This may help explain the fundamentalist Christians' feeling of isolation and the persistent claim that they are "under attack" even as 76 percent of Americans call themselves Christians.

At any rate, conservative Christians crave their objective truth, and they believe it has been spelled out for them in the Bible. As you might expect, C.W. God has something to say about this. He explains the "popularity of human religions" thus:

> It almost doesn't matter what the belief system is, as long as it's firm, consistent, clear in its expectation of the follower, and rigid. Given those characteristics, you can find people who believe in almost anything. The strangest behavior and belief can be—has been—attributed to God. It's God's way, they say. God's word.
>
> And there are those who will *accept* that. *Gladly.* Because, you see, *it eliminates the need to think.* (152–153)

Hitting below the belt? Well, it's nothing that hasn't been said before. And reading between the lines of *Left Behind* suggests it's a very famil-iar argument indeed.

FAITH, REASON, AND MOCKERY

An enduring theme in the *Left Behind* series is the tension between thinking and believing, between rationality and faith. The desire to reason—the *inability to escape* the desire to reason—is a source of difficulty for many of the characters and, we would argue, for the series itself.

We are confronted with this tension at the very beginning of *Left Behind*, when Rayford, Buck, and Chloe begin to entertain the possibility that the fundamentalist Christians *have* been Raptured and were right all along. The three characters viewed themselves as intellectuals, too educated and smart for religion, and they find themselves questioning not only their beliefs, but also their self-identities. Fascinatingly, it's a fear of ridicule that bothers them most: "I've been convinced," [Chloe] said, "but I'm still fighting. I'm supposed to be an intellectual. I have critical friends to answer to. Who's going to believe this? Who's going to think I haven't lost my mind?" (*Left Behind*, 404).

Now we're getting to the heart of things. These characters have directly defined themselves as smarter, and ultimately better, than believers. Now they are the ones being called ignorant and wrong—and there's proof to back it up! Rayford frets: "How could he have missed this? God had tried to warn his people by putting his Word in written form centuries before. For all Rayford's education and intelligence, he felt he had been a fool. . . . After a lifetime of achieving, of excelling, of being better than most and the best in most circles, he had been as humbled as was possible in one stroke" (*Left Behind*, 312, 102).

We have no proof of this (call it a matter of faith), but there seems to be genuine authorial pain here. Consider these two quotes, the first explaining why Bruce, the left-behind pastor, failed to make the grade; the second describing Buck's experience as he explores Christianity:

> "When people found out I [Bruce] was on the pastoral staff at New Hope, I would tell them about the cool pastor and

the neat church, but I was shy about telling them about Christ. If they challenged me and asked if New Hope was one of those churches that said Jesus was the only way to God, I did everything but deny it. I wanted them to think I was OK, that I was with it. I may be a Christian and even a pastor, but don't lump me with the weirdos. Above all, don't do that." (*Left Behind,* 197)

Was it possible? Could he be on the cusp of becoming a born-again Christian? . . . Buck had read and even written about "those kinds" of people, but even at his level of worldly wisdom he had never quite understood the phrase. He had always considered the "born-again" label akin to "ultrarightwinger" or "fundamentalist." Now, if he chose to take a step he had never dreamed of taking, if he could not somehow talk himself out of this truth he could no longer intellectually ignore, he would also take upon himself a task: educating the world on what that confusing little term really meant. (*Left Behind,* 396)

Of course, the authors *are* "those kinds" of people. They are born again, and they are fundamentalists; they are the "weirdos." So no doubt they have been the targets of arrogance and pity, have been mocked as ignorant and disregarded as unintelligent. (And no doubt this series is itself an attempt to "educate the world" on the meaning of "born again.") How satisfying would it be to have the tables turned, to have nonbelievers (and believer-fakes) kicking themselves while the Christians kicked back in heaven? How satisfying would it be to have . . . proof?

It's a sticky wicket—they know that faith is the ultimate, and yet it doesn't quite fulfill; there's a human longing for more. Without proof, without an event like the Rapture, there's no way to silence the "intellectuals" and the patronizing voices. In the books, however, as prophecy after prophecy comes true, believers have proof for the very first time. The characters, then, get to experience what real-life Christians never have: the objective verification of their faith.

Reason must be addictive, because the characters can't seem to let it go, even when it hurts their argument. Throughout the series, as the main characters grapple with nonbelievers, they can't resist trying to prove the rational purpose and moral correctness of God's choices, an exercise that (as we have seen already in regard to God's cruelty) consistently rings hollow. If faith is what is required, it is inadvisable to resort to flimsy argument. But it's very revealing that even the most devout believers can't stifle the rational impulse—there must be something in ourselves, or at least our society, that makes us long for logic, fairness, and sense in a way that makes faith very difficult indeed.

To read both *Left Behind* and *Conversations with God* is to watch the dynamics of the two groups unfold: the Christians state their beliefs, the New Agers call them uneducated hillbillies, and the Christians sit steaming until the Rapture comes. Still, we would not say the *Left Behind* series is primarily about revenge. It is, in many ways, about redemption, courage, and commitment to ideals, embracing the opportunity to change when wrong, reaching out with all of one's being to love and serve and fight for what's right. But the ambivalence toward nonbelievers cannot be dismissed, nor can the struggle between faith and reason. If two quotes could represent the thematic fiber of these 5,000 pages (all of which, as we might have mentioned, we read), it would be these, from *Glorious Appearing,* the twelfth book:

"Understand it?" Chang said. "I can't say I do. But I believe it." (53)

"Sad."

"Yes, it is. Very. And yet I believe all these judgments will demonstrate to the whole world God's justice and righteousness and will finally silence all who have scoffed." (369)

WHO'S READING THIS STUFF, ANYWAY?

If these authors are so sure that they know the truth, why do they spend so much time obsessing about the other viewpoint? For *Conversations with God* and other New Age titles, that's obvious: Christianity is the dominant religion in the United States, and New Age philosophies arose in response to it. But what about the Christians? Do they really have anything to fear from a handful of New Age bestsellers?

A glance at a few religious-affiliation surveys taken in the past few years reveals that around 76 percent of Americans say they practice Christianity, whereas only .03 percent (that's *point-oh-three,* less than 100,000 people) associate themselves with a New Age religion. That doesn't sound very threatening. Still, Americans made the New Age books major bestsellers; these millions of readers have to come from somewhere. Some of those readers were undoubtedly "secular or non-religious," which is the second-largest "religious" group, including around 13 percent of Americans. But the rest could very likely be unhappy or unconvinced Christians looking for an alternative (or a "clarification," such as that provided in *The Celestine Prophecy*).

Given these numbers, it really *is* extraordinary that four New Age books made it so big. Judaism, Islam, and Buddhism are all more populous religions than New Age in the United States (although not by much), but no huge bestseller—or *any* bestseller, as far as we are aware—has sprung from those faiths. As different as the New Age books are from one another, their commonalities must have resonated with Americans in this time period. So perhaps Christianity *is* at risk of some slippage. Not everyone has the stamina to defend a locust-happy God.

But it also goes the other way. The *Left Behind* series has been described as a "crossover success," and with seventy-five million books sold, it has to have reached some non-Christians. According to the website leftbehind.com, Jenkins and LaHaye have personally heard from thousands of new Christians who converted after reading the books.

We don't have the data to reveal which side is winning this battle, but we can see why it rages on. Though the values and premises of each camp are utterly different, they are equally appealing and equally in step with those we have seen reflected in bestselling books so far. The conservative Christian viewpoint provides order, clarity, instruction, black and white ideas, and rules that don't bend. All this appeals to the side of our American soul that craves simplicity and immediate answers. The New Age viewpoint promises endless opportunities to change and evolve, new ways of viewing the world that emphasize the nurturance and guidance of a loving, noncritical universe. This appeals to the part of us that wants to feel good about human nature and our own endless possibilities. Both provide opportunities for redemption. And—perhaps most importantly—both assure us that we are not alone, tell us that life has meaning, and emphasize how very important we are.

These messages are not exactly unpredictable: they're what we anxious mortals want to hear. But one of the most fascinating and counterintuitive aspects of these books is their underlying assertion that life's discomforting complexity—its apparent chaos, randomness, and tragedy—can be simplified, indeed *remedied,* by even more complicated explanations. The basic concepts of Christian salvation or guiding coincidences may be easy to summarize in a few words, but describing and justifying all the details of each vision takes hundreds if not thousands of pages. We can't help but think of the low-carb diet phenomenon, in which people preferred the seeming complexity of the program over the very simple, free weight-loss advice that everyone knows. It seems that readers do the same thing in the religious sphere: we're happy to exchange all the weird stuff we can't explain for even weirder and more convoluted explanations of the world, as long as those explanations provide order and comfort. Nobody wants to hear just how simple it all could be, needing but a sentence to explain: perhaps we are born, and then we die, the meaning of everything in between ours to choose.

RELIGIOUS READING: WHAT'S THE POINT?

In the introduction to this chapter, we raised the point that all instructive religious writing demands faith from readers. We didn't want to harp on it too much then, but really, why *do* millions of people look to books to learn about things that can't actually be known? Why trust a Betty Eadie, a Gary Zukav, or a Rick Warren? Why trust anyone who stands to make a buck off your faith?

Or more than a buck. All of the books we reviewed are very well merchandised, often attended by extras such as seminars and tapes. Don Miguel Ruiz, author of *The Four Agreements,* sells a companion book, CD, calendar, and card set, in addition to several related books, and an assortment of seminars and "journeys" costing anywhere from $25 to $1,300. *Seat of the Soul's* Gary Zukav offers a variety of methods to absorb his beliefs, including a three-year program costing $300 a month. James Redfield offers an "experiential guide," a pocket guide, tapes, and CDs to accompany *The Celestine Prophecy.* Neale Donald Walsch helps seekers put the principles of *Conversations with God* into practice by selling nineteen spin-off titles (including two meditation guides and a *Conversations with God for Teens*), plus retreat opportunities and a "Life Education Program" that cost over a thousand dollars each. Rick Warren sells *Meditations on the Purpose Driven Life,* a companion journal, a "pocket tool" for proselytizing (sold ambitiously in sets of 250), a Bible cover, and a "scripture keeper," as well as videos and CDs. Bruce

Wilkinson offers CDs, devotionals, journals, and spin-off titles including *The Prayer of Jabez for Women,* written by his wife Darlene. The *Left
Behind* authors are busy writing prequels and sequels and kids' series
and selling videos, greeting cards, calendars, and a controversial video
game. Even Betty J. Eadie offered up *Embraced by the Light: Prayers &
Devotions for Daily Living* and two follow-up books.

Now we're not saying that it's wrong to make money off religious
products or guidance. We're not saying that sincere people wouldn't,
and we're not suggesting anything about these particular authors—we
have no reason to think they don't believe what they write. Selling a
bunch of merchandise simply seems to be the thing to do for anyone
who's written a bestselling spiritual book, and hey, maybe all the stuff
helps people.

We *are* saying that there's a strong financial incentive to break into
this market (we're hurrying to finish *The Purpose-Driven Seat of Celestine
Conversations* as we speak!), that it's not always possible to determine
the source of the author's knowledge, and that it's *never* possible to know
the author's motives. And well, historically, peddling God has hardly
been an untainted occupation.

Does that really matter? Does it make a difference if God really
played Ouija board with Neale Donald Walsch, or if Don Miguel
Ruiz accurately crystallized the Toltec viewpoint? Conveniently, C. W.
God doesn't seem to think it's that important: "Even if everything I've
said is 'wrong,' can you think of a better way to live?" (108). And if
readers are only looking for inspiration, ideas, or curiosities, perhaps
he is right. (Those so inclined might also want to check out Mitch
Albom's *The Five People You Meet in Heaven* for its interesting speculation on the afterlife.)

But what about those really searching for answers, or those who just
start out curious and end up believing? Christians are enormously sensitive about this issue, and concerned reviewers pick apart any religious

or spiritual work that might send an incorrect message about God and salvation—including (especially?) works by other Christians. In online reviews—including one titled "My friends all pray the prayer of Jabez . . . and all I got was this lousy t-shirt!"—they raise myriad concerns about Wilkinson's book, disapproving of its gimmicky promises (e.g., "Your life will become marked by miracles," 24–25). They call the book shallow, formulaic, silly, and even dangerous—after all, a new believer might chant the prayer of Jabez for a month, see no territory expansion, and give up on Christ forever.

The Purpose Driven Life also draws many critics. Their main complaint is Warren's paraphrasing and trimming of scripture, though they also call the book faddish and simplistic. With a level of sarcasm uncommon for believers, one reviewer said, "If you want to fill your head with meaningless 'Christianese,' then this is the book for you! If you want 'feel good' religion without true depth, then this is the book for you! If you want simplistic and misleading teaching, then this is the book for you!" Some Christian critics contend that Warren uses Bible verses out of context, selecting those translations that support his points—and snipping them when convenient. Warren, for his part, claims that using a variety of translations helps believers approach scripture in fresh ways. (Interestingly, every Christian book reviewed in this chapter draws on numerous translations of the New Testament, selectively paraphrasing and pruning. There is no evidence in any of these books that the authors can read the original Greek. Maybe we're just being snotty—one of us teaches Greek. Still, would you trust an authority on Shakespeare who couldn't read English?)

In a review of *Left Behind,* pastor Rich Vincent attributes the series' success to a "sadistic streak in evangelicals" and raises concerns about the books' sensationalism and theological inconsistencies, saying,

Some defend the value of this series by emphasizing that it is a good evangelistic tool. Sadly, this is proof that the Beast truly has possessed us—for we care more for pragmatism (what works) than truth. If the series is not true, then any conversions to Christ are not *because* of the series, but *in spite* of the series. Our concern for truth should take precedence over our concern for what works. (http://www.theocentric.com/theology/eschatology/left_behind_stephen_king_for_c.html)

It goes without saying that Christian reviewers also condemn the New Age titles. But of course, these critical voices can't possibly drown out those of the millions of happy readers who love and take comfort in these Christian and New Age bestsellers.

That bestselling religious books even exist brings up a larger issue. No matter what the theology, there's an inherent and unavoidable problem in the very concept of looking to a fallible human for universal truth. Yet it seems that we in America have this "religious" mentality not only about religion, but about everything else too—our diet, our relationships, our politics. We look to other people—to *writers,* no less, who barely even qualify—to tell us how to live. We don't go out in the world trusting our experience, as C.W. God would have us do; and we very readily discard our experiences and take advice from "experts" instead. We don't even trust our own reading of the Bible, a great book (and perennial bestseller) that will outlive every one of its bestselling interpreters. Why are we so religiously challenged?

Ironically, *Reading Lolita in Tehran* is a book all about religion, and yet its topics are very different from what we've covered in this chapter. But of course we are not religiously oppressed here in the United States, dismantled civic crèches notwithstanding, and so naturally what shows up in our religious books is the *conflict* between competing views, not the imposition of any particular one. Still, in many ways we do seem to be religiously oppressed—not by our society or by our government, but by our willingness to look to gurus and holy men to tell us what is healthy, what is normal, what is good. We are oppressed by a religious *mentality;* we would clearly rather listen to someone else than think for ourselves. *Conversations with God* has that much right. And although some aspects of life do require expert guidance—finances, working with fondant, even (as many would argue) spiritual matters—we think this tendency is in general a serious societal problem.

LITERARY EXPLORATIONS

There's another, though far less common, way to approach religion in bestselling books: through literature that invites the intellectual participation of the reader. We don't mean fictionalized nonfiction like *The Celestine Prophecy* and *Left Behind.* We mean literature that is out to explore, not tell. There's a certain gentleness in this kind of fiction, a polite offering of ideas that one need not accept to move forward, that makes novels wonderfully well-suited for thinking about issues of all kinds, even religious ones.

Jan Karon, for example, is the epitome of politeness in *Light from Heaven,* the final book in her Mitford series, which was #7 for fiction in 2005. This deeply Christian book tells the story of Father Tim (an Episcopalian priest) and his simple life of faith and service. Although the "issues" in the novel aren't necessarily complex ones, we think that Karon's depiction of a Christian life—marked by humility, good humor, and profound kindness—speaks more highly of Christianity than any semi-biblical lecture or vengeful divine massacre ever could.

On the more cerebral end of the scale is Yann Martel's *Life of Pi,* a literary novel about a teenage boy who is a practicing Hindu, Christian, and Muslim—all at once. Seeing the beauty in all three religions and in faith itself, Pi explains to his discomfited critics, "I just want to love God" (69). This faith shines forth even when Pi and a 450-pound

Bengal tiger end up in a lifeboat together—for seven months—after their vessel sinks in the middle of the Pacific. Alternating between practical and fantastical, *Life of Pi* has the character of a religious fable. Martel uses the unlikely premise to explore such issues as the relationships between animals and humans, the universal need for survival and companionship (often competing urges when stranded at sea), and the importance of faith in understanding deeper truths and embracing life's "better story" rather than the "dry, yeastless factuality" of a solely rational worldview (64).

Life of Pi may not "make you believe in God," as the book's prologue suggests (x), but it will certainly make you think about the ideas raised within its pages. And although novels like it don't serve the same purpose as the instructive religious titles we've reviewed in this chapter, we would suggest that they offer a nice balance to all that preaching and goading.

Indeed, as books slide toward the literary end of the scale, they customarily tend to offer more explorative visions of the world: more sophisticated analysis in the nonfiction and deeper themes and fewer straight answers in the novels. Have the bestselling literary books from the recent past continued this proud tradition? We find out as we climb the final rungs of popular American reading in our next chapter.

READING FOR REDEMPTION: TRIALS AND TRIUMPHS IN LITERARY FICTION AND NONFICTION

"Em-pa-thy." Carefully, Maizy pronounced each syllable. "I want to feel what she feels—completely, utterly, totally. What I mean is, I want to love her."

I was dumbfounded. My jaw fell and my lips parted. "But you do love her."

"Not really," she said. "Not until I feel her pain like I feel my own."

Icy Sparks

We keep yammering on about empathy, particularly the lack of it in many of the bestselling books from the recent past. Well, there's a big group out there that doesn't need the lecture.

Today's readers of "literary" fiction and nonfiction—a label of somewhat nebulous meaning that implies non-formulaic, higher-quality books on any topic—are all *over* empathy. They seem to have taken Azar Nafisi to heart when she said, "A novel . . . is the sensual experience of another world. If you don't enter that world, hold your breath with the characters and become involved in their destiny, you won't be able to empathize" (111). Nafisi's focus is novels, but much of the bestselling nonfiction from this time period, especially of the creative and journalistic sort, also provides that "sensual experience" if readers will only take a gulp and dive in.

Taking a glance at the top literary books from the past sixteen years—of which we read around fifty—it's clear that readers are eagerly donning their bathing-caps and plunging into all sorts of new worlds. But empathy, even here, takes its own revealing course. We take a peek at yet another facet of America's soul as we examine the bestsellers of literary fiction and nonfiction in this chapter.

But before we begin, we have to make a pit stop at Oprah's Book Club.

Help Me, Oprah Winfrey!

Between 1996 and 2002, Oprah Winfrey picked forty-three different works of literary fiction (and five works of nonfiction) for her televised Book Club. After reading each selection, participants were to tune in for the discussion on the *Oprah Winfrey Show*, which generally included Oprah, the author, and a handful of lucky readers who had found the book especially meaningful and had sent in letters describing why.

Every single one of these books became a bestseller. Each of Oprah's 1996–1999 selections sold an average of 1.4 million copies; not a week went by during the entire six-year period without at least one of Oprah's books on the bestseller lists. In some years, the *only* debut novelists to make it into the top thirty on an annual list were those chosen by Oprah. So though we really do not want or need to examine the inner workings of Oprah's Book Club, we can't ignore her remarkable influence on recent bestselling literary fiction. (We will, however, ignore most of her post-2002 picks, because at that time Oprah decided to reinvigorate the classics, highlighting such authors as John Steinbeck, William Faulkner, and Elie Wiesel.)

It's funny the things you hear about Oprah books. "They're all the same," various critics claim, though each seems to mean something slightly different. Some say they're all about African Americans, or all about women, or all about *feeeeelings*. Listening to the rumors—or even reading the published criticisms by some professional (and comparatively impotent) reviewers—you get the idea that every one of her books is about black women weeping over retarded babies.

It's true that Oprah intentionally looked for books written by African Americans, but even so, only about one-quarter of the authors were minorities. It's also true that three-quarters of the selected authors were women (and almost all the novels penned by men have a central female character or narrator). And it's true that she picked at least one book about a retarded baby. But none of those claims is *exactly* on the mark when you take a look at Oprah's whole canon—or even her biggest hits, which are the ones that we read. (Although every one of her choices has been a bestseller, we focused on the most popular of these—the ones on the annual lists.) There are commonalities, important ones, but they are both grander and more revealing than concerns of race or gender. And more significantly, they apply equally well to most of the bestselling literary works of this period that Oprah *didn't* choose. Ultimately, literary readers both inside and outside Oprah's domain are choosing works with startling similarities.

We also found no qualitative difference between Oprah books and the other literary titles that hit the top of the charts. Some people have called Oprah the "Midas of the mid-list" and her books "middlebrow," usually with the implication that they aren't quite real literature. We really don't want to get involved in this one. In fact, most of the titles had positive reviews in the *New York Times Book Review* before Oprah picked them. And having read the books, we know it's untrue, and unfair, to declare sweepingly that all Oprah books possess the same quality and potential for intellectual consideration. They don't.

Finally, we think the middlebrow–highbrow debate to be largely irrelevant: we admire any quest for high standards, and we hope that the reading public at large will be literate enough to have that kind of nitpicky discussion someday, but we doubt that the Oprah-snubbers have a clue what the rest of America is reading. If they did, they just might get down on their knees and kiss Oprah's feet for getting books with some depth, penned by talented writers, on the list at all.

And yes, maybe we're biased; when you've read Danielle Steel, Michael Savage, and Betty Eadie's near-death ramblings in close succession, even a book about retarded babies starts to look like a darn fine read. Still, battle-weary or not, we contend that getting more people to read more complex books—and, by extension, to accept the complexity of life and tolerate more viewpoints—is truly important. Oprah should be praised for these efforts! And though we personally expect more from books than she and her club members (and many other readers) seem to have demanded, ultimately we're just happy that people are reading literature. We also can't help but be fascinated by the incredible influence Oprah has had on what Americans read—and even more importantly, *how* they read.

With that tease, let's get to the books. In our analysis of literary fiction, we flit back and forth between Oprah picks and those bestsellers not selected for her book club. When it matters, we've tried to make it clear which are which, but as we've said, there is really no point in maintaining this false dichotomy, and most of the time, we simply ignore it. Call it compassion fatigue.

Don't Want to Be a Mongolian Idiot

Our first stop is the literature that focuses on "difference," especially in the form of handicaps and diseases—what some call "affliction fiction." Come one, come all, see the dwarfs and freaks, the chubby and the "special" on parade! Many of these are Oprah's doing. She started in 1997 with Ursula Hegi's *Stones from the River,* which became the

#6 trade paperback for the year. So begins this tale of a German *Zwerg* (dwarf): "As a child Trudi Montag thought everyone knew what went on inside others. That was before she understood the power of being different. The agony of being different" (9).

That pretty much sums it up. These books cultivate empathy by treating readers to the horrible loneliness of the misunderstood, misshapen, and rejected. Another 1997 Oprah selection was Wally Lamb's *She's Come Undone* (#3 trade paperback), the life story of a young woman struggling with weight and self-esteem (which some critics have seen as the ultimate Oprah book in that it seems to parallel her own life story). Then came *Jewel* in 1999 (#12 trade paperback), Bret Lott's novel about a mother of six who learns that her youngest child is, as the doctor so compassionately puts it, a "Mongolian Idiot"—that is, physically and mentally retarded. The year 2001 brought *Icy Sparks* to Oprah's list, Gwyn Hyman Rubio's book about a girl with Tourette's syndrome (#5 trade paperback).

We were hoping for killer albinos, but it looks like only Dan Brown is into that scene.

With the exception of *Jewel*, which focuses on the difficulty of raising a retarded child rather than the child's experience, these books are all thematically similar, and the characters' outcastiness tends to blend together. Yes, it's tough being a misfit. (Don't we know it! How come there aren't any Oprah books about *nerds*?) To be fair, though, the books have plenty of thought-provoking moments. After Trudi stops wailing about her dwarfdom, for example, *Stones from the River* becomes a fascinating portrait of Germany during the Hitler years. And who in rural Kentucky in 1956 would know what to make of Tourette's syndrome? No one in *Icy Sparks*. Not understanding she has a disorder, Icy explains her situation thus: "I reckon I got a touch of pokeweed inside me, the poison parts. . . . This poison builds up, get stronger and stronger, until it has to get out. If it don't, it'll eat me up . . . So

I have to let this poison out. A jerk here. A croak there. A cuss word. A nasty thought" (122). Less compelling are Icy's seemingly endless encounters with other misfits—fat people, "sissies," kids with cerebral palsy—that teach her not to fear and judge, and eventually, to accept herself. It all starts to look a bit too much like the fraternity reject-room in *Animal House*.

There's nothing *wrong* with self-love and respect for difference and all that, of course, but it just gets a little redundant and strikes us as a little too . . . simple? Obvious? Manipulative? How easy it is to empathize with a good person who's been dealt a nasty fate. Reading any one of these books would make a fine literary jaunt, but we wouldn't recommend a back-to-back affliction fest. It's just all too similar.

You can try to blame Oprah for foisting so much of this on us, but ultimately it's the readers who want it. The majority of Oprah's books *don't* have these themes, but the ones that do have been the top-sellers. Moreover, non-Oprah books on similar topics have also been extremely popular, three of them in the past few years: Jodi Picoult's *My Sister's Keeper,* about a teenage girl's lifetime fight against leukemia (#10 trade paperback in 2005); Mark Haddon's *The Curious Incident of the Dog in the Night-Time,* told from the perspective of a fifteen-year-old autistic boy (#10 trade paperback in 2004, #7 in 2005); and Jeffrey Eugenides's Pulitzer Prize-winning *Middlesex,* the captivating if slow-starting story of a hermaphrodite and his painful adolescent transition from girl to man (talk about your differences!). Even the plot of *The Memory Keeper's Daughter,* the #2 trade paperback in 2006, hinges on the existence of a baby with Down's syndrome, though the book's themes lie elsewhere.

The Curious Incident of the Dog in the Night-Time, however, is quite different from many of the other books of this type because it attempts to demonstrate the thought processes of the autistic rather than cat-alogue the sadness of those with disabilities. We don't know if it's accurate, but we don't really care: it's very interesting, very funny, and refreshingly free of self-pity. If we like Christopher, it's because of his unflagging, charming logic and unwitting sense of humor; if we feel for him, it's because he ends up facing some immense challenges for a person of his abilities. This is a book that really plunges the reader into a different world, a world of mental and social limitations that is at once foreign and fascinating. It succeeds without platitudes, without goopy reminders that we may seem different, but we're really all the same. In fact, Christopher *isn't* the same as regular folk—he can't tell lies, interpret facial expressions, or touch anything yellow without having a meltdown. *Curious Incident* is noteworthy because it offers the full, fleshed-out perspective of someone *truly* different—a claim that few bestsellers in any genre can make.

Sucks to Be You

But we all know that being different isn't the only thing that can bring a person down. A lot can go wrong in life, and we readers want to know all the details of every marrow-melting scenario.

Your son might get kidnapped. Your father might sign you up to be an African missionary. Your boyfriend might abandon you, pregnant, in a Wal-Mart parking lot. Your grandfather could head up a nutty fundamentalist religion. Your ex could be a worthless drunk whose habit condemns you to constant public humiliation and snickering. Your expedition might reach the summit of Mt. Everest just as a huge storm hits. Your husband could have another wife and family across the Atlantic.

Extreme scenarios such as those just mentioned are the norm in literary fiction and nonfiction alike. They're the equivalent of the pulse-pumping "good and evil" titles, in which every move has worldwide significance. These are the high-octane librettos of the heart.

Weird Coincidences

Ever since we read *The Celestine Prophecy,* we see coincidences everywhere. Here are some of our favorites from the books in this chapter.

- Both Trudi Montag and Icy Sparks befriend an effeminate blond boy and sing like "an angel."

- Both *The Deep End of the Ocean* and *The Curious Incident of the Dog in the Night-Time* discuss a famous probability puzzle called the Monty Hall Problem.

- Both Nathan in *The Poisonwood Bible* and Grandpa Herman in *The Rapture of Canaan* go crazy for God after going to war.

- Both Dinah in *The Red Tent* and Sybil in *Midwives* get burned for attempting to free live newborns from dead mothers with emergency C-sections.

Though occasionally tottering on the precipice of the melodramatic, many of these titles are intriguing and well written, and because their topics are so different, so are their themes. Barbara Kingsolver's *The Poisonwood Bible,* for example, explores the consequences of Christian hubris, each member of a missionary family finding transformation or destruction in the land they hoped to shape to their own devices (#3 trade paperback in 2000). Joyce Carol Oates's *We Were the Mulvaneys,* on the other hand, introduces the perfect American family and chronicles its crumbling into alcoholism and exile (#2 trade paperback in 2001). And *The Deep End of the Ocean* details the unraveling of a not-so-perfect American family after the kidnapping of its three-year-old (#11 for hardcover fiction in 1996).

The drama, however, is different from that of adventure-thriller fiction. No matter how uncommon these fictional plots might be, they are still more likely to happen to the average reader than a whirlwind crime-fighting tour. The sheer possibility of such events, such suffering, invites morbid curiosity—how *would* someone handle that? What would it feel like?

But with the curiosity comes a certain comfort. We readers seem to have a grim fascination with misfortunes—even invented ones—as long as they fall in other people's laps. Both *My Sister's Keeper* and *The Deep End of the Ocean* describe how people flock to assist the afflicted out of "secret joy" that they themselves were spared (*Sister's Keeper*, 81). Perhaps we also harbor the idea that heaving ourselves along on another's catastrophe will free us from our own, hoping that "if I feel this entire, if I let this wound me, my own will be spared. I will be absolved, by lent and prior pain, from destruction in the first person" (*Deep End*, 349).

As if! But even as we take from these books the comfort of *not* having lived these calamities, we can also admire the characters that make it through them—and sometimes even come out better in the end. This inspirational element is particularly apparent in the "hard times" literature—stories that transport us to tough times and hostile places, setting us in the shadows of an escaping soldier or lacing us into a farmer's ever-laboring boots.

WHAT DO THE SIMPLE FOLK DO?

We mentioned in the introduction the success of Charles Frazier's *Cold Mountain,* a weighty Civil War novel that became a word-of-mouth smash, rising to #2 for hardcover fiction in 1997. The tremendous popularity of this book was a surprise to almost everyone. That's not to say it isn't fine writing—it is—but it's slow and dark and does an excellent job of scraping the war free of all its potential glory. There aren't any battles or hoop skirts to be seen, and the main character—Inman, a deserting Southerner—never owned slaves and can't even figure out what he and his kinsmen were fighting for all those years. Sure, there's a love story, but even that gets doused from time to time with an icy splash of nineteenth-century practicality. As she assures Inman of her perpetual regard, for example, his sweetie Ada privately wonders, "Is anything remembered forever?" (196).

But what this book has in spades is suffering. Inman faces the worst of human nature as he picks his way through the North Carolina mountains to get home to Ada, dodging both vengeful Confederates (he's a deserter, remember) and invading Federalists. What emerges is a world without justice or order, a world in which "every man that died in that war on either side might just as soon have put a pistol against the soft of his palate and blown out the back of his head for all the meaning it had" (240).

And so the simple effort to survive, the endurance of the human spirit—even when it is terribly confused and disheartened—is all that remains in this muddy world. Inman doesn't really know what he'll find at home, but the idea of making it there is what sustains him; he hopes that "Ada might save him from his troubles and redeem him from the past four years" (314).

Ada waits at home, but she has her own trials. Finding herself destitute and alone, she must give up the life of a privileged lady and learn to work her land if she is to survive. In doing so, she finds meaning and contentment that she never knew before.

This is a major part of the romance of *Cold Mountain*. Though the story has been stripped of much of the Civil War's traditional drama, Ada's journey from idle to industrious has its own powerful draw. Readers seem to be entranced by the idea of simpler, humbler times, where the currency of hard labor brings us everything we need. This theme gets fleshed out to the max in Robert Morgan's *Gap Creek,* the #15 hardcover fiction title in 2000.

MIND THE GAP

Gap Creek is the kind of book you give to someone having a really bad year. Caustic breakup? Back pain? Tax audit? That's nothing compared to the slew of horrors that Julie faces in this novel. The story, set in South Carolina around the turn of the century, is guaranteed to make anybody feel better about life.

In just one year, Julie loses her younger brother and her father, gets decked by her husband, causes a fire that kills her landlord, gets swindled twice, nearly drowns, barely escapes starvation, has to deliver her own baby on the kitchen floor, loses said baby, and then gets evicted. And all through it, she has to deal with a persnickety mother-in-law!

Times are tough, but Julie is a hard worker. In fact, it's her primary personality trait. Julie has spent much of her life handling the serious jobs usually performed by men—chopping wood, butchering hogs— and though she resents it sometimes, she also admits, "It was work that made me think clear, and it was work that made me humble" (122). It is work that enables her to keep going after the death of her daughter.

What's Grosser than Gross?

"Papa held the lantern closer and we seen that Masenier was throwing up. White stuff come out of his mouth and lines of white stuff. 'My god,' I said. For I thought he was throwing up milk or some white gravy. But what come out of his mouth was gobs of squirming things. They was worms, wads and wads of white worms." (14)

Welcome to *Gap Creek,* suckas!

This attitude is important, for Julie entertains no illusions about a loving universe. After her brother dies, she realizes, "People could be born and they could suffer, and they could die, and it didn't mean a thing. The moon was shining above the trees and the woods was peaceful . . . The world was exactly like it had been and would always be, going on about its business" (15). She believes in God, but mostly she demonstrates time and time again that she has the strength to endure anything and keep trying to make life good no matter what comes her way. Despite her many trials, she can still enjoy the simplest things, such as eating delicious food and dancing in the fallen leaves. Nothing can permanently break this woman's spirit.

As we know by now, today's readers love inspiration, so it's not a surprise that this mother of all inspirational stories hit the charts. But we also think that readers find an underlying romance in *Gap Creek*—not in the conditions, which are just too wretched to romanticize, but in our forgotten capabilities, the collective strength and self-sufficiency that working people possessed not so long ago. A book like this reminds us how dependent we are on modern conveniences and technology. We don't render lard. We don't deliver our own babies. Face it—we wouldn't survive a week in Gap Creek. And so the story is all the more inspirational because it is also so humbling.

STORM STORIES

We also like inspiration of the nonfictional variety, books full of real-life folks scaling equally heart-stopping peaks . . . sometimes literally. Jon Krakauer's *Into Thin Air* is just what its subtitle declares: "A Personal Account of the Mt. Everest Disaster." Krakauer was part of the May 1996 Everest expedition that encountered a deadly storm just at its members attempted the final stage of the ascent. It's an outstanding journalistic accomplishment (#7 nonfiction in 1997, #11 mass-market paperback in 1998), combining many of the elements found in much popular literary fiction: a first-person narrator, an alien location described in detail and placed in historical context, vibrant characters with great strengths and tragic flaws, and survival in the face of tragedy.

The year 1997 turned out to be a bountiful season for disaster books; Sebastian Junger's *The Perfect Storm* also appeared that year, eventually becoming the 42nd bestselling book for the entire decade from 1993 to 2003. Junger tells the story of the "Storm of Century" of October 1991, focusing on the disappearance of the *Andrea Gail,* a swordfishing boat out of Gloucester. The journalistic challenge here was the absence of information—no one knows what happened, exactly, to the *Andrea Gail.* So Junger, with a good deal of research, imaginatively reconstructs what was likely to have occurred. In the process, he threads through his tale the backgrounds of the six fishermen on the boat, the history of the fishing industry, and famous shipwrecks, while also recounting other (much better documented) calamities related to the same storm. Junger is heavier on the details than Krakauer, partly because of the dearth of real information about the fate of his protagonists (and perhaps partly because of the author's lack of personal connection with either fishing or the specific disasters). Mention a hurricane, and you get pages of textbook-like explanation of how they form and what they do. Interested in the physiological details of drowning (and who isn't)? You got it—*CSI* has nothing on Junger's anatomical exactness. In one paragraph, more than thirty individual tools and spare parts are listed, a cornucopia of boat accoutrements for the landlubber. Just pray there isn't a quiz.

Twenty-nine thousand feet up or 1,000 miles out to sea; hundred-foot waves or freezing temperatures, no visibility, and little oxygen. The journalistic books present us with vocations and avocations most of us will never experience. Indeed, the conclusion of any sane reader would have to be that swordfishing is no way for a human to make a living under *any* circumstances, and that it would be better for the gene pool if stranded mountain climbers were left there. Although both books attempt to peer inside the psyches of the characters (real people, in this case), a question still leaps out so starkly that it grabs readers by the shoulders and slaps them on both cheeks: why would anyone ever do these things? What is *wrong* with these people?

That's a question for another book to answer, but one thing is sure—all these "hard times" books, fiction and nonfiction, capture the general tenor of today's literary reading. In some ways, these titles attempt the opposite of *Chicken Soup for the Soul*. "Oh *yeah?*" you can hear the authors fume. "You think life is like *that?* Well, I'll show you!" And then they write long books about how awful life can be. Readers get to share in the suffering of slavery or family tragedy or life-threatening disaster. They can step into other times and other places, experiencing life's brutality through another's (usually first-person) eyes. These books acknowledge, if not revel in, life's unfairness and unpredictability.

But in other ways, many of these books are simply extended versions of chicken-soupy stories. Even though the journeys are long and fraught with trouble, they usually end with some admiring look at the human spirit, its power to endure and find meaning despite terrible circumstances. Readers get to empathize with the ailing characters and also walk away uplifted, perhaps even more so because of the intensity of the characters' plight and thus the catharsis.

It's not, in fact, entirely different from the experience of reading typical "good and evil" fiction in which the protagonists are being tormented by some creep. In both types of books, readers share in the characters' extreme trials, rooting for their eventual triumph. Does it make a huge difference whether those trials come in the form of a flinty-eyed terrorist or a hard Carolina winter? Pick your poison.

The improvement here, though, is that when the creep in the story is life itself—as in *Into Thin Air* or *Gap Creek*—the authors don't try to view the situation from the antagonist's perspective. ("I blinded her with whirling snowflakes of death," the blizzard chuckled to itself. "I froze her up good! Bwa ha ha!") Many of the literary titles emphasize that "evil" is generally just hardship, poor choices, irreconcilable differences, or simple bad luck, and that it is very much part of who we are—not a separate, cackling monster, but an inevitability, something we can never truly vanquish but can only hope to survive with some measure of dignity.

Guilty and Guiltier

If there's one emotion that preoccupies literary authors and readers of the recent past, it is guilt. It is nearly impossible to make it through a single literary novel without stepping in a pile of the stuff.

And sure, that's realistic. Who isn't feeling guilty about something? But it goes way beyond acknowledging our collective dirty laundry. These characters aren't just a little guilty; they are *really* guilty, and they are desperately seeking redemption.

The novel that demonstrates this obsession most explicitly is Khaled Hosseini's *The Kite Runner,* the #11 trade paperback in 2004, #2 in 2005, and #5 in 2006. The novel follows Amir, the son of a wealthy Afghan merchant. Out of cowardice, jealousy, and embedded prejudice, Amir allows his best friend and servant to suffer an unspeakable crime. His inaction has serious consequences, and the guilt tortures Amir throughout his life, until he has the opportunity to rescue the son of his old friend from the Taliban, thereby earning his redemption.

Though in some ways *The Kite Runner* is a classic "good and evil" book, with the Taliban representing pure, crazy evil and the abused servant representing pure, selfless good, Hosseini diverges from that well-worn path by exploring the middle ground—Amir—in great detail. From the very beginning, the protagonist is aware of his dark side, the small cruelties he inflicts on his adoring servant-friend, his willingness to do *anything* for the love and approval of his father. He must face and overcome these tendencies, finally risking his own life, to earn his atonement.

A novel with similar themes, although a very different setting, is Kim Edwards's *The Memory Keeper's Daughter*. As in *The Kite Runner*, Edwards's plot hinges on a split-second decision with permanent and rippling consequences. It's 1964, and David Henry is present at the birth of his son—who is followed unexpectedly into the light by a twin, a girl with Down's syndrome. David, wishing to spare his wife the grief and hardship of raising a disabled child, tells her that the second baby was born dead. He asks the nurse to take the infant to an institution, but she decides to keep and raise the child herself. David is unable to confess the truth, and the secret ultimately devours his marriage and keeps him frozen in time, full of regret for his hasty error. Like Amir in *The Kite Runner*, he attempts to assuage his guilt by helping others in need.

The list goes on. Characters suffer guilt for things they did as adults, things they did as children, and things they could not possibly have done at any time (see "Guilty Until Proven Innocent" for a tasty sample). All are significantly shaped by these feelings, and they usually try to make up for the events or actions somehow. But the authors don't claim that pure redemption is possible. Even Amir, who is able to make a more direct exchange than most—hurt the father, save the son—doesn't succeed with flying colors. More importantly, he can never erase his past deeds.

None of us can, of course. These authors are addressing a serious and apparently quite pressing human problem: we can't undo the past, so what is the next best thing? How do we go on? In *The Kite Runner*, a family friend says to Amir, "Good, *real* good, was born out of your father's remorse. Sometimes, I think everything he did, feeding the poor on the streets, building the orphanage, giving money to friends in need, it was all his way of redeeming himself. And that, I believe, is what true redemption is, Amir jan, when guilt leads to good" (302).

Guilty Until Proven Innocent

Greed may have been good in the '80s, but since then it's been all about guilt. Come, climb into some of our literary characters' guilty consciences . . .

- I brought home the flu that killed my parents! (Amanda, *Drowning Ruth*)
- I caused my infant brother's death by eating sugar cubes left on the windowsills for the stork! (Trudi, *Stones from the River*)
- I didn't prevent my son/brother from being kidnapped! (Beth/Vincent, *The Deep End of the Ocean*)
- I failed to rescue my wife from our burning home! (Alan, *Here on Earth*)
- I caused a neighbor's miscarriage by fantasizing about the father of the child! (Dolores, *She's Come Undone*)
- I disappointed my parents by getting raped! (Marianne, *We Were the Mulvaneys*)
- I exist, and therefore tie my mother down to a pedestrian life! (Astrid, *White Oleander*)
- I'm having an affair with a priest, and I don't even love him! (Alice, *Songs in Ordinary Time*)
- I accidentally killed my father and failed to prevent my mother from chopping off her own finger! (Jessie, *The Mermaid Chair*)

Another bestseller has a different answer. *The Reader,* by Bernard Schlink (#3 trade paperback in 1999), is the intriguing story of a German boy who becomes involved, and falls passionately in love, with an older woman named Hanna. Later, as a law student, he encounters Hanna again in court, where he learns that she served as a guard for the Nazi SS. He must try to reconcile these two visions of his former lover, ultimately coming to terms with her inextricable presence in his life. More cerebral and philosophical than any other book on the bestseller lists during this time period, this is both a story about human complexity and an allegory of sorts for collective German guilt. *The Reader* concludes that escaping guilt is impossible; the narrator can't free himself from his past with Hanna, and Hanna's own attempts to atone for her Nazi involvement do not bring redemption. The narrator learns that living with guilt, even as we attempt good works as penance, is the only possible course.

Despite the popularity of Christian reading, simple forgiveness—whether human or divine—is rarely offered up in these books as a solution to our guilt. Perhaps, as we see in David Guterson's beautiful *Snow Falling on Cedars* (the #10 trade paperback in 1995), forgiveness can prevent us from making mistakes that will haunt us forever. But there seems to be no easy absolution for crimes already committed. Even Krakauer's *Into Thin Air* is steeped in guilt:

> Of the six climbers on Hall's expedition who reached the summit, only Mike Groom and I made it back down: four teammates with whom I'd laughed and vomited and held long intimate conversations lost their lives. My actions—or failure to act—played a direct role in the death of Andy Harris. And while Yasuko Namba lay dying on the South Col, I was a mere 350 yards away, huddled inside a tent, oblivious to her struggle, concerned only with my own safety. The stain this has left on my psyche is not the sort of thing that washes off after a few months of grief and guilt-ridden self-reproach. (271)

Our fascination with these topics suggests that we are, like the real and fictional people who fill our bestselling pages, restlessly seeking a cure for our own lingering regrets.

Me, Myself, and I

One of the major criticisms of Oprah's club is that her books are exercises in self-indulgence. The discussions on the show feature earnest women sitting around a table, saying things such as "Oh, it was so *moving*" and "I just sobbed when he went back to Poughkeepsie" and "I really related to Ernestina's Slavic wanderlust."

It's not hard to see why serious lit people would be a little bit appalled.

But as Kathleen Rooney points out in *Reading with Oprah,* critics have mistakenly confused the themes of the books with the interpretive approach of the discussion-leader. It is Oprah who demands that kind of reading: not only a highly emotional reading, but also the deliberate imposition of self on the text. To Oprah, fiction is meant to conjure up our own memories and lives. Oprah's literary conversations continually show her and her audience reading the text as an autobiographical journey—Oprah's, their own, and the author's. This kind of reading can elicit empathy, but mostly in the sense that it minimizes the differences between us. It is not necessarily Azar Nafisi's "sensual experience of another world," but rather the sensual experience of our *own* world—over and over again. The idea that good fiction can be reflective and discomforting, rather than sentimentalizing and triumphant, is not really on Oprah's radar.

This insistence on the "realness" of fiction, and thus especially the realness of the characters, sheds some light on Oprah's emotional response to the controversy over *A Million Little Pieces,* James Frey's supposedly nonfictional account of his life of addiction. So overwhelmed was Oprah by the triumphant tome that in October of 2005 she took a break from the classics to make *A Million Little Pieces* her next selection. Frey's graphic description of his wretched life as an addict and his near-impossible recovery in a rehab clinic ended up selling almost five million copies. Within just a few months of his appearance on *Oprah,* however, an online journal announced that Frey had made up substantial chunks of his story. Eventually, a semi-contrite Frey was compelled to confess on air to Oprah that he had, in fact, invented many parts of his memoir. His lying was, he pleaded, a "coping mechanism."

Frey might have sidestepped the entire brouhaha if he had appended the usual "cover-your-butt" note to his text, the kind of thing John Berendt does in his autobiographical account of life amid the quirky characters of Savannah in *Midnight in the Garden of Good and Evil* (#3 nonfiction in 1997, #38 for 1993–2003):

> The characters in this book are real, but it bears mentioning that I have used pseudonyms for a number of them in order to protect their privacy, and in a few cases I have gone a step further by altering their descriptions. Though this is a work of nonfiction, I have taken certain storytelling liberties, particularly having to do with the timing of events. Where the narrative strays from strict nonfiction, my intention has been to remain faithful to the characters and to the essential drift of events as they really happened.

But Frey, alas, had claimed his story was all true (even though he apparently first shopped it around to publishers as fiction!), and now Oprah was angry; she felt "conned." She had chosen Frey's book mainly because it was amazing that so many horrible things could "happen to one person" and he could survive. And indeed, Frey's rejection of the twelve-step Alcoholics Anonymous program and his insistence on being brutally honest and taking responsibility for everything had apparently made him a bit of hero in the recovery world: he claimed in the memoir to have overcome his addiction by force of will alone (aided by a book of Tao and some influential friends). Typical is this passage, when he is appalled by an addiction lecture from a "Rock Star" (Frey's style can at times evoke a nearly Germanic frenzy for capitalization):

> The life of the Addict is always the same. There is no excite-
> ment, no glamour, no fun. There are no good times, there is
> no joy, there is no happiness. There is no future and no escape.
> There is only an obsession. An all-encompassing, fully
> enveloping, completely overwhelming obsession. To make
> light of it, brag about it, or revel in the mock glory of it is
> not in any way, shape or form related to its truth, and that
> is all that matters, the truth. That this man is standing in front
> of me and everyone else in this room lying to us is heresy.
> The truth is all that matters. This is fucking heresy. (159)

Truth. Ah, there's the rub. Oprah and all Frey's readers before January 2006 perhaps had a right to feel cheated. They bought a memoir, and it turned out to be partially fictionalized. Okay, shame on Frey, although he is not the first and will not be the last to reinvent himself in a memoir. (The book is now published with notes indicating its slippery hold on facts, and a class action suit may give readers a full refund if they sign a sworn statement that they bought the book on the assumption it was nonfiction. It is still listed on the Random House website, however, under "Biography and Autobiography.")

Frey's real mistake was that he undermined Oprah's way of reading. In this type of literary analysis, fictional characters are "real"—primarily, they are vehicles for exploring the lives of readers and authors. Authors who write explicitly about their own struggles, then, are even more pow-erful because they are "real" and also, well, real. But Frey's lies threatened this whole interpretive foundation, the entire edifice of the Book Club's manner of reading: If a real-life character might not be real, what would that say about the "fictional" characters? Could it *all* be, well, purely fictional? Could there be a little conman lurking underneath every authorial wizard, a hot-air balloonist merely pulling levers and cranking wheels? For Oprah, the link between character and author/reality had to be preserved: pay no attention to that man behind the curtain.

Frey was skewered on national TV.

For comparison's sake, consider the story of Rigoberta Menchú Tum, who received the 1992 Nobel Peace Prize for her campaign against the Guatemalan civil war. Much of her notoriety derived from a 1983 biography—really an autobiography composed of taped interviews—titled (in the English translation) *I, Rigoberta Menchú.* Afterward, it was discovered that her memoir was full of lies, with many of its most significant episodes distorted, inverted, or completely invented. Frey may have exaggerated about his crimes and his toughness—the root canal without any anesthesia or painkillers should have been a tip-off—but Menchú claimed to have watched her brother die of malnutrition when in fact he was alive and well and running a homestead nearly twenty years later! Nonetheless, the Nobel committee did not revoke her award or demand that she come back and explain herself. As one of her critics concedes, the story—even with its numerous misleading and false statements—"enabled her to focus international condemnation on an institution that deserved it, the Guatemalan army." To this day, the book remains a staple in college courses, and Menchú is an internationally admired advocate for indigenous people's rights. She might have lied, but nobody cares. Lucky for her, she didn't mess with Oprah.

Oprah's overwhelming sincerity makes one of her choices, Jonathan Franzen's *The Corrections,* a bit of a head-scratcher. It's a hilarious and thoroughly enjoyable novel, to be sure (and was the #5 hardcover fiction title for 2001), but its bald presentation of family life and human nature at their least inspirational doesn't exactly scream out "Oprah." (Apparently Franzen thought so too; he rather haughtily opposed his book's inclusion on Oprah's list, which got him "disinvited" to her show.

Still, *The Corrections* remained an Oprah pick—although some of the books were printed without the OBC endorsement on the cover—and Franzen later thanked Lady Book Club for her support.) According to the book review in *O, the Oprah Magazine,* "there's something thrilling, heartening, and inspiring about seeing life revealed so accurately, so transparently—and finally, so forgivingly. . . . we feel (as we do in real life) awe and profound respect for the bravery and resilience of the deeply flawed human beings who manage to be born, and die, and survive all the moments between."

This review demonstrates the essence of Oprah-vision. Although we would agree with the "accurately" and "transparently" part of the review—the book is deliciously honest—we don't think *The Corrections* is particularly forgiving or awe-inspiring or that the characters display much bravery. And we think that's the point. Franzen's novel suggests that humor and irony, not sincerity and awe, are the tools with which to face our bumbling, neurotic selves (and relatives).

Nonetheless, although we strongly believe that literature can be much more than therapy and that novels (and life) can be more than unyieldingly sincere, we're also certain that Oprah's approach has provided a safe, welcoming introduction to the world of books for a great many of her viewers. As she made clear in her announcement of *Anna Karenina* in 2004, many people are literally afraid to read books, especially classics. But Oprah assures her viewers, as she did then, "Let's not be scared of it." She got people reading *Tolstoy,* for heaven's sake; she got people reading at all. And that, any way you slice it, is an admirable achievement.

Girl Power

We all know that most Oprah TV viewers are female. It's also been estimated that 70 percent of readers of all literary fiction are female. Thus, it's easy to assume that most of her books are "for women." But we're not even sure what that means.

There's a weird underlying assumption in our culture that says books about men are appropriate for humanity, and books about women are for women alone. That seems wrong, especially for "literary" fiction, which is supposed to shed light on the human experience; that should be a fine activity for both sexes. But then it's not clear at what point men should be reasonably allowed to tune out. What *is* "chick lit"? Books about female friends, books about mothers and daughters? But women read about male friends and about fathers and sons. What about a novel like *Midwives* (#12 trade paperback in 1998), which is about, you know, midwives? Chick lit, right? But a man—Chris Bohjalian—wrote it.

In fact, men write a lot of these books. Oprah favors female authors, but many of her most popular selections were written by men, and about half of the non-Oprah books we read were also male offerings.

But we still get the feeling that, as a rule, the guys just aren't picking these books up. Certain novels are obviously exclusionary, such as *The Divine Secrets of the Ya-Ya Sisterhood* by Rebecca Wells (#2 trade paperback in 1998) or *The Red Tent* by Anita Diamant (#6 trade paperback in 2001). (And in fact we would advise most anyone to avoid "sisterhoods" of all kinds and any use of the word "red" that might refer to stained underpants.) But most literary bestsellers do not contain scrapbooks, excessive weeping, or menstrual tents. They should not be inherently unappealing to male readers.

How do we know they are? Well, it all goes back to subjects and themes, what really boils down to a lack of variety and an obsession with certain topics that can, in all honesty, only be female. The bestsellers from this time period aren't all *about* women. But the vast majority of them are about families, relationships, and personal journeys. They emphasize feelings and dynamics rather than actions and events. And as varied as they are in plot and writing style, they overlap in weird ways: the sheer number of birth scenes we read, for example, could easily have sent us whimpering back to John Grisham if we weren't incredibly brave. (Massage the perineum, indeed!)

But there's more.

To a bizarre degree, the bestselling literary fiction features child or adolescent protagonists. Ninah in *The Rapture of Canaan* (#12 trade paperback in 1997). Benjy, Norm, and Alice in *Songs in Ordinary Time* (#10 trade paperback in 1997). Pi in, you know, *Life of Pi*. Even Alice Sebold's enormously popular page-turner, the relatively theme-free *The Lovely Bones,* has a fourteen-year-old narrator. Yeah, she's dead, but she's still only fourteen. And the unnamed, vampire-hunting narrator is sixteen at the start of Elizabeth Kostova's *The Historian* (#8 fiction in 2005). In fact, of the thirty-six literary novels we reviewed, twenty-three of these are told, to a significant extent, from a child's point of view. (And that doesn't include memoirs such as *Angela's Ashes* and *A Child Called "It,"* both child-driven narratives.)

Now consider this. In over a third of the books, those children don't have parents. Specifically mothers. March was raised by a housekeeper in *Here on Earth* (#10 trade paperback in 1998). Both the eponymous heroines Jewel and Icy Sparks lost their parents early in life. Amir's mother died in childbirth in *The Kite Runner;* Ada is orphaned early in *Cold Mountain;* the famous geisha is sent to learn her exotic trade upon the death of her mother.

What are these, Disney movies? At least they spared us the nasty step-mothers.

These two conditions—child narrators without mothers—come together explicitly in books such as *The Secret Life of Bees* by Sue Monk Kidd (#2 trade paperback in 2003, #3 in 2004, #6 in 2005) and *White Oleander* by Janet Fitch (#11 fiction in 1999). In *Secret Life,* fourteen-year-old Lily has spent her whole life longing for the mother whom she accidentally shot and killed as a small child. Fleeing her abusive father, Lily goes searching for more information about her mother and ulti-mately finds a new, nurturing home with surrogate mothers galore.

White Oleander is the hardcore version of this search. Twelve-year-old, fatherless Astrid finds herself in the juvenile dependency system when her self-absorbed poet mother goes to prison for murder. Scrappy little Astrid has to adjust to piteous conditions as she's shuffled from one trashy foster home to another, latching on to every adult she meets in an attempt to replace the mother she lost, find the love she never really had, and escape the influence of her mother, who even from prison has the power to destroy Astrid's fragile victories.

These books could hardly be more different in style and audience: whereas Lily seeks acceptance through bee-keeping and goddess worship (*Secret Life* is a young-adult novel), Astrid seduces her foster father and takes a gander at prostitution and drugs. But the driving force of each book is the emptiness of an adolescent girl without a mother.

The loss of a parent is not an uncommon literary plot device, of course, but the overwhelming focus on children in these books, especially so many motherless ones, calls for analysis. Although it's possible that a huge group of adult orphans is keeping these titles afloat, it seems more reasonable to assume that the ones doing most of the reading are the mothers (and wannabe mothers) themselves. So many of these books take pains to reinforce the absolute necessity of mothering; Sidda, in *Divine Secrets of the Ya-Ya Sisterhood,* can't even stand to get married until she solves the riddle of her mother's life and love. *Drowning Ruth's* title character gives up her city-dwelling aspirations to return to her Aunt Mandy, the only mother she's ever known, asking, "How could I leave someone who loved me that much?" (330). Books such as *My Sister's Keeper* and *The Nanny Diaries* ask us to consider what mothering really is—and when it fails. Even Terry McMillan's *A Day Late and a Dollar Short,* a breath of fresh unsentimental air ("All kids don't like their parents, you know. And ain't no rule that say you gotta like your kids either,"149), ultimately celebrates the wisdom of a mother and her ability to unite a splintered family.

Even though literary bestsellers are not as repetitive or predictable as romance novels, could it be that the reasons people read them are not so different? Do mothers feel so unappreciated that they must read book after book that assures them of their importance? (As Mitch Albom soothes at the end of *For One More Day,* "behind your stories is always your mother's story, because hers is where yours begins," 194.) And what of the bestsellers that celebrate female friendship and fellowship, such as *Divine Secrets* and *The Red Tent, The Secret Life of Bees,* and Toni Morrison's *Paradise?* Perhaps women just find such topics comforting and heartwarming—but we wonder if the extreme popularity of these subjects exposes a real longing for connections with absent children and distant friends.

All told, it hints at a far-reaching loneliness that, in combination with what we know about romance readers, makes women out to be the saddest bunch of bookworms you ever did see. Sociological studies of book clubs (one of the best is revealingly subtitled "Women and the Uses of Reading in Everyday Life") show that most participants are female and, though educated, still read fiction experientially; that is, they value the emotional proximity to characters, just as they rely on the friendship of the group itself.

The studies also suggest that those darn romance heroines were right: men *don't* read much, at least not literary fiction. (Or perhaps they do, but—because women buy more of it—the novels men prefer don't make it to the bestseller lists.) Maybe men have been leery of literary fiction in general since Oprah came to town, fearing a candle-lighting ceremony or a birth scene behind every cover. Maybe they are simply less interested in people, preferring the facts of nonfiction, the action of thrillers, or the technological fantasies of science fiction. Maybe they are too busy hunting, fishing, and racing cars.

Whatever the reason, it seems sad to us. With many women super-imposing themselves on the books they read, and most men potentially not reading literary fiction at all, it seems that relatively few people are looking to literature for its ideas. In her study of the Book-of-the-Month Club, Janice A. Radway refers to this kind of approach to literature—an approach that applies to both genders—as "middle-brow personalism," a reading that emphasizes identification, connection, communion, and sentiment. Although finding oneself in a book is a legitimate way to read, we would argue that novels can be much more than mirrors. Instead of just celebrating who we already are, books can refine us by inspiring us to question what we assume and believe. And we do that in part by *removing* our own histories and feelings from the story, allowing ourselves to become the characters rather than the other way around.

Books can also prompt us to think about more than just families and relationships. Although these certainly are critical aspects of the human experience, the literary fiction from the recent past is missing the rest of the picture—it's notably silent on topics that lie outside the most personal realms. In the world of recent bestsellers, one must look to the *non-*fiction titles to step beyond the hearth and out into a larger world.

JUST THE FACTS, MA'AM

We were pleased to discover that there is a market out there for a thoughtful appraisal of ideas, culture, history, and science. For example, a handful of well-researched books about how we think (and don't) and why we act the way we do have shot up the recent annual best-seller lists. These bestsellers have a bit of a formula of their own: summarize academic studies of a topic but humanize them by briefly outlining the scholar's career or appearance or controversial place in the field; include numerous case studies (the more, and weirder, the better—attention spans wane); bring in interviews with leading figures; add some personal anecdotes, especially of places (businesses or locations visited while doing research); bring all of this together into a provocative thesis; come up with a short, catchy title (followed by a longer subtitle that explains it); and, most wonderfully and mysteriously, make it all seem interesting and important.

The current master of this genre is Malcolm Gladwell, who has combined studies from social and cognitive psychology, marketing, anthropology, and sociology in two fascinating explorations of human behavior: *The Tipping Point: How Little Things Can Make a Big Difference* (#8 trade paperback in 2005) and *Blink: The Power of Thinking without Thinking* (#8 nonfiction in 2005). Also interested in how we make decisions are Steven D. Levitt and Stephen J. Dubner, who cogently apply the laws of incentives to such seemingly divergent topics as real estate, day care, Sumo wrestlers, the Ku Klux Klan, crime, and parenting in *Freakonomics. A Rogue Economist Explores the Hidden Side of Everything* (#8 nonfiction in 2005, #12 in 2006). Though the book doesn't quite live up to its impishly bombastic subtitle, who could resist a book that juxtaposes "rogue" with "economist"?

Readers are equally concerned about the bigger picture, especially changes forced onto the world by leaps in technology. *The World is Flat: A Brief History of the Twenty-First Century* (#6 nonfiction in 2005), a study of (and argument for) globalization by *New York Times* columnist Thomas Friedman, was so popular that it was issued in an updated and even flatter version just one year after its initial publication. And perhaps our favorite in this group is Eric Schlosser's *Fast Food Nation: The Dark Side of the All-American Meal* (#9 trade paperback in 2002), an uncomfortable look at one prime example of modern America's union of technology, consumerism, and big business. Anyone who reads this book and continues to pack up the kids for a Happy Meal may just be deranged.

It's not only journalistic analyses that strike oil; occasionally an academic popularizer breaks through. Jared Diamond's *Guns, Germs, and Steel: The Fates of Human Societies* (#3 trade paperback in 2005)—a brilliant, if not completely convincing, attempt to explain why Western culture has differed from non-Western cultures (talk about your big pictures)—won a Pulitzer Prize for nonfiction. David McCullough has won two Pulitzers for his biographies in the past fifteen years, one for *Truman* in 1993 (#8 in nonfiction in 1992) and the other for *John Adams* in 2002 (#4 in nonfiction in 2001). And he continues to bridge the gap between scholarship and the masses: his *1776* was the fifth bestselling nonfiction book in 2005. Even if you're not a fan of historical writing (which we are), it's not hard to see why McCullough has met with so much success. His clear prose and absolute mastery of detail, particularly of primary sources, transforms even the most complicated and potentially arid issues into riveting narrative. Although history textbooks and ideological agendas do their best to suck the joy out of studying history in American schools, apparently many of us eventually recover.

Most of the bestselling literary nonfiction, then, is as fixated on big external issues as the fiction is on small internal ones. Though we have not found any studies of book-reading habits that reveal whether the same people read nonfiction and fiction, we have a feeling—and after reading the books covered in this chapter, we're all over this feeling stuff—that most people have a strong preference for one or the other. Almost everyone we know lists sharply toward one side of the bookstore or the other. Maybe this is just the way life has to be: fictionites can get some facts from historical novels; nonfiction readers can learn about people from popular summaries of studies in the social sciences. Still, we can't help thinking that the two are complementary and equally necessary for a thoughtful life—that to answer our questions, we need to combine the emotive with some facts, the personal with the objective, the experiential with the experimental. Perhaps the truth we are seeking will emerge from that complex intersection. But is that what we are really looking for?

TRAGEDY TOMORROW, COMEDY TONIGHT

We said in the introduction that there was no one similarity linking all the bestselling books of this time period. And we meant it. But if we had to find the one characteristic that fits all the books the best, it would not be the perpetuation of simple answers to complex questions, or the desire to drown out alternative perspectives, or even the desperate need for inspiration in its various forms. It would be this one commonality that shines forth across the genres and audiences and writing styles:

We have no taste for tragedy.

You might have laughed at the no-budge "happy ending" rule in the world of romance novels, but be careful not to feel too smug. Think back on all the books we've examined so far. From *Chicken Soup* to *The Poisonwood Bible,* how many had a truly tragic ending? Well, none. We want to read that marriages work out, that diets succeed, and that people can heal from even the worst of fortune's flukes. Sure, we can stomach some mixed endings—as long as there's *something* hopeful in the conclusion, some whisper that the characters have grown and will go on to good things, or a confirmation of the power and persistence of love (such as in the tragic romances). But almost never will we embrace a pure tragedy, one in which the inherent weaknesses of the characters lead to their doom, one in which their best efforts to make restitution fail, one that reminds us just how close we are at every moment to disaster and that that perhaps luck is the only thing that keeps us from plunging into that chasm.

And so we must applaud Oprah once again, who was brave enough to get (at least) one on the list.

House of Sand and Fog is a superb book and a superb example of the power of tragedy that is missing from the rest of our reading. A novel by Andre Dubus III, which was the #9 trade paperback in 2000, *House of Sand and Fog* weaves together the stories of three struggling characters: Colonel Behrani, a Persian immigrant desperate to make it in

America; Kathy Nicolo, a former addict attempting to scrape her life together after a failed marriage; and Lester Burdon, an unhappily married police officer willing to do almost anything for the hope of a new, passionate life. A simple mistake—a clerical error, a fluke—yokes these characters together in a series of events that, fueled by their own insecurities and dreams, ultimately destroys them.

The power of this story lies in its characters: believable, fractured people who are likeable one moment and frustrating, even repugnant, the next. Each is the protagonist of his or her own story; each is the antagonist to another. The narrative captures the essence of real life, where strength and weakness and desire and fear—not good or evil—determine the course of events. This is a book that demands empathy even for people who create many of their own problems, a real willingness to set aside the self and look through another's eyes.

Some of Oprah's readers weren't happy about that at first. Commented discussion member "George," "At first, I was outraged that Oprah would recommend a dark novel with no characters to truly like"—but that characteristic is exactly why this type of book is so important. Empathizing with heroes is easy, but how many of us emerge heroic from our tangles of real-life triumphs and mistakes? Whether grounded in a fictional landscape or a real one, the ability to sympathize with very different people—while retaining our ability to analyze and critique events—can be a major step toward hauling ourselves out of the divisive "tell me what I want to hear" mentality in which our collective American soul is currently so enmeshed.

We know what you're thinking. Who has time for another bummer? But reading a tragic book isn't the same experience as watching a sad litany on the evening news. Books have *context*, and they explore how and why things happen. Through that exploration the events gain depth and meaning, and most importantly, they evoke thought.

The experiences of reading comedy and tragedy are fundamentally different. We end a chipper book, and we bop outside for rollerblading. We finish a sad book, and we can't help but think about it—even if we try the rollerblading anyway and end up in a ditch. Why *did* those things happen to those characters? Could those events have been avoided? What does this book say about life, and does it ring true? Tragedy makes us think about the nature of the human struggle, the nature of the universe. Generally, it's the most disturbing stories— whether books or films—that stay with us the longest and push us to consider and reconsider the most.

That kind of thinking can even be inspiring. For some reason, as a culture we seem to have misunderstood and misappropriated the concept of "inspiration," often assigning it to our most predictable and one-dimensional works of art. But inspiration is not supposed to be a lantern that we shine to pretend there is no darkness; it is supposed to be the lantern in our hands as we plunge into the darkness. And so exploring where characters went wrong can be a fine way to help readers decide what's right. One of Oprah's *House of Sand and Fog* readers, for example, claimed to have given up smoking because "Kathy's endless desperate smoking disgusted [her]." Reading tragedy may not result in such noticeable (or life-saving) changes for everyone, but it can still, in subtler ways, help us consider and choose what not to be.

Of course, many of the books on the lists, especially the literary ones, are disturbing and thought-provoking, even if they end with hopeful notes. And we think that's swell. But we have to wonder what is so hard, so arm-twistingly bone-chillingly hard, about taking that next little baby step and being willing to admit that happiness just isn't always on the menu?

Tragedy is a reality check. People shouldn't actually be allowed to purchase a volume of *Chicken Soup* without a companion book of, say, *Rancid Bratwurst for the Soul (if There Is One)*. Only the smallest fraction of life involves paraplegic children hitting home runs, and the fact that we avoid that basic reality in every literary genre bespeaks a terrible fear lurking in our souls—not necessarily a fear of that truth itself, but of acknowledging and thinking seriously about it.

There is a place in this world for *Chicken Soup for the Soul,* just as there is a place for romantic comedies and Hallmark Hall of Fame movies and any art that uplifts and reminds us what is important. But there is a place, too, for sorrow, for honesty, and for thought. If recent American bestsellers are any indication, we readers *want* to find answers in books to humanity's most pressing questions. But to do so, we must invite to our bookshelves the other half of truth. The wisdom we seek lies in the balance.

DECIPHERING DA CODE:

CONCLUSIONS

They looked down at the burgundy rectangle on the desk, its arresting swatch of Mona Lisa.

A book, they thought. *The Da Vinci Code.*

They fingered the cover of the bestselling mystery novel. *A novel. With mysteries.* Dan Brown had written it.

An author.

They delved into the book, expecting an intriguing read. But nothing could have prepared them for the *shocking* twists they would find inside its pages. And the most shocking truth of all . . . *they could have waited for the movie!*

Don't worry. We won't write this final chapter in DanBrownese. But maybe we should, because it obviously works: *The Da Vinci Code* is *the* bestselling phenomenon of this millennium, the #1 seller in hardback fiction in 2003 and 2004, and second only to John Grisham's latest thriller in 2005. (In fact, to be fair—and we are nothing if not fair when it comes to Dan Brown—the combined sales of *The Da Vinci Code* and *The Da Vinci Code: Special Illustrated Edition* surpassed those of Grisham's *The Broker.*) In 2006, *Da Vinci* took the top spot in trade paperbacks (7,500,000 copies, trade and mass market combined). Over 60 million copies of the book are now in print!

Why? What makes it so special? Publishers have been turning themselves inside out trying to figure out that one. The only thing they're certain about is that Brown's next novel, *The Solomon Key*, will sell well. Damn well. (Several books have already surfaced with the single, happy agenda of predicting what *The Solomon Key* is going to be about. And debunking it.)

For those two or three of you who have not read *Da Vinci*, and who may have forgotten its summary in the introduction of this book, here's an even briefer one: Harvard professor and "religious symbologist" Robert Langdon gets called in to solve creepy murder of Louvre curator. Granddaughter of victim accompanies him on journey to find murderer and escape bad guys. Journey becomes quest for Holy Grail. Secrets and codes are discovered and cracked. Mystery is solved; albino dies. The end.

There appear to be as many answers to the mystery of *Da Vinci*'s success as there are holes in its historicity. One of the better balanced best-selling explorations of the history behind the story—*Secrets of the Code: The Unauthorized Guide to the Mysteries Behind the Da Vinci Code*—offers nine different reasons the novel has attracted so many readers: (1) interesting ideas, (2) consummate artistry, (3) spiritual aspects, (4) the "quest," (5) feminist sensitivities, (6) anti-fundamentalism, (7) scientific "research," (8) symbolism, and (9) conspiracy theories.

That's an excellent start. A thriller with religious content, *The Da Vinci Code* also exhibits several traits typical of bestsellers in this period, making it the perfect culmination of our study. Ultimately, the novel's popularity—and the multifarious reasons for its popularity—reveals a reading public in need of a different kind of education.

Mastering the Formula

As we mentioned in the introduction (you're still smarting from that bar bet, aren't you?), *The Da Vinci Code* and *Angels & Demons* are basically the same book. The similarities between the two novels are *so* remarkable—especially when it comes to structure and style—as to suggest that *The Da Vinci Code*'s success has mostly everything to do with its highly controversial content and little to do with its masterful manipulation of generic topoi or any looming literary qualities. Oh sure, it's a great vacation read. But so are *Angels & Demons* and the hundreds if not thousands of similar detective thrillers published every year that don't become mega-sellers.

Separated at Birth

Take the Dan Brown challenge! Each of the following nine quotes is a chapter cliffhanger from either *The Da Vinci Code* or *Angels & Demons*. Can you tell which is which?

1. "[He] peered into the study and immediately felt his skin crawl. *Holy mother of Jesus,* he said to himself."
2. "Finally, he felt the blood begin to flow."
3. "The horrifying answer was only a moment away."
4. "*The wheels are in motion.*"
5. "Then . . . the little girl began to scream."
6. "The world had yet to hear the most shocking news of all."
7. "With that, the connection went dead."
8. "They stole his *eye?*"
9. "What you see in this photograph . . . Monsieur Saunière did that to himself."

Answers:

A & D: 1, 3, 5, 6, 8, *Da Vinci:* 2, 4, 7, 9

Simply, *Da Vinci's* controversial and titillating particulars set it apart from its twin. First, the cast of characters and nature of the quest: *Angels & Demons* features Galileo and Bernini, Rome, and a murdered pope. *Da Vinci's* got, well, da Vinci, Paris, England, and Jesus. The frantic effort to prevent the obliteration of the Vatican, as dramatic as it is, can't hold a candle to the search for the Holy Grail. Ask Indiana Jones, or his father. (Or the protagonist of both *Angels* and *Da Vinci,* for that matter, who is sort of a poor-man's Indiana. Maybe in the next installment, Dan Brown could exchange his hero's Mickey Mouse watch for a whip and a John Williams theme song.)

Second, and more importantly, *The Da Vinci Code* made Christianity's fans *and* foes stand up and pay attention.

If you haven't read the book, be warned: we have to give away the big answer here. The Holy Grail is not a snazzy goblet, not an object at all. The "Grail," through some linguistic and symbolic tussle, actually refers to the chalice shape that represents the womb. More concretely, it means those suppressed gospels (the Gnostic ones) not included in the Bible, which acknowledge Jesus's marriage to Mary Magdalene and the fruit of their union. Jesus had *sex!* Had *kids!* The Grail, is, ultimately, Mary Magdalene herself, the documents that "prove" her motherhood, and her progeny.

Some people didn't like that at all. Some of them really *did.* And the rest of the world wondered what the fuss was about and checked it out.

And here's the little sentence on the page before the prologue that made them care so much in the first place:

> All descriptions of artwork, architecture, documents, and secret rituals in this novel are accurate.

Brown included virtually the same mark of authenticity in the beginning of *Angels & Demons,* but people didn't quite take it the same way.

Popes, Galileo—who cares? Once he started talking about Jesus, though, Christians leapt from the woodwork in outrage. At last count (and we actually counted), we found over forty books devoted to debunking (or, much less frequently, bunking) the historicity of *Da Vinci*. A vast majority of these "explorations" of the novel are patent defenses of traditional Christianity against the blasphemies of the novel.

Two of these became bestsellers. They take on not just *Da Vinci* itself, but *Holy Blood, Holy Grail* (the book on which much of Dan Brown's "scholarship" depends—the authors lost a well-publicized lawsuit against Brown for plagiarism), Elaine Pagels (a genuine scholar of the Gnostics), the Jesus Seminar, and modernity in general. Darrel Bock claims to have discovered "the real secret and code behind *The Da Vinci Code . . .* It is nothing less than a conscious effort to obscure the uniqueness and vitality of the Christian faith and message" (*Breaking the Da Vinci Code: Answers to the Questions Everyone's Asking,* 127). Two ministers attack Dan Brown in *Cracking Da Vinci's Code: You've Read the Fiction, Now Read the Facts;* the novel denies, they conclude, "in such an engrossing way," the traditional values of "patriarchy, doctrinal precision, canons, confessions, clearly defined sexual morality, church institutions and authority" while celebrating "neo-pagan" values such as a "personal spiritual quest, diversity, individualism, egalitarianism, and sexual liberation" (168). For the two code-cracking ministers, these icons of modernity pretty much spell the end of civilization as we have come to cherish it.

Others delighted in *Da Vinci's* supposed irreverence. Like *Conversations with God,* the novel pits Christian fundamentalism against a less restrictive spirituality, claiming that man muddied up religion. It thus became a novel of great hope for those trying to reconcile what has been perceived as an oppressive male-centered Christian (especially Catholic) tradition with their own connections to the Church. It also supplied plenty of welcome fodder to anyone hungry for a little Church-bashing.

Careful about the Coitus

Despite the hoopla, there have been few public protests against *The Da Vinci Code*—even the Christian debunkers almost universally give it a favorable review as far as summertime reading goes. Contrast this with the reception of Kazantzakis's *The Last Temptation of Christ*, both the book and the subsequent movie. In that work, a chaste Jesus does not actually have sex with Mary Magdalene, but merely fantasizes about it. The psychological trials of Jesus as he struggles to accept the cost of his divinity—a truly interesting novel of ideas—nearly got its author excommunicated from the Church; the movie was banned from Blockbuster because it had a "dream sequence" of Jesus having sex. But Tom Hanks didn't suffer the same fate in the *Da Vinci* movie. Even though *Da Vinci* theology annoys readers, it's the actual depiction of divine relations that gets you burned at the box office.

Yet *all* of these reactions reveal a startlingly unsophisticated reading public. *The Da Vinci Code* is a novel. Despite its claims of accurate detail, it is patently a work of fiction. Feeling profoundly shaken *or* gleeful about its pronouncements is feeling way too much. How could readers get their shorts in such a bundle over this plot?

The entire Christian story is a matter of faith. Scholars can help us determine when and how the New Testament was put together (something else Dan Brown, alas, gets mostly wrong), but no amount of scholarship can tell us the truth about the life and death of Jesus. The *preference* of Gnostic texts, no matter how they are interpreted, to the canonical books of the New Testament—or vice versa—is ultimately not a matter of scholarship but one of belief. One *chooses* to accept the varied and conflicting accounts of the birth, life, death, and resurrection of Jesus put together decades after the fact. Or not. Or partly.

And—let us repeat—*The Da Vinci Code* is not even a religious text or work of scholarship! It's a *novel!*

Moreover, readers seemed to have misread what the novel actually says about Jesus. The book claims that Jesus was a father; it *never* claims that he is not divine. (The movie-makers wised up, making this distinction explicit in the closing moments of the film.) In fact, the ethical, theological, spiritual, and cultural ramifications of Jesus's sexuality are virtually absent from the text. And although we understand that some fundamentalists may be too uncomfortable with sex to make that distinction, it is a significant one. *The Da Vinci Code* is about the *Church,* not about the Christian faith. The book is about the Church's supposed efforts to hide the "truth" from the world for twenty centuries. Churchgoers might not like that, but ascribing such secrecy to the Church is hardly a new idea—and surely not worth a cultural freak-out.

People are simply taking this book far too seriously and interpreting it far too sloppily. While searching along with Professor Langdon for the Holy Grail, they are finding answers they already want to believe. Dislike the Church? Well, you should—they're a secretive, lying, and murderous bunch of thugs and pretty much always have been (this despite the fact that the immediate villains in the piece are not from mainstream Catholic institutions, but a renegade bishop of Opus Dei and a scholar who will *do anything* to bring the truth to light). Convinced that institutionalized Christianity, especially in its more conservative leanings, has somehow lost touch with its roots? You were right. Or want proof the world is anti-Christian and going to hell? Just read this mystery! (And then—quickly—take one of the antidotal "guides" to its devilish charms.) Feel that Western culture has suppressed women? Here's why. (Indeed, one of the brilliant twists of *Da Vinci* is that its thesis attracts women readers to a genre rife with car chases and corpses.) Certain that history has been written by the winners? Here's what really happened. Instead of questioning Dan Brown's claim to truth—or even reading the statement closely to see that "artwork, architecture, documents, and secret rituals" do not equal "theology" or "history"—many readers took the book as true (or at least good) if they liked the ideas about the Church, and false if they didn't.

These readers are not stupid; we personally know lots of smart people who enjoyed—even loved—the novel, some who thought it might be true, a couple who were mildly offended. *Da Vinci* readers aren't lacking in brains; we're just not reading the book very carefully if we come away from the experience with anything more than a few hours of escapist fun and a suntan. In fact, we're reading *Da Vinci* the same way we're reading political books: assuming truth if the ideas comfort us and screaming out "liar!" if they don't.

We're also finding in it the same pleasures we get from other popular fiction. *The Da Vinci Code* is a high-octane epic battle with global repercussions. The characters tell us that it's important. The quasi-historical setting shouts out that it's important. Dan Brown's style screams, *This is really, really important!* (never before have italics been so abused). The resolution of the mystery has ramifications not just for the characters but for the reader as well. Get this Jesus thing wrong—and we've apparently been getting it wrong from the beginning—and bad things will happen. *Horrible things!*

The bad guys display as well the archetypal lack of empathy we have come to expect from our formula fiction. Silas, the homicidal albino, relishes his duties. The mastermind of the entire sanguinary plan to uncover the goblet, the Teacher (as Grail scholar Sir Leigh Teabing is known to his accomplices), even poisons his own aide-de-camp. Isn't that just the way with villains these days? Only Bishop Manuel Aringarosa, the duped and pathetically desperate leader of the soon-to-be-decommissioned Opus Dei, has any regrets—"no one was supposed to die"—but it's much too late. So much for middlemen.

The Da Vinci Code also adds a delicious dimension that most other bestselling fiction does not: the book makes readers feel like they are being educated. What Dan Brown does best is fill the novel with pseudo-scholarly details and intriguing tidbits about high art and history. A lot of it seems plausible, and all of it seems cool. Brown should really consider writing textbooks because he is a genius at making learning fun. (Next time he could try it with some real facts. Imagine the possibilities: Dan Brown meets David McCullough! The Founding Fathers were all Masons, weren't they? Oh, wait a minute. That was *National Treasure.*)

Here's the giveaway: genuine research is never so relentlessly explanatory. Brown seems terrified by the thought that someone, somewhere, might not fully grasp one of his references:

> The keystone, however, bore the simplest of inscriptions.
> Job 38:11
> *A Bible verse?* Silas was stunned with the devilish simplicity.
> . . .
> *Job. Chapter thirty-eight. Verse eleven.* (128)

So *that's* what that colon means? Thanks, Dan! You can almost feel him hovering over your shoulder, suffering little paroxysms at the unspeakable idea that you might be confused by an erudite (or in this case, not-so-erudite) tidbit. It can come off as unnecessary and even a bit insulting, but one thing is certain: no one will walk away confused.

We don't know how calculated Dan Brown was, but he has played American culture brilliantly. He found the perfect way to launch his formulaic conspiracy tale to infamy: Hinge the plot on Jesus's bloodline, but focus on Mary Magdalene, and be sure to avoid all theological implications. Make the Catholics guilty, but shine the spotlight on a conservative branch known for its bizarre rituals of self-mutilation. Claim that all "descriptions are accurate," and stand by your "scholarship," but finally insist it's a work of fiction. The result? Enough Christian annoyance without absolute condemnation to get more publicity than the Pope himself—and sell more books than the Pope does.

Brown is not just a master of American cultural pathologies; he also played readers brilliantly. Once we heard about the controversy, sixty million of us obeyed our curiosity and bought the book. We plunged enthusiastically into Brown's world of crime fighting, secret societies, religious cover-ups, and code-loving painters. We let his cliffhangers seize our hearts, forgiving the blatant manipulation, because we *had to know*. We graciously went along with the lame romance between Langdon and Sophie, and in some cases we even let the story seep into our souls and change our beliefs. This book truly held our culture in its sway over the past few years; it was the one, more than any other, that we simply couldn't put down.

THE TWO C'S

But our lust for controversy and conspiracy goes beyond *Da Vinci*. Were readers disgusted by James Frey's deception when he foisted off his fiction as a memoir? Sure, a little. But they still bought the book. The vice president and director of publicity for Anchor Books observed that Frey's public humiliation "actually propelled sales" of *A Million Little Pieces*. Indeed, the combined sales of Frey's debunked memoir and its sequel, *My Friend Leonard*, approached one million in 2006.

But the prime proof of our addiction to the two C's has to be the popularity of Kevin Trudeau's *Natural Cures "They" Don't Want You to Know About*. His super-selling thesis—the book was the #1 nonfiction title in 2005— is that "medical science has absolutely, 100 percent, failed in the curing and prevention of illness, sickness and disease" (11) and that there "are all-natural cures for virtually every disease and ailment, suppressed and hidden by the pharmaceutical industry, FDA, and Federal Trade Commission" (15). The conspiratorial "they" that have perpetrated this "great lie" are the drug companies, the food companies, the trade associations, every medical group from A to V (the Alzheimer's Association to the Vestibular Disorders Association, including the American Red Cross and American Rhinologic Society—damn those nose doctors!), charities and foundations (he singles out the Jerry Lewis Telethon), lobbyists, and government agencies.

Frankly, this is the last person anyone should trust when it comes to, well, anything. Before *Natural Cures,* Trudeau peddled a variety of products in "reality" style infomercials: dietary supplements, real estate investment, and memory-improvement courses. For some of these previous efforts, he pled guilty to larceny and spent two years in prison. His "Nutrition for Life" program got him banned from operating in Michigan. Ever. In 1998 he was forced to pay $500,000 to the Federal Trade Commission (FTC) for false and misleading claims in six infomercials. He also paid $2 million to settle charges for claiming coral calcium cures cancer, among other things. Eventually the FTC banned Trudeau (as summarized by Consumeraffairs.com) "from appearing in, producing, or disseminating future infomercials that advertise any type of product, service, or program to the public, except for truthful infomercials for informational publications. In addition, Trudeau cannot make disease or health benefits claims for any type of product, service, or program in any advertising, including print, radio, Internet, television, and direct mail solicitations, regardless of the format and duration." He is, however, allowed to advertise (but not sell) his book. (His "co-hosts" on these infomercials, by the way, are former televangelists accused of fraud.) Most of his claims lack any supporting evidence or basis in research (and some are simply false). After all, he quite openly admits, "All my conclusions and statements of fact are, in most cases, opinions." Read that again. Yes, he actually says that on page 5.

But the more the world learned of Trudeau's shady background and unfounded pronouncements, the more copies of *Natural Cures* they bought. Like *The Da Vinci Code,* Trudeau's book appeals to the belief that there is a truth out there that somehow has been kept hidden from us. It appeals so much that people would rather take medical advice from a proven liar and convicted criminal than face that there may not be any "natural cures," not to mention any mysterious "they."

We live in an *X-Files* world. Americans have taken the ubiquitous human hope that there is something beyond our immediate awareness and reduced it to comfortable formulas. Religious books are based on the premise that ultimate truth can be found—truth that the secular world, and other religions, tries to suppress. Diet and get-rich books offer the reader a previously unknown secret to success, a code cracked and revealed to the reader (for only twenty bucks!) by the latest guru. Romance readers feed off the belief that somewhere out there, beyond their own experience but unveiled in their books, exists a perfect relationship. Liberal authors discuss the hidden agenda of the Right ("no blood for oil"); conservatives counter that Democrats secretly want the terrorists to win. And one of the main attractions of Harry Potter, of course, is the wonderfully detailed alternative universe lying right under the noses of us non-magical Muggles.

Ironically, the more we seek the secrets, the more we hide from the one real truth that most of these books try to suppress: that there are no easy answers to humanity's complex problems, whether they manifest themselves in cancer, loneliness, terrorism, a beer gut, or an apparently indifferent universe.

WE DID THIS TO OURSELVES?

It seems that we readers may be looking for answers in all the wrong places. The mystery of Jesus—and of Christianity itself—is not to be found in the pages of a thriller. Really. But we seem to need a guru, an expert, to steer us ahead. Whether we want firmer abs, better marriages, deader terrorists, or tighter connections with the powers of the cosmos, we turn to the latest purveyor of the truth: Dr. Atkins, John Gray, Michael Moore, Rick Warren, Morrie Schwartz. And now Dan Brown. Ouch.

Is truth really so ephemeral? And is it even reasonable to look to the book-of-the-day for such deeply needed wisdom?

What a strangely medieval world American readers seem to live in. For hundreds of years, it was common practice to pick a line at random from some authoritative book—the Bible was a favorite, of course, but so was the *Aeneid*—and follow the advice buried in the verse. Anyone familiar with Augustine's tale of his own conversion will remember the process. One glance at the page—Luke 18:22 to be exact (that's the book of Luke, chapter 18, verse 22; but you knew that)—and there was "no need" to read further. All of life's tensions dissolved; his lengthy struggle was over.

Now we seem to turn to popular books for the same easy resolution of life's tensions and ambiguities. And oh what books! We may have climbed out of the Middle Ages, but one may doubt our progress in having swapped the Bible for *The Purpose Driven Life,* or Virgil for Dan Brown.

Of course, in those days the actual problem was not the texts themselves—the *Aeneid* and the Bible are brilliant and richly complex works—but how they were abused by their readers. In the modern world both readers and books seem to be to blame. We're behaving as abusively as ever, but today's books seem to like it. So many of them are written not to explore issues, as our timeless texts were, but to encourage readers to look to them for—and expect nothing more than—straightforward answers and reassurance. Our reading too often simplifies, rather than enriches; validates, rather than undermines; explains, rather than adumbrates; commands, rather than suggests; answers, rather than questions; pardons, rather than challenges; and accuses, rather than seeks to understand. It's a vicious circle that simply cannot cure what ails.

Of course, bestselling books are not the only sign of our increasing cultural balkanization. The blogs we visit, the television news we choose to watch, the radio stations we listen to, and the schools and universities we attend are increasingly monochromatic, offering whatever vision of life reinforces rather than challenges our preconceptions. We stare at the amazing bandwidth of modern life with a remote in our hands, quickly changing stations until we find the "truth" we already know. PBS too secular? Park it at FOX. Hate *The National Review?* Subscribe to *The Nation.* Emotionally disturbed by elephants? There's bound to be a chatroom for you. Find Christians annoying? Just avoid them—a support group for omphaloskeptics meets on Tuesdays in the community center. An American can easily make it through every single minute of a busy life without ever honestly confronting difference, without being challenged to defend a point of view. Should some well-articulated thoughts of a coworker furrow your brow, Rush Limbaugh is right there on the drive home, dittoheads, to smooth out the wrinkles.

Ironically, our Western freedom has won for us the opportunity to close out *all* competing voices, not just those of a ruling "regime." It's not so surprising, perhaps, but sad, that our book choices for the most part follow this same pattern. We have often been taught not to believe everything we read, but it is equally true that we should not read everything we believe.

Most distressing to us is that this kind of reading, especially of fiction, is almost exclusively pursued by the most highly educated Americans. Remember, only 57 percent of adult Americans say they have read a single book in the past year. That's *any* book at all. Less than half of Americans read any literary fiction, or what might be called "literature"—novels, poetry, or drama. The percentage of those who read books is directly proportional to years of education. So the readers buying books are, for the most part, products of the American educational system. Our findings in this book—which match our impressions after a combined thirty-eight years in higher education—thus suggest that this system is failing to teach people how and why to read. The decline of basic literacy is certainly an immediate problem, but what may be even more detrimental to our democratic experiment in the long run is our diminishing ability to read *well*. If we cannot do that, we may ultimately lose our ability to sift through complex information, to walk safely through the quagmire of indeterminacy, to work together in a world of difference to find common ground and progress. As the authors of the NEA-sponsored 2002 report *Reading at Risk* put it, "If literacy is the baseline for participation in social life, then reading—and reading of literary work in particular—is essential to a sound and healthy understanding of, and participation in, a democratic society" (1).

It used to be thought that an education—especially a college education—was the place where all ideas were up for grabs. Although President Bush has called for a reinvigoration of the kind of science and mathematics instruction that will make the country economically and technologically strong, an even louder cry should be raised for a renewed emphasis on the kinds of humanistic education that can strengthen our country's democratic soul. Good reading evokes a kind of transformation, and that, ultimately, is what any good education should do too. The study of art, philosophy, religion, language, culture, and especially literature—whether native or foreign, past or current—sharpens (and changes) minds, opens hearts, and emboldens souls. A literary immersion in different worlds and powerful ideas—whether through fiction or nonfiction—is unsettling, challenging, inspirational, and healthily subversive. Great (as in "very good") books are the very heart of a curriculum that teaches and reinforces rational, critical, and self-critical thinking about the world and one's place in it, of an education that encourages an empathetic response to the human condition and instills a desire to act on that response. The ability to read well—whether a novel, a newspaper, or a website—is exactly the talent that Americans of the twenty-first century must possess if they are to sift critically through mounds of information and competing claims of truth.

Increasingly, however, the American educational system has narrowed its goals, focusing on test scores at the K-12 level and nourishing the particular ideology du jour in colleges and universities. The resulting demotion of rich and multivocal texts in the humanities and social sciences has often reduced reading to a political activity more likely to produce boredom or visceral advocacy than reflection. Whether there is a cause and effect here (fewer and fewer Americans have been taught how to read or think critically as bestsellers become repetitively one-dimensional), or whether the overlapping trends are merely two sides of the same cultural coin, is a question we can't answer. But it's an uncomfortable and unhappy coincidence.

Still, all is not lost. There remain those, like Professor Nafisi, who believe that in the mind-numbing pace of the modern world, a book can still provide our best shot at a transformative experience, altering our opinions and enlarging our sensitivities. We've harped so much on *Reading Lolita in Tehran* in these pages because it is a perfect flashlight of a book: one that both illuminates the value of reading and, in doing so (however unintentionally), exposes how easily we Americans can overlook the artistic freedom we have. *Reading Lolita* is a story of people without choices who put themselves at great risk to have them. It's a story of people who were not satisfied with the one-sided, fear-driven, simplistic material they were told to read and believe.

It's a story that made us feel deeply troubled by what our culture has done with its own freedom. As a society we more closely resemble the antagonists in Nafisi's book—the students and government representatives who hate and fear complicated, ambiguous literature—than the courageous and thoughtful students who believed in such literature's power and importance. Imagine Americans risking their lives to read great Western literature, let alone ancient Persian poetry. We won't even risk the metamorphosis of our thoughts.

Every day, we pay lip service to democratic values and then again and again and again make undemocratic choices in the marketplace. Bestsellers are bestsellers because we buy them: nothing more. If we can wean ourselves from the destructive and useless quest for easy answers, devoting ourselves instead to a genuine search for truth in all its complexity, we can change the substance of these lists. Of course, we need not weed out formulaic, didactic, and simplistic titles entirely. There's always a place for relaxation and fun and the latest cultural craze, whether it be the stare-inducing *Magic Eye* books or the addictive challenge of sudoku (sales of these puzzle books reached nearly six million in 2006—score one for the nerds!). We just need to strike a better balance, using our reading time not only for comfort and thrills but for honest exploration and reflection as well. Not to be overly epic, but the health of our souls and society might very well depend on it.

Provocative, well-written, well-researched choices are out there, both on the bestseller lists and far from them. There are so many wonderful books that can send readers spinning into new realms of intellectual and emotional contemplation, both those that have withstood the test of time and some of the nearly 200,000 offered up each year to the free market of ideas. We already have the passion for what they have to offer. We simply need to realize that they are what we have been seeking all along.

APPENDIX: BESTSELLER LISTS

Publishers Weekly Bestselling Books 2006

Fiction

1. *For One More Day,* Mitch Albom
2. *Cross,* James Patterson
3. *Dear John,* Nicholas Sparks
4. *Next,* Michael Crichton
5. *Hannibal Rising,* Thomas Harris
6. *Lisey's Story,* Stephen King
7. *Twelve Sharp,* Janet Evanovich
8. *Cell,* Stephen King
9. *Beach Road,* James Patterson and Peter de Jonge
10. *The 5th Horseman,* James Patterson and Maxine Paetro
11. *Judge & Jury,* James Patterson and Andrew Gross
12. *At Risk,* Patricia Cornwell
13. *Wild Fire,* Nelson DeMille
14. *Treasure of Khan,* Clive Cussler and Dirk Cussler
15. *Brother Odd,* Dean Koontz

Nonfiction

1. *The Innocent Man,* John Grisham
2. *You: On a Diet—The Owner's Manual for Waist Management,*

Michael F. Roizen, MD, and Mehmet C. Oz, MD
3. *Marley & Me*, John Grogan
4. *The Audacity of Hope*, Barack Obama
5. *Culture Warrior*, Bill O'Reilly
6. *Guinness World Records 2007*, Guinness World Records
7. *The Best Life Diet*, Bob Greene
8. *Cesar's Way: The Natural Everyday Guide to Understanding and Correcting Common Dog Problems*, Cesar Millan and Melissa Jo Peltier
9. *The World Is Flat*, Thomas L. Friedman
10. *State of Denial: Bush at War, Part III*, Bob Woodward
11. *The Purpose Driven Life*, Rick Warren
12. *Freakonomics*, Steven D. Levitt and Stephen J. Dubner
13. *Inside My Heart: Choosing to Live with Passion and Purpose*, Robin McGraw
14. *Paula Deen Celebrates! Best Dishes and Best Wishes for the Best Times of Your Life*, Paula Deen and Martha Nesbit
15. *Godless: The Church of Liberalism*, Ann Coulter

Trade Paperbacks
1. *The Da Vinci Code*, Dan Brown
2. *The Memory Keeper's Daughter*, Kim Edwards
3. *Night*, Elie Wiesel
4. *Rachael Ray Express Lane Meals*, Rachael Ray
5. *The Kite Runner*, Khaled Hosseini
6. *The Mermaid Chair*, Sue Monk Kidd
7. *The Five People You Meet in Heaven*, Mitch Albom
8. *Cameras in Narnia*, Ian Brodie
9. *90 Minutes in Heaven*, Don Piper
10. *Glass Castle*, Jeannettte Walls
11. *Sudoku for Dummies*, Andrew Heron and Edmund James
12. *Rachael Ray 2, 4, 6, 8*, Rachael Ray

13. *Rachael Ray 365*, Rachael Ray
14. *True Believer*, Nicholas Sparks
15. *Jerusalem Countdown*, John Hagee

Mass-Market Paperbacks
1. *Morrigan's Cross*, Nora Roberts
2. *Dance of the Gods*, Nora Roberts
3. *Valley of Silence*, Nora Roberts
4. *Blue Smoke*, Nora Roberts
5. *4th of July*, James Patterson
6. *Lifeguard*, James Patterson
7. *Mary, Mary*, James Patterson
8. *Predator*, Patricia Cornwell
9. *Eleven on Top*, Janet Evanovich
10. *Angels & Demons*, Dan Brown
11. *Cell*, Stephen King
12. *The Camel Club*, David Baldacci
13. *No Place Like Home*, Mary Higgins Clark
14. *Chill Factor*, Sandra Brown
15. *Sam's Letters to Jennifer*, James Patterson

Publishers Weekly Bestselling Books 2005

Fiction
1. *The Broker*, John Grisham
2. *The Da Vinci Code*, Dan Brown
3. *Mary, Mary*, James Patterson
4. *At First Sight*, Nicholas Sparks
5. *Predator*, Patricia Cornwell
6. *True Believer*, Nicholas Sparks
7. *Light from Heaven*, Jan Karon

8. *The Historian*, Elizabeth Kostova
9. *The Mermaid Chair*, Sue Monk Kidd
10. *Eleven on Top*, Janet Evanovich
11. *Honeymoon*, James Patterson and Howard Roughan
12. *4th of July*, James Patterson and Maxine Paetro
13. *Lifeguard*, James Patterson and Andrew Gross
14. *S Is for Silence*, Sue Grafton
15. *The Camel Club*, David Baldacci

Nonfiction
1. *Natural Cures "They" Don't Want You to Know About*, Kevin Trudeau
2. *Your Best Life Now: 7 Steps to Living at Your Full Potential*, Joel Osteen
3. *The Purpose-Driven Life*, Rick Warren
4. *You: The Owner's Manual*, Michael F. Roizen, MD, and Mehmet C. Oz, MD
5. *1776*, David McCullough
6. *The World Is Flat*, Thomas L. Friedman
7. *Love Smart: Find the One You Want— Fix the One You Got*, Dr. Phil McGraw
8. *Blink: The Power of Thinking without Thinking*, Malcolm Gladwell
9. *Freakonomics: A Rogue Economist Explores the Hidden Side of Everything*, Stephen D. Levitt and Stephen J. Dubner
10. *Guinness World Records 2006*, Guinness World Records
11. *French Women Don't Get Fat*, Mireille Guiliano
12. *Teacher Man*, Frank McCourt
13. *Our Endangered Values*, Jimmy Carter
14. *700 Sundays*, Billy Crystal
15. *Team of Rivals: The Political Genius of Abraham Lincoln*, Doris Kearns Goodwin

Trade Paperbacks
1. *A Million Little Pieces*, James Frey

2. *The Kite Runner*, Khaled Hosseini

3. *Guns, Germs and Steel*, Jared Diamond

4. *Rachael Ray 365*, Rachael Ray

5. *Wicked*, Gregory Maguire

6. *The Secret Life of Bees*, Sue Monk Kidd

7. *The Curious Incident of the Dog in the Night-Time*, Mark Haddon

8. *The Tipping Point*, Malcolm Gladwell

9. *South Beach Diet*, Arthur Agatston, MD

10. *My Sister's Keeper*, Jodi Picoult

11. *Bad Cat*, Jim Edgar

12. *Lady & Sons: Savannah Country*, Paula H. Deen

13. *Sudoku Easy, Vol. 1*, Will Shortz

14. *Memoirs of a Geisha*, Arthur Golden

15. *Why Do Men Have Nipples*, Mark Leyner and Billy Goldberg, MD

Mass-Market Paperbacks

1. *The Broker*, John Grisham

2. *Red Lily*, Nora Roberts

3. *Black Rose*, Nora Roberts

4. *Angels & Demons*, Dan Brown

5. *3rd Degree*, James Patterson and Andrew Gross

6. *Life Expectancy*, Dean Koontz

7. *South Beach Diet*, Arthur Agatston, MD

8. *Trace*, Patricia Cornwell

9. *State of Fear*, Michael Crichton

10. *London Bridges*, James Paterson

11. *Northern Lights*, Nora Roberts

12. *Nighttime Is My Time*, Mary Higgins Clark

13. *The Calhouns: Catherine, Amanda and Lilah*, Nora Roberts

14. *The Calhouns: Suzanna & Megan*, Nora Roberts

15. *Hour Game*, David Baldacci

Publishers Weekly Bestselling Books 2004

Fiction

1. *The Da Vinci Code,* Dan Brown
2. *The Five People You Meet in Heaven,* Mitch Albom
3. *The Last Juror,* John Grisham
4. *Glorious Appearing,* Tim LaHaye and Jerry B. Jenkins
5. *Angels & Demons,* Dan Brown
6. *State of Fear,* Michael Crichton
7. *London Bridges,* James Patterson
8. *Trace,* Patricia Cornwell
9. *The Rule of Four,* Ian Caldwell and Dustin Thomason
10. *The Da Vinci Code: Special Illustrated Collector's Edition,* Dan Brown
11. *I Am Charlotte Simmons,* Tom Wolfe
12. *Night Fall,* Nelson De Mille
13. *A Salty Piece of Land,* Jimmy Buffett
14. *Ten Big Ones,* Janet Evanovich
15. *Black Wind,* Clive Cussler and Dirk Cussler

Nonfiction

1. *The Purpose Driven Life,* Rick Warren
2. *The South Beach Diet,* Arthur Agatston, MD
3. *My Life,* Bill Clinton
4. *America (The Book),* Jon Stewart and the *Daily Show* writers
5. *The South Beach Diet Cookbook,* Arthur Agatston, MD
6. *Family First,* Dr. Phil McGraw
7. *He's Just Not That Into You,* Greg Behrendt and Liz Tuccillo
8. *Eats, Shoots & Leaves,* Lynne Truss
9. *Your Best Life Now,* Joel Osteen
10. *Guinness World Records 2005,* Guinness World Records Ltd.
11. *Unfit for Command,* John O'Neill and Jerome R. Corsi

12. *The Automatic Millionaire,* David Bach
13. *The Proper Care and Feeding of Husbands,* Dr. Laura Schlessinger
14. *The Family,* Kitty Kelley
15. *Plan of Attack,* Bob Woodward

Trade Paperbacks

1. *The South Beach Diet Good Fats/Good Carbs Guide,* Arthur Agatston
2. *The 9/11 Commission Report,* The 9/11 Commission
3. *The Secret Life of Bees,* Sue Monk Kidd
4. *The Lovely Bones,* Alice Sebold
5. *The Wedding,* Nicholas Sparks
6. *Anna Karenina,* Leo Tolstoy
7. *Reading Lolita in Tehran,* Azar Nafisi
8. *1,000 Places to See Before You Die,* Patricia Schultz
9. *One Hundred Years of Solitude,* Gabriel García Márquez
10. *The Curious Incident of the Dog in the Night-Time,* Mark Haddon
11. *The Kite Runner,* Khaled Hosseini
12. *Atkins for Life,* Robert C. Atkins, MD
13. *The Good Earth,* Pearl S. Buck
14. *The Heart Is a Lonely Hunter,* Carson McCullers
15. *The Devil in the White City,* Erik Larson

Mass-Market Paperbacks

1. *Angels & Demons,* Dan Brown
2. *Bleachers,* John Grisham
3. *The Last Juror,* John Grisham
4. *Deception Point,* Dan Brown
5. *Skipping Christmas,* John Grisham
6. *Safe Harbour,* Danielle Steel
7. *Blue Dahlia,* Nora Roberts
8. *Digital Fortress,* Dan Brown

9. *Dr. Atkins New Diet Revolution,* Robert C. Atkins, MD
10. *The Notebook,* Nicholas Sparks
11. *The Guardian,* Nicholas Sparks
12. *Prey,* Michael Crichton
13. *Birthright,* Nora Roberts
14. *Blow Fly,* Patricia Cornwell
15. *The Big Bad Wolf,* James Patterson

Publishers Weekly Bestselling Books 2003

Fiction
1. *The Da Vinci Code,* Dan Brown
2. *The Five People You Meet in Heaven,* Mitch Albom
3. *The King of Torts,* John Grisham
4. *Bleachers,* John Grisham
5. *Armageddon,* Tim LaHaye and Jerry B. Jenkins
6. *The Teeth of the Tiger,* Tom Clancy
7. *The Big Bad Wolf,* James Patterson
8. *Blow Fly,* Patricia Cornwell
9. *The Lovely Bones,* Alice Sebold
10. *The Wedding,* Nicholas Sparks
11. *Shepherds Abiding,* Jan Karon
12. *Dark Tower V: Wolves of the Calla,* Stephen King
13. *Safe Harbour,* Danielle Steel
14. *Babylon Rising,* Tim LaHaye and Greg Dinallo
15. *Trojan Odyssey,* Clive Cussler

Nonfiction

1. *The Purpose-Driven Life,* Rick Warren
2. *The South Beach Diet,* Arthur Agatston, MD
3. *Atkins for Life,* Robert C. Atkins, MD
4. *The Ultimate Weight Solution,* Dr. Phil McGraw
5. *Living History,* Hillary Rodham Clinton
6. *Lies: And the Lying Liars Who Tell Them . . . ,* Al Franken
7. *Guinness World Records 2004,* Guinness World Records
8. *Who's Looking Out for You?* Bill O'Reilly
9. *Dude, Where's My Country?* Michael Moore
10. *A Royal Duty,* Paul Burrell
11. *Good to Great,* Jim Collins
12. *Kate Remembered,* A. Scott Berg
13. *The Essential 55,* Ron Clark
14. *Treason,* Ann Coulter
15. *The World According to Mister Rogers,* Fred Rogers

Trade Paperbacks

1. *Dr. Atkins' New Carbohydrate Gram Counter,* Robert C. Atkins, MD
2. *The Secret Life of Bees,* Sue Monk Kidd
3. *East of Eden,* John Steinbeck
4. *Seabiscuit,* Laura Hillenbrand
5. *Dr. Atkins' New Diet Revolution,* Robert C. Atkins, MD
6. *Life of Pi,* Yann Martel
7. *Self Matters,* Dr. Phil McGraw
8. *The Nanny Diaries,* Emma McLaughlin and Nicola Kraus
9. *Ladies' Detective Agency,* Alexander McCall Smith
10. *Trading Spaces Behind the Scenes,* Meredith Books Editors
11. *What to Expect When You're Expecting,* Heidi Murkoff
12. *Fix-It and Forget-It Cookbook,* Dawn J. Ranck and Phyllis Pellman Good
13. *Cold Mountain,* Charles Frazier

14. *The Atkins Journal,* Robert C. Atkins, MD
15. *The Hours,* Michael Cunningham

Mass-Market Paperbacks

1. *Dr. Atkins' New Diet Revolution,* Robert C. Atkins, MD
2. *The King of Torts,* John Grisham
3. *Seabiscuit,* Laura Hillenbrand
4. *Key of Light,* Nora Roberts
5. *Key of Knowledge,* Nora Roberts
6. *Key of Valor,* Nora Roberts
7. *Three Fates,* Nora Roberts
8. *Angels & Demons,* Dan Brown
9. *Red Rabbit,* Tom Clancy
10. *The Beach House,* James Patterson
11. *Prey,* Michael Crichton
12. *Daddy's Little Girl,* Mary Higgins Clark
13. *Four Blind Mice,* James Patterson
14. *Truly Madly Manhattan,* Nora Roberts
15. *Engaging the Enemy,* Nora Roberts

Publishers Weekly Bestselling Books 2002

Fiction

1. *The Summons,* John Grisham
2. *Red Rabbit,* Tom Clancy
3. *The Remnant,* Tim LaHaye and Jerry B. Jenkins
4. *The Lovely Bones,* Alice Sebold
5. *Prey,* Michael Crichton
6. *Skipping Christmas,* John Grisham
7. *The Shelters of Stone,* Jean M. Auel
8. *Four Blind Mice,* James Patterson

9. *Everything's Eventual*, Stephen King

10. *The Nanny Diaries*, Emma McLaughlin and Nicola Kraus

11. *From a Buick 8*, Stephen King

12. *The Beach House*, James Patterson and Peter de Jonge

13. *Star Wars: Attack of the Clones*, R. A. Salvatore

14. *Nights in Rodanthe*, Nicholas Sparks

15. *Answered Prayers*, Danielle Steel

Nonfiction

1. *Self Matters*, Dr. Phil McGraw

2. *A Life God Rewards*, Bruce Wilkinson with David Kopp

3. *Let's Roll!* Lisa Beamer with Ken Abraham

4. *Guinness World Records 2003*, Guinness World Records

5. *Who Moved My Cheese?* Spencer Johnson

6. *Leadership*, Rudolph W. Guiliani

7. *The Prayer of Jabez for Women*, Darlene Wilkinson

8. *Bush at War*, Bob Woodward

9. *Portrait of a Killer*, Patricia Cornwell

10. *Body for Life*, Bill Phillips

11. *I Hope You Dance*, Mark D. Sanders and Tia Sillers

12. *Stupid White Men*, Michael Moore

13. *Bringing Up Boys*, James Dobson

14. *Good to Great*, Jim Collins

15. *Get with the Program*, Bob Greene

Trade Paperbacks

1. *Fix-It and Forget-It Cookbook*, Dawn J. Ranck and Phyllis Pellman Good

2. *The Two Towers*, J.R.R. Tolkien

3. *The Lord of the Rings*, J.R.R. Tolkien

4. *The Return of the King*, J.R.R. Tolkien

5. *The Fellowship of the Ring,* J.R.R. Tolkien
6. *What to Expect When You're Expecting,* 3rd ed., Heidi Murkoff, Arlene Eisenberg, and Sandee Hathaway
7. *Sula,* Toni Morrison
8. *Empire Falls,* Richard Russo
9. *Fast Food Nation,* Eric Schlosser
10. *The Last Time They Met,* Anita Shreve
11. *The Hobbit,* J.R.R. Tolkien
12. *A Common Life,* Jan Karon
13. *Suzanne's Diary for Nicholas,* James Patterson
14. *Chicken Soup for the Mother's Soul II,* edited by Canfield and Hansen, et al.
15. *Fix-It and Forget-It Recipes for Entertaining,* Phyllis Pellman Good and Dawn J. Ranck

Mass-Market Paperbacks
1. *The Summons,* John Grisham
2. *The Lord of the Rings: The Two Towers,* J.R.R. Tolkien
3. *Face the Fire,* Nora Roberts
4. *The Villa,* Nora Roberts
5. *Midnight Bayou,* Nora Roberts
6. *On the Street Where You Live,* Mary Higgins Clark
7. *The Lord of the Rings: The Fellowship of the Ring,* J.R.R. Tolkien
8. *The Hobbit,* J.R.R. Tolkien
9. *1st to Die,* James Patterson
10. *The Kiss,* Danielle Steel
11. *Violets Are Blue,* James Patterson
12. *Isle of Dogs,* Patricia Cornwell
13. *Table for Two,* Nora Roberts
14. *The Lord of the Rings: The Return of the King,* J.R.R. Tolkien
15. *The Black House,* Stephen King and Peter Straub

Publishers Weekly Bestselling Books 2001

Fiction
1. *Desecration,* Tim LaHaye and Jerry B. Jenkins
2. *Skipping Christmas,* John Grisham
3. *A Painted House,* John Grisham
4. *Dreamcatcher,* Stephen King
5. *The Corrections,* Jonathan Franzen
6. *Black House,* Stephen King and Peter Straub
7. *The Kiss,* Danielle Steel
8. *Valhalla Rising,* Clive Cussler
9. *A Day Late and a Dollar Short,* Terry McMillan
10. *Violets Are Blue,* James Patterson
11. *P Is for Peril,* Sue Grafton
12. *He Sees You When You're Sleeping,* Mary Higgins Clark
13. *A Common Life,* Jan Karon
14. *Isle of Dogs,* Patricia Cornwell
15. *Suzanne's Diary for Nicholas,* James Patterson

Nonfiction
1. *The Prayer of Jabez,* Bruce Wilkinson
2. *Secrets of the Vine,* Bruce Wilkinson
3. *Who Moved My Cheese?* Spencer Johnson
4. *John Adams,* David McCullough
5. *Guinness World Records 2002,* Guinness World Records Ltd.
6. *Prayer of Jabez Devotional,* Bruce Wilkinson
7. *The No Spin Zone,* Bill O'Reilly
8. *Body for Life,* Bill Phillips
9. *How I Play Golf,* Tiger Woods
10. *Jack,* Jack Welch
11. *I Hope You Dance,* Mark D. Sanders and Tia Sillers

12. *Self Matters*, Dr. Phil McGraw
13. *The Blue Day Book*, Bradley Trevor Greive
14. *The Road to Wealth*, Suze Orman
15. *America's Heroes: Inspiring Stories of Courage, Sacrifice, and Patriotism*, editors at SP LLC

Trade Paperbacks

1. *Life Strategies*, Dr. Phil McGraw
2. *We Were the Mulvaneys*, Joyce Carol Oates
3. *The Indwelling*, Jerry B. Jenkins and Tim LaHaye
4. *The Lord of the Rings*, J.R.R. Tolkien
5. *Icy Sparks*, Gwyn Hyman Rubio
6. *The Red Tent*, Anita Diamant
7. *Girl with a Pearl Earring*, Tracy Chevalier
8. *The Fellowship of the Ring*, J.R.R. Tolkien
9. *The Mark*, Jerry B. Jenkins and Tim LaHaye
10. *Left Behind*, Jerry B. Jenkins and Tim LaHaye
11. *Bridget Jones's Diary*, Helen Fielding
12. *The Hobbit*, J.R.R. Tolkien
13. *Band of Brothers*, Stephen Ambrose
14. *The Four Agreements*, Don Miguel Ruiz
15. *Tribulation Force*, Jerry B. Jenkins and Tim LaHaye

Mass-Market Paperbacks

1. *A Painted House*, John Grisham
2. *Hannibal*, Thomas Harris
3. *Dance Upon Air*, Nora Roberts
4. *Heaven and Earth*, Nora Roberts
5. *Bear and Dragon*, Tom Clancy
6. *Carolina Moon*, Nora Roberts
7. *The Lord of the Rings: The Fellowship of the Ring*, J.R.R. Tolkien

8. *Last Precinct,* Patricia Cornwell
9. *Before I Say Goodbye,* Mary Higgins Clark
10. *Time and Again,* Nora Roberts
11. *Reflections and Dreams,* Nora Roberts
12. *Journey,* Danielle Steel
13. *Stanislavsky Sisters,* Nora Roberts
14. *The Hobbit,* J.R.R. Tolkien
15. *Dreamcatcher,* Stephen King

Publishers Weekly Bestselling Books 2000

Fiction

1. *The Brethren,* John Grisham
2. *The Mark,* Jerry B. Jenkins and Tim LaHaye
3. *The Bear and the Dragon,* Tom Clancy
4. *The Indwelling,* Tim LaHaye and Jerry B. Jenkins
5. *The Last Precinct,* Patricia Cornwell
6. *Journey,* Danielle Steel
7. *The Rescue,* Nicholas Sparks
8. *Roses Are Red,* James Patterson
9. *Cradle and All,* James Patterson
10. *The House on Hope Street,* Danielle Steel
11. *The Wedding,* Danielle Steel
12. *Drowning Ruth,* Christina Schwartz
13. *Before I Say Good-Bye,* Mary Higgins Clark
14. *Deck the Halls,* Mary and Carol Higgins Clark
15. *Gap Creek,* Robert Morgan

Nonfiction

1. *Who Moved My Cheese?* Spencer Johnson
2. *Guinness World Records 2001,* Guinness World Records Ltd.
3. *Body for Life,* Bill Phillips
4. *Tuesdays with Morrie,* Mitch Albom
5. *The Beatles Anthology,* The Beatles
6. *The O'Reilly Factor,* Bill O'Reilly
7. *Relationship Rescue,* Dr. Phil McGraw
8. *The Millionaire Mind,* Thomas J. Stanley
9. *Ten Things I Wish I'd Known—Before I Went Out into the Real World,* Maria Shriver
10. *Eating Well for Optimum Health,* Andrew Weil, MD
11. *The Prayer of Jabez,* Bruce Wilkinson
12. *Flags of Our Fathers,* James Bradley with Ron Powers
13. *A Short Guide to a Happy Life,* Anna Quindlen
14. *On Writing,* Stephen King
15. *Nothing Like It in the World,* Stephen E. Ambrose

Trade Paperbacks

1. *A Child Called "It,"* Dave Pelzer
2. *Left Behind,* Jerry B. Jenkins and Tim LaHaye
3. *The Poisonwood Bible,* Barbara Kingsolver
4. *Chicken Soup for the Couple's Soul,* Jack Canfield, Mark Victor Hansen, et al.
5. *Apollyon,* Jerry B. Jenkins and Tim LaHaye
6. *Tribulation Force,* Jerry B. Jenkins and Tim LaHaye
7. *Chicken Soup for the Teenage Soul III,* Jack Canfield, Mark Victor Hansen, et al.
8. *While I Was Gone,* Sue Miller
9. *House of Sand and Fog,* Andre Dubus III
10. *Talking Dirty with the Queen of Clean,* Linda Cobb

11. *The Lost Boy,* Dave Pelzer
12. *The Worst Case Scenario Survival Handbook,* Joshua Piven and David Borgenicht
13. *Chicken Soup for the Golfer's Soul,* Jack Canfield, Mark Victor Hansen, et al.
14. *Nicolae,* Jerry B. Jenkins and Tim LaHaye
15. *The Millionaire Next Door,* William Danko and Thomas Stanley

Mass-Market Paperbacks
1. *The Testament,* John Grisham
2. *The Brethren.* John Grisham
3. *Hannibal,* Thomas Harris
4. *The Green Mile,* Stephen King
5. *Heart of the Sea,* Nora Roberts
6. *Tears of the Moon,* Nora Roberts
7. *Black Notice,* Patricia Cornwell.
8. *Irresistible Forces,* Danielle Steel
9. *Timeline,* Michael Crichton
10. *The Girl Who Loved Tom Gordon,* Stephen King
11. *We'll Meet Again,* Mary Higgins Clark
12. *Pop Goes the Weasel,* James Patterson
13. *River's End,* Nora Roberts
14. *False Memory,* Dean Koontz
15. *A Walk to Remember,* Nicholas Sparks

Publishers Weekly Bestselling Books 1999

Fiction
1. *The Testament,* John Grisham
2. *Hannibal,* Thomas Harris
3. *Assassins,* Tim LaHaye and Jerry B. Jenkins

4. *Star Wars: Episode 1, The Phantom Menace,* Terry Brooks
5. *Timeline,* Michael Crichton
6. *Hearts in Atlantis,* Stephen King
7. *Apollyon,* Tim LaHaye and Jerry B. Jenkins
8. *The Girl Who Loved Tom Gordon,* Stephen King
9. *Irresistible Forces,* Danielle Steel
10. *Tara Road,* Maeve Binchy
11. *White Oleander,* Janet Fitch
12. *A Walk to Remember,* Nicholas Sparks
13. *Pop Goes the Weasel,* James Patterson
14. *Black Notice,* Patricia Cornwell
15. *Granny Dan,* Danielle Steel

Nonfiction
1. *Tuesdays with Morrie,* Mitch Albom
2. *The Greatest Generation,* Tom Brokaw
3. *Guinness World Records 2000 Millennium Edition,* Guinness World Records Ltd.
4. *'Tis,* Frank McCourt
5. *Who Moved My Cheese?* Spencer Johnson
6. *The Courage to Be Rich,* Suze Orman
7. *The Greatest Generation Speaks,* Tom Brokaw
8. *Sugar Busters!* H. Leighton Steward, Morrison C. Bethea, et al.
9. *The Art of Happiness,* the Dalai Lama and Howard C. Cutler
10. *The Century,* Peter Jennings and Todd Brewster
11. *Body for Life,* Bill Phillips
12. *Life Strategies,* Dr. Phil McGraw
13. *Have a Nice Day!* Mick Foley
14. *Suzanne Somers' Get Skinny on Fabulous Food,* Suzanne Somers
15. *Don't Sweat the Small Stuff in Love,* Richard and Kristine Carlson

Trade Paperbacks

1. *The Pilot's Wife,* Anita Shreve
2. *Memoirs of a Geisha,* Arthur Golden
3. *The Reader,* Bernard Schlink
4. *Angela's Ashes,* Frank McCourt
5. *Chicken Soup for the Couple's Soul,* Jack Canfield, Mark Victor Hansen, et al.
6. *Don't Sweat the Small Stuff at Work,* Richard Carlson
7. *Where the Heart Is,* Billie Letts
8. *Soul Harvest,* Jerry B. Jenkins and Tim LaHaye
9. *Nicolae,* Jerry B. Jenkins and Tim LaHaye
10. *Chicken Soup for the Golfer's Soul,* Jack Canfield, Mark Victor Hansen, et al.
11. *Here on Earth,* Alice Hoffman
12. *Jewel,* Bret Lott
13. *I Know This Much Is True,* Wally Lamb
14. *Chicken Soup for the Teenage Soul II,* Jack Canfield, Mark Victor Hansen, et al.
15. *Windows 98 for Dummies,* Andy Rathbone

Mass-Market Paperbacks

1. *The Street Lawyers,* John Grisham
2. *The Testament,* John Grisham
3. *Bag of Bones,* Stephen King
4. *Point of Origin,* Patricia Cornwell
5. *Rainbow Six,* Tom Clancy
6. *Jewels of the Sun,* Nora Roberts
7. *Summer Sister,* Judy Blume
8. *You Belong to Me,* Mary Higgins Clark
9. *Southern Cross,* Patricia Cornwell
10. *Op Center VI: State of Siege,* Tom Clancy and Steve Pieczenik

11. *Homeport,* Nora Roberts
12. *The Reef,* Nora Roberts
13. *Power Play: Shadow Watch,* Tom Clancy and Martin Greenberg
14. *Mirror Image,* Danielle Steel
15. *All Through the Night,* Mary Higgins Clark

Publishers Weekly Bestselling Books 1998

Fiction

1. *The Street Lawyer,* John Grisham
2. *Rainbow Six,* Tom Clancy
3. *Bag of Bones,* Stephen King
4. *Man in Full,* Tom Wolfe
5. *Mirror Image,* Danielle Steel
6. *The Long Road Home,* Danielle Steel
7. *The Klone and I,* Danielle Steel
8. *Point of Origin,* Patricia Cornwell
9. *Paradise,* Toni Morrison
10. *All Through the Night,* Mary Higgins Clark
11. *I Know This Much Is True,* Wally Lamb
12. *Tell Me Your Dreams,* Sidney Sheldon
13. *The Vampire Armand,* Anne Rice
14. *The Loop,* Nicholas Evans
15. *You Belong to Me,* Mary Higgins Clark

Nonfiction

1. *The 9 Steps to Financial Freedom,* Suze Orman
2. *The Greatest Generation,* Tom Brokaw
3. *Sugar Busters!* H. Leighton Steward, Morrison C. Bethea, et al.
4. *Tuesdays with Morrie,* Mitch Albom

5. *Guinness World Records 1999,* Guinness World Records Ltd.

6. *Talking to Heaven,* James Van Praagh

7. *Something More: Excavating Your Authentic Self,* Sarah Ban Breathnach

8. *In the Meantime,* Iyanla Vanzant

9. *A Pirate Looks at Fifty,* Jimmy Buffett

10. *If Life Is a Game These Are the Rules,* Cherie Carter-Scott

11. *Angela's Ashes,* Frank McCourt

12. *For the Love of the Game: My Story,* Michael Jordan

13. *The Day Diana Died,* Christopher Andersen

14. *The Century,* Peter Jennings and Todd Brewster

15. *Eat Right 4 Your Type,* Peter J. D'Adam

Trade Paperbacks

1. *Don't Sweat the Small Stuff . . . And It's All Small Stuff,* Richard Carlson

2. *Divine Secrets of the Ya-Ya Sisterhood,* Rebecca Wells

3. *Chicken Soup for the Teenage Soul,* Jack Canfield, Mark Victor Hansen, et al. (dual edition)

4. *Chicken Soup for the Teenage Soul,* Jack Canfield, Mark Victor Hansen, et al. (dual edition)

5. *Don't Sweat the Small Stuff with Your Family,* Richard Carlson

6. *Chicken Soup for the Kid's Soul,* Jack Canfield, Mark Victor Hansen, et al.

7. *Chicken Soup for the Pet Lover's Soul,* Jack Canfield, Mark Victor Hansen, et al.

8. *Chicken Soup for the Mother's Soul,* Jack Canfield, Mark Victor Hansen, et al.

9. *A 2nd Helping of Chicken Soup for the Woman's Soul,* Jack Canfield, Mark Victor Hansen, et al.

10. *Here on Earth,* Alice Hoffman

11. *Prescription for Nutritional Healing,* James F. Balch, MD, and Phyllis A. Balch, CNC
12. *Midwives,* Chris Bohjalian
13. *Cold Mountain,* Charles Frazier
14. *James Cameron's Titanic,* Ed W. Marsh
15. *A 5th Portion of Chicken Soup for the Soul,* Jack Canfield, Mark Victor Hansen, et al.

Mass-Market Paperbacks
1. *The Partner,* John Grisham
2. *The Ghost,* Danielle Steel
3. *The Ranch,* Danielle Steel
4. *Special Delivery,* Danielle Steel
5. *Unnatural Exposure,* Patricia Cornwell
6. *Pretend You Don't See Her,* Mary Higgins Clark
7. *Power Plays: Ruthless.com,* Tom Clancy
8. *Rising Tides,* Nora Roberts
9. *Wizard and Glass,* Stephen King
10. *Dr. Atkins' New Diet Revolution,* Robert C. Atkins, MD
11. *Into Thin Air,* Jon Krakauer
12. *Tom Clancy's Op-Center V,* created by Tom Clancy and Steve Pieczenik
13. *The Notebook,* Nicholas Sparks
14. *Fear Nothing,* Dean Koontz
15. *Sanctuary,* Nora Roberts

Publishers Weekly Bestselling Books 1997

Fiction
1. *The Partner,* John Grisham
2. *Cold Mountain,* Charles Frazier
3. *The Ghost,* Danielle Steel

4. *The Ranch,* Danielle Steel

5. *Special Delivery,* Danielle Steel

6. *Unnatural Exposure,* Patricia Cornwell

7. *The Best Laid Plans,* Sidney Sheldon

8. *Pretend You Don't See Her,* Mary Higgins Clark

9. *Cat & Mouse,* James Patterson

10. *Hornet's Nest,* Patricia Cornwell

11. *The Letter,* Richard Paul Evans

12. *Flood Tide,* Clive Cussler

13. *Violin,* Anne Rice

14. *The Matarese Countdown,* Robert Ludlum

15. *Plum Island,* Nelson DeMille

Nonfiction

1. *Angela's Ashes,* Frank McCourt

2. *Simple Abundance,* Sarah Ban Breathnach

3. *Midnight in the Garden of Good and Evil,* John Berendt

4. *The Royals,* Kitty Kelley

5. *Joy of Cooking,* Irma S. Rombauer, Marion Rombauer Becker, et al.

6. *Diana: Her True Story,* Andrew Morton

7. *Into Thin Air,* Jon Krakauer

8. *Conversations with God, Book 1,* Neale Donald Walsch

9. *Men Are from Mars, Women Are from Venus,* John Gray

10. *Eight Weeks to Optimum Health,* Andrew Weil

11. *Just As I Am,* Billy Graham

12. *The Man Who Listens to Horses,* Monty Roberts

13. *The Millionaire Next Door,* Thomas J. Stanley and William D. Danko

14. *The Perfect Storm,* Sebastian Junger

15. *Kids Are Punny,* Rosie O'Donnell

Trade Paperbacks

1. *Don't Sweat the Small Stuff . . . and It's All Small Stuff,* Richard Carlson
2. *Chicken Soup for the Woman's Soul,* Jack Canfield, Mark Victor Hansen, et al.
3. *She's Come Undone,* Wally Lamb
4. *Chicken Soup for the Mother's Soul,* Jack Canfield, Mark Victor Hansen, et al.
5. *Wizard and Glass,* Stephen King
6. *Stones from the River,* Ursula Hegi
7. *Prescription for Nutritional Healing,* James F. and Phyllis A. Balch
8. *Windows 98 for Dummies,* 2nd ed., Andy Rathbone
9. *Chicken Soup for the Christian Soul,* Jack Canfield, Mark Victor Hansen, et al.
10. *Songs in Ordinary Time,* Mary McGarry Morris
11. *A 4th Course of Chicken Soup for the Soul,* Jack Canfield, Mark Victor Hansen, et al.
12. *Rapture of Canaan,* Sheri Reynolds
13. *Heart of a Woman,* Maya Angelou
14. *Petals on the River,* Kathleen E. Woodiwiss
15. *Undaunted Courage,* Stephen E. Ambrose

Mass-Market Paperbacks

1. *The Runaway Jury,* John Grisham
2. *Five Days in Paris,* Danielle Steel
3. *Malice,* Danielle Steel
4. *Silent Honor,* Danielle Steel
5. *Executive Orders,* Tom Clancy
6. *Moonlight Becomes You,* Mary Higgins Clark
7. *Desperation,* Stephen King
8. *My Gal Sunday,* Mary Higgins Clark

9. *Airframe*, Michael Crichton

10. *Cause of Death*, Patricia Cornwell

11. *The Deep End of the Ocean*, Jacquelyn Mitchard

12. *Ticktock*, Dean Koontz

13. *The Regulators*, Richard Bachman

14. *The Lost World*, Michael Crichton

15. *The Hornet's Nest*, Patricia Cornwell

Publishers Weekly Bestselling Books 1996

Fiction

1. *The Runaway Jury*, John Grisham

2. *Executive Orders*, Tom Clancy

3. *Desperation*, Stephen King

4. *Airframe*, Michael Crichton

5. *The Regulators*, Richard Bachman

6. *Malice*, Danielle Steel

7. *Silent Honor*, Danielle Steel

8. *Primary Colors*, Anonymous

9. *Cause of Death*, Patricia Cornwell

10. *The Tenth Insight*, James Redfield

11. *The Deep End of the Ocean*, Jacquelyn Mitchard

12. *How Stella Got Her Groove Back*, Terry McMillan

13. *Moonlight Becomes You*, Mary Higgins Clark

14. *My Gal Sunday*, Mary Higgins Clark

15. *The Celestine Prophecy*, James Redfield

Nonfiction

1. *Make the Connection*, Oprah Winfrey and Bob Greene

2. *Men Are from Mars, Women Are from Venus*, John Gray

3. *The Dilbert Principle*, Scott Adams

4. *Simple Abundance,* Sarah Ban Breathnach
5. *The Zone,* Barry Sears with Bill Lawren
6. *Bad As I Wanna Be,* Dennis Rodman
7. *In Contempt,* Christopher Darden
8. *A Reporter's Life,* Walter Cronkite
9. *Dogbert's Top Secret Management Handbook,* Scott Adams
10. *My Sergei: A Love Story,* Ekaterina Gordeeva with E. M. Swift
11. *Gift and Mystery,* Pope John Paul II
12. *I'm Not Really Here,* Tim Allen
13. *Rush Limbaugh Is a Big Fat Idiot and Other Observations,* Al Franken
14. *James Herriot's Favorite Dog Stories,* James Herriot
15. *My Story,* Sarah, Duchess of York

Trade Paperbacks
1. *A Third Serving of Chicken Soup for the Soul,* Jack Canfield, Mark Victor Hansen, et al.
2. *Snow Falling on Cedars,* David Guterson
3. *It's a Magical World: A Calvin and Hobbes Collection,* Bill Watterson
4. *There's Treasure Everywhere: A Calvin and Hobbes Collection,* Bill Watterson
5. *Chicken Soup for the Woman's Soul,* Jack Canfield, Mark Victor Hansen, et al.
6. *A Journal of Daily Renewal: The Companion to Make the Connection,* Bob Greene and Oprah Winfrey
7. *Windows 95 for Dummies,* Andy Rathbone
8. *Fugitive from the Cubicle Police: A Dilbert Book,* Scott Adams
9. *The Last Chapter and Worse: A Far Side Collection,* Gary Larson
10. *The English Patient,* Michael Ondaatje
11. *Reviving Ophelia,* Mary Pipher
12. *Microsoft Windows 95 Resource Kit,* Microsoft Publishers
13. *Still Pumped from Using the Mouse: A Dilbert Book,* Scott Adams

14. *SSN: A Strategy Guide to Submarine Warfare*, Tom Clancy
15. *Dr. Atkins' New Diet Revolution*, Robert Atkins

Mass-Market Paperbacks
1. *The Rainmaker*, John Grisham
2. *The Green Mile, Part 1: The Two Dead Girls*, Stephen King
3. *The Green Mile, Part 2: The Mouse on the Mile*, Stephen King
4. *The Green Mile, Part 3: Coffey's Hands*, Stephen King
5. *The Green Mile, Part 5: Night Journey*, Stephen King
6. *The Green Mile, Part 4: The Bad Death of Eduard Delacroix*, Stephen King
7. *The Green Mile, Part 6: Coffey on the Mile*, Stephen King
8. *The Gift*, Danielle Steel
9. *Lightning*, Danielle Steel
10. *The Lost World*, Michael Crichton
11. *Let Me Call You Sweetheart*, Mary Higgins Clark
12. *The Horse Whisperer*, Nicholas Evans
13. *Rose Madder*, Stephen King
14. *Tom Clancy's Op Center III: Games of the State*, Tom Clancy and Steve Pieczenik
15. *From Potter's Field*, Patricia Cornwell

Publishers Weekly Bestselling Books 1995

Fiction
1. *The Rainmaker*, John Grisham
2. *The Lost World*, Michael Crichton
3. *Five Days in Paris*, Danielle Steel
4. *The Christmas Box*, Richard Paul Evans
5. *Lightning*, Danielle Steel
6. *The Celestine Prophecy*, James Redfield

7. *Rose Madder,* Stephen King
8. *Silent Night,* Mary Higgins Clark
9. *Politically Correct Holiday Stories,* James Finn Garner
10. *The Horse Whisperer,* Nicholas Evans
11. *Politically Correct Bedtime Stories,* James Finn Garner
12. *Memnoch the Devil,* Anne Rice
13. *Beach Music,* Pat Conroy
14. *From Potter's Field,* Patricia Cornwell
15. *Morning, Noon and Night,* Sidney Sheldon

Nonfiction
1. *Men Are from Mars, Women Are from Venus,* John Gray
2. *My American Journey,* Colin Powell with Joseph Persico
3. *Miss America,* Howard Stern
4. *The Seven Spiritual Laws of Success,* Deepak Chopra
5. *The Road Ahead,* Bill Gates
6. *Charles Kuralt's America,* Charles Kuralt
7. *Mars and Venus in the Bedroom,* John Gray
8. *To Renew America,* Newt Gingrich
9. *My Point . . . and I Do Have One,* Ellen DeGeneres
10. *The Moral Compass,* William J. Bennett
11. *The Book of Virtues,* William J. Bennett
12. *I Want to Tell You,* O. J. Simpson with Laurence Schiller
13. *In the Kitchen with Rosie,* Rosie Daley
14. *Emotional Intelligence,* Daniel Goleman
15. *David Letterman's Book of Top Ten Lists,* David Letterman

Trade Paperbacks
1. *A Second Helping of Chicken Soup for the Soul,* Jack Canfield, Mark Victor Hansen, et al.
2. *The Calvin and Hobbes Tenth Anniversary Book,* Bill Watterson

3. *The Far Side Gallery 5*, Gary Larson
4. *Ten Stupid Things Women Do to Mess Up Their Lives*, Laura Schlessinger
5. *What to Expect: The Toddler Years*, A. Eisenberg, H. Murkoff, et al.
6. *The Stone Diaries*, Carol Shields
7. *Microsoft Windows 95 Resource Kit*, Microsoft Press
8. *Aladdin Factor*, Jack Canfield and Mark Victor Hansen
9. *The Promise*, Thomas Nelson
10. *Snow Falling on Cedars*, David Guterson
11. *Illuminata: A Return to Prayer*, Marianne Williamson
12. *Chicken Soup for the Soul Cookbook*, Jack Canfield, Mark Victor Hansen, et al.
13. *Dianetics*, L. Ron Hubbard
14. *The Celestine Prophecy: An Experiential Guide*, James Redfield and Carol Adrienne
15. *Secrets of Fat-Free Cooking*, Sandra Woodruff

Mass-Market Paperbacks
1. *The Chamber*, John Grisham
2. *Tom Clancy's Op-Center*, Tom Clancy and Steve Pieczenik
3. *Accident*, Danielle Steel
4. *Wings*, Danielle Steel
5. *Debt of Honor*, Tom Clancy
6. *Insomnia*, Stephen King
7. *Tom Clancy's Op-Center II: Mirror Image*, Tom Clancy and Steve Pieczenik
8. *Nothing Lasts Forever*, Sidney Sheldon
9. *Remember Me*, Mary Higgins Clark
10. *Icebound*, Dean Koontz
11. *The Body Farm*, Patricia Cornwell
12. *Lottery Winner*, Mary Higgins Clark

13. *Key to Midnight*, Dean Koontz
14. *Dark Rivers of the Heart*, Dean Koontz
15. *All That Glitters*, V. C. Andrews

Publishers Weekly Bestselling Books 1994

Fiction

1. *The Chamber*, John Grisham
2. *Debt of Honor*, Tom Clancy
3. *The Celestine Prophecy*, James Redfield
4. *The Gift*, Danielle Steel
5. *Insomnia*, Stephen King
6. *Politically Correct Bedtime Stories*, James Finn Garner
7. *Wings*, Danielle Steel
8. *Accident*, Danielle Steel
9. *The Bridges of Madison County*, Robert James Waller
10. *Disclosure*, Michael Crichton
11. *Nothing Lasts Forever*, Sidney Sheldon
12. *Taltos*, Anne Rice
13. *Dark Rivers of the Heart*, Dean Koontz
14. *The Lottery Winner*, Mary Higgins Clark
15. *Remember Me*, Mary Higgins Clark

Nonfiction

1. *In the Kitchen with Rosie*, Rosie Daley
2. *Men Are from Mars, Women Are from Venus*, John Gray
3. *Crossing the Threshold of Hope*, John Paul II
4. *Magic Eye I*, N. E. Thing Enterprises
5. *The Book of Virtues*, William J. Bennett
6. *Magic Eye II*, N. E. Thing Enterprises
7. *Embraced by the Light*, Betty J. Eadie with Curtis Taylor

8. *Don't Stand Too Close to a Naked Man,* Tim Allen

9. *Couplehood,* Paul Reiser

10. *Magic Eye III,* N. E. Thing Enterprises

11. *Dolly,* Dolly Parton

12. *James Herriott's Cat Stories,* James Herriott

13. *Barbara Bush,* Barbara Bush

14. *Nicole Brown Simpson,* Faye D. Resnick

15. *The Bubba Gump Shrimp Co. Cookbook,* Oxmoor House/Leisure Arts

Trade Paperbacks

1. *Schindler's List,* Thomas Keneally

2. *Homicidal Psycho Jungle Cat,* Bill Watterson

3. *Chicken Soup for the Soul,* Jack Canfield and Mark Victor Hansen

4. *The T-Factor Fat Gram Counter,* Jamie Pope-Cordle and Martin Katahn

5. *Care of the Soul,* Thomas Moore

6. *The Curse of Madame "C,"* Gary Larson

7. *The Shipping News,* Annie Proulx

8. *Butter Busters: The Cookbook,* Pam Mycoskie

9. *Gumpisms,* Winston Groom

10. *Magic Eye Poster Book,* N. E. Thing Enterprises

11. *Magic Eye Book of Postcards,* N. E. Thing Enterprises

12. *Lasher,* Anne Rice

13. *Beavis & Butthead's Ensucklopedia,* Mike Judge

14. *The Pocket Powter,* Susan Powter

15. *Pigs in Heaven,* Barbara Kingsolver

Mass-Market Paperbacks

1. *The Client,* John Grisham

2. *Disclosure,* Michael Crichton

3. *Without Remorse,* Tom Clancy

4. *Vanished*, Danielle Steel
5. *I'll Be Seeing You*, Mary Higgins Clark
6. *Interview with the Vampire*, Anne Rice
7. *Nightmares & Dreamscapes*, Stephen King
8. *A Case of Need*, Michael Crichton
9. *Winter Moon*, Dean Koontz
10. *Pleading Guilty*, Scott Turow
11. *The Door to December*, Dean Koontz
12. *Mr. Murder*, Dean Koontz
13. *Ruby*, V. C. Andrews
14. *Pearl in the Mist*, V. C. Andrews
15. *Slow Waltz in Cedar Bend*, Robert James Waller

Publishers Weekly Bestselling Books 1993

Fiction

1. *The Bridges of Madison County*, Robert James Waller
2. *The Client*, John Grisham
3. *Slow Waltz at Cedar Bend*, Robert James Waller
4. *Without Remorse*, Tom Clancy
5. *Nightmares and Dreamscapes*, Stephen King
6. *Vanished*, Danielle Steel
7. *Lasher*, Anne Rice
8. *Pleading Guilty*, Scott Turow
9. *Like Water for Chocolate*, Laura Esquivel
10. *The Scorpio Illusion*, Robert Ludlum
11. *The Golden Mean*, Nick Bantock
12. *I'll Be Seeing You*, Mary Higgins Clark
13. *A Dangerous Fortune*, Ken Follett
14. *Mr. Murder*, Dean Koontz
15. *Gai-Jin*, James Clavell

Nonfiction

1. *See I Told You,* Rush Limbaugh
2. *Private Parts,* Howard Stern
3. *Seinlanguage,* Jerry Seinfeld
4. *Embraced by the Light,* Betty J. Eadie with Curtis Taylor
5. *Ageless Body, Timeless Mind,* Deepak Chopra
6. *Stop the Insanity,* Susan Powter
7. *Women Who Run with the Wolves,* Clarissa Pinkola
8. *Men Are from Mars, Women Are from Venus,* John Gray
9. *The Hidden Life of Dogs,* Elizabeth Marshall Thomas
10. *And If You Play Golf, You're My Friend,* Harvey Penick with Bud Shrake
11. *The Way Things Ought to Be,* Rush Limbaugh
12. *Beating the Street,* Peter Lynch with John Rothchild
13. *Harvey Penick's Little Red Book,* Harvey Penick with Bud Shrake
14. *Wouldn't Take Nothing for My Journey Now,* Maya Angelou
15. *Further Along the Road Less Traveled,* M. Scott Peck

Trade Paperbacks

1. *The T-Factor Fat Gram Counter,* Dr. Martin Katahn and Jamie Pope-Cordle
2. *Life's Little Instruction Book,* H. Jackson Brown Jr.
3. *The Days Are Just Packed,* Bill Watterson
4. *The Age of Innocence,* Edith Wharton
5. *The Far Side Gallery 4,* Gary Larson
6. *Rare Air: Michael on Michael,* Michael Jordan
7. *The Chickens Are Restless,* Gary Larson
8. *Schindler's List,* Thomas Keneally
9. *Live and Learn and Pass It On,* H. Jackson Brown Jr.
10. *Beavis & Butthead: This Book Sucks,* Mike Judge
11. *A Return to Love,* Marianne Williamson
12. *Submarine,* Tom Clancy

13. *A Thousand Acres,* Jane Smiley
14. *On the Pulse of the Morning,* Maya Angelou
15. *Not for Sale at Any Price,* Ross Perot

Mass-Market Paperbacks
1. *The Pelican Brief,* John Grisham
2. *The Firm,* John Grisham
3. *Jurassic Park,* Michael Crichton
4. *A Time to Kill,* John Grisham
5. *Rising Sun,* Michael Crichton
6. *Jewels,* Danielle Steel
7. *Mixed Blessings,* Danielle Steel
8. *Gerald's Game,* Stephen King
9. *All Around Town,* Mary Higgins Clark
10. *Dolores Claiborne,* Stephen King
11. *The Waste Lands,* Stephen King
12. *Congo,* Michael Crichton
13. *Stars Shine Down,* Sidney Sheldon
14. *Darkest Hour,* V. C. Andrews
15. *Dragon Tears,* Dean Koontz

Publishers Weekly Bestselling Books 1992

Fiction
1. *Dolores Claiborne,* Stephen King
2. *The Pelican Brief,* John Grisham
3. *Gerald's Game,* Stephen King
4. *Mixed Blessings,* Danielle Steel
5. *Jewels,* Danielle Steel
6. *The Stars Shine Down,* Sidney Sheldon

7. *Tale of the Body Thief,* Anne Rice
8. *Mexico,* James A. Michener
9. *Waiting to Exhale,* Terry McMillan
10. *All Around the Town,* Mary Higgins Clark
11. *Scruples Two,* Judith Krantz
12. *Sahara,* Clive Cussler
13. *Hideaway,* Dean R. Koontz
14. *The Road to Omaha,* Robert Ludlum
15. *Star Wars: Dark Force Rising,* Timothy Zahn

Nonfiction
1. *The Way Things Ought to Be,* Rush Limbaugh
2. *It Doesn't Take a Hero,* H. Norman Schwarzkopf
3. *How to Satisfy a Woman Every Time,* Naura Hayden
4. *Every Living Thing,* James Herriott
5. *A Return to Love,* Marianne Williamson
6. *Sam Walton,* Sam Walton
7. *Diana,* Andrew Morton.
8. *Truman,* David McCullough
9. *Silent Passage,* Gail Sheehy
10. *Sex,* Madonna
11. *The Juiceman's Power of Juicing,* Ray Kordich
12. *Harvey Penick's Little Red Book,* Harvey Penick
13. *More Wealth without Risk,* Charles Givens
14. *I Can't Believe I Said That,* Kathie Lee Gifford
15. *Creating Love,* John Bradshaw

Trade Paperbacks
1. *Life's Little Instruction Book,* H. Jackson Brown Jr.
2. *Forever in Your Embrace,* Kathleen Woodiwiss
3. *Live and Learn and Pass It On,* H. Jackson Brown Jr.

4. *The T-Factor Fat Gram Counter,* Dr. Martin Katahn and Jamie Pope-Cordle
5. *Attack of the Deranged Mutant Killer Monster Snow Goons,* Bill Watterson
6. *The Indispensable Calvin and Hobbes,* Bill Watterson
7. *Mrs. Fields Cookie Book,* Debbie Fields and the editors of Time-Life Books
8. *Cows of Our Planet,* Gary Larson
9. *Prophet,* Frank Peretti
10. *Juicing for Life,* Cherie Calbom and Maureen Keane
11. *The Complete & Up-to-Date Fat Book,* Karen J. Bellerson
12. *Daisy Faye and the Miracle Man,* Fannie Flagg
13. *You Just Don't Understand,* Deborah Tannen
14. *America: What Went Wrong,* Donald L. Barlett and James B. Steele
15. *Don't Know Much about History,* Kenneth Davis

Mass-Market Paperbacks
1. *The Firm,* John Grisham
2. *The Silence of the Lambs,* Thomas Harris
3. *A Time to Kill,* John Grisham
4. *Scarlett,* Alexandra Ripley
5. *Heartbeat,* Danielle Steel
6. *Message from Nam,* Danielle Steel
7. *The Sum of All Fears,* Tom Clancy
8. *Four Past Midnight,* Stephen King
9. *Needful Things,* Stephen King
10. *No Greater Love,* Danielle Steel
11. *Secrets of the Morning,* V. C. Andrews
12. *September,* Rosamunde Pilcher
13. *Jurassic Park,* Michael Crichton
14. *The Stand,* Stephen King

15. *Loves Music, Loves to Dance*, Mary Higgins Clark

Publishers Weekly Bestselling Books 1991

Fiction
1. *The Firm*, John Grisham
2. *Loves Music, Loves to Dance*, Mary Higgins Clark
3. *Possession: A Romance*, A. S. Byatt
4. *As the Crow Flies*, Jeffrey Archer
   Star Wars: Heir to the Empire, Timothy Zahn
5. *The Kitchen God's Wife*, Amy Tan
   The Sum of All Fears, Tom Clancy
6. *Damage*, Josephine Hart
   Heartbeat, Danielle Steel

Nonfiction
1. *Iron John: A Book about Men*, Robert Bly
2. *Wealth without Risk*, Charles J. Givens
3. *Financial Self-Defense*, Charles J. Givens
4. *Homecoming*, John Bradshaw.
5. *Parliament of Whores*, P. J. O'Rourke
6. *Chutzpah*, Alan Dershowitz
7. *Toujours Provence*, Peter Mayle
8. *Fire in the Belly: On Being a Man*, Sam Keen
9. *Final Exit*, Derek Humphrey
10. *DO IT! Let's Get Off Our Buts*, John-Roger and Peter McWilliams
11. *Uh-Oh: Some Observations from Both Sides of the Refrigerator*, Robert Fulghum
12. *You Just Don't Understand: Women and Men in Conversation*, Deborah Tannen
13. *The Civil War: An Illustrated History*, Geoffrey C. Ward with Ric

Burns & Ken Burns
14. *A Life on the Road*, Charles Kuralt
15. *The Prize: The Epic Quest for Oil, Money and Power*, Daniel Yergin

Trade Paperbacks
1. *7 Habits of Highly Effective People*, Stephen Covey
2. *The T-Factor Fat Gram Counter*, Jamie Pope and Martin Katahn
3. *Codependent No More*, Melody Beattie
4. *All I Need to Know I Learned from My Cat*, Suzy Becker
5. *You Just Don't Understand*, Deborah Tannen
6. *From Beirut to Jerusalem*, Thomas Friedman
7. *A Year in Provence*, Peter Mayle
8. *The Revenge of the Baby-Sat*, Bill Watterson
9. *The Education of Little Tree*, Forrest Carter
10. *Life's Little Instruction Book*, H. Jackson Brown Jr.
11. *What Color Is Your Parachute*, Richard N. Bolles
12. *Men at Work: The Craft of Baseball*, George F. Will
13. *Scientific Progress Goes "Boink,"* Bill Watterson
14. *A Peace to End All Peace*, David Fromkin

Mass-Market Paperbacks
1. *The Silence of the Lambs*, Thomas Harris
2. *The Joy Luck Club*, Amy Tan
   Dances with Wolves, Michael Blake
3. *Red Dragon*, Thomas Harris
4. *The Burden of Proof*, Scott Turow
5. *Four Past Midnight*, Stephen King
6. *Sleeping with the Enemy*, Nancy Price
   September, Rosamunde Pilcher
7. *Memories of Midnight*, Sidney Sheldon
   The Women in His Life, Barbara Taylor

It Was on Fire When I Lay Down on It, Robert Fulghum
8. *The Price of Tides,* Pat Conroy
9. *"G" Is for Gumshoe,* Sue Grafton
   Not without My Daughter, Betty Mahmoody with William Hoffer
10. *The Mummy,* Anne Rice
11. *Buffalo Girls,* Larry McMurtry
12. *The Bourne Ultimatum,* Robert Ludlum
13. *The Gold Coast,* Nelson DeMille
14. *The Voice of the Night,* Dean R. Koontz

USA TODAY—Top 100 Books 1993–2003

1. *Harry Potter and the Sorcerer's Stone,* J. K. Rowling; art, Mary GrandPré
2. *Dr. Atkins' New Diet Revolution,* Robert C. Atkins
3. *Harry Potter and the Chamber of Secrets,* J. K. Rowling; art, Mary GrandPré
4. *Harry Potter and the Order of the Phoenix,* J. K. Rowling; art, Mary GrandPré
5. *Harry Potter and the Prisoner of Azkaban,* J. K. Rowling; art, Mary GrandPré
6. *Harry Potter and the Goblet of Fire,* J. K. Rowling; art, Mary GrandPré
7. *Who Moved My Cheese?* Spencer Johnson
8. *Tuesdays with Morrie,* Mitch Albom
9. *Men Are from Mars, Women Are from Venus,* John Gray
10. *Don't Sweat the Small Stuff . . . and It's All Small Stuff,* Richard Carlson
11. *What to Expect When You're Expecting,* Heidi Murkoff, Arlene Eisenberg, and Sandee Hathaway
12. *The 7 Habits of Highly Effective People,* Stephen R. Covey
13. *The Da Vinci Code,* Dan Brown

14. *Angela's Ashes*, Frank McCourt
15. *Body-for-Life*, Bill Phillips, Michael D'Orso
16. *Chicken Soup for the Soul*, Jack Canfield and Mark Victor Hansen
17. *The Greatest Generation*, Tom Brokaw
18. *The Celestine Prophecy*, James Redeld
19. *Divine Secrets of the Ya-Ya Sisterhood*, Rebecca Wells
20. *Rich Dad, Poor Dad*, Robert T. Kiyosaki with Sharon L. Lechter
21. *In the Kitchen with Rosie*, Rosie Daley
22. *Simple Abundance*, Sarah Ban Breathnach
23. *The South Beach Diet*, Arthur Agatston
24. *The Testament*, John Grisham
25. *To Kill a Mockingbird*, Harper Lee
26. *Chicken Soup for the Teenage Soul*, Jack Canfield, Mark Victor Hansen, and Kimberly Kirberger
27. *The Brethren*, John Grisham
28. *The Catcher in the Rye*, J. D. Salinger
29. *What to Expect the First Year*, Heidi Murkoff, Arlene Eisenberg, and Sandee Hathaway
30. *The Four Agreements*, Don Miguel Ruiz
31. *A Painted House*, John Grisham
32. *The Rainmaker*, John Grisham
33. *The Summons*, John Grisham
34. *Life Strategies*, Phillip C. McGraw
35. *Oh, the Places You'll Go!* Dr. Seuss
36. *Seabiscuit: An American Legend*, Laura Hillenbrand
37. *Dr. Atkins' New Carbohydrate Gram Counter*, Robert C. Atkins
38. *Midnight in the Garden of Good and Evil*, John Berendt
39. *Memoirs of a Geisha*, Arthur Golden
40. *The Runaway Jury*, John Grisham
41. *The Hobbit*, J.R.R. Tolkien
42. *The Perfect Storm*, Sebastian Junger

APPENDIX: BESTSELLER LISTS

43. *Snow Falling on Cedars*, David Guterson
44. *Embraced by the Light*, Betty J. Eadie
45. *The Chamber*, John Grisham
46. *The Prayer of Jabez*, Bruce Wilkinson
47. *The Lovely Bones*, Alice Sebold
48. *Cold Mountain*, Charles Frazier
49. *Holes*, Louis Sachar
50. *Chicken Soup for the Woman's Soul*, Jack Canfield, Mark Victor Hansen, Jennifer Read Hawthorne, and Marci Shimoff
51. *The Notebook*, Nicholas Sparks
52. *The Partner*, John Grisham
53. *The Street Lawyer*, John Grisham
54. *The Poisonwood Bible*, Barbara Kingsolver
55. *The Seat of the Soul*, Gary Zukav
56. *The Horse Whisperer*, Nicholas Evans
57. *Hannibal*, Thomas Harris
58. *A Child Called It*, Dave Pelzer
59. *Sugar Busters!* H. Leighton Steward, Sam S. Andrews, Morrison C. Bethea, and Luis A. Balart
60. *Skipping Christmas*, John Grisham
61. *Left Behind*, Tim LaHaye and Jerry B. Jenkins
62. *The Christmas Box*, Richard Paul Evans
63. *The Red Tent*, Anita Diamant
64. *The Bridges of Madison County*, Robert James Waller
65. *Where the Heart Is*, Billie Letts
66. *Love You Forever*, Robert Munsch; art, Sheila McGraw
67. *The Five People You Meet in Heaven: A Novel*, Mitch Albom
68. *The Fellowship of the Ring*, J.R.R. Tolkien
69. *Protein Power*, Michael R. Eades and Mary Dan Eades
70. *Chicken Soup for the Mother's Soul*, Jack Canfield, Mark Victor Hansen, Jennifer Read Hawthorne, and Marci Shimoff

71. *John Adams,* David McCullough
72. *Into Thin Air,* Jon Krakauer
73. *She's Come Undone,* Wally Lamb
74. *Self Matters,* Phillip C. McGraw
75. *The Millionaire Next Door,* Thomas J. Stanley and William D. Danko
76. *The Zone,* Barry Sears and Bill Lawren
77. *The Pilot's Wife,* Anita Shreve
78. *The Secret Life of Bees,* Sue Monk Kidd
79. *The Lost World,* Michael Crichton
80. *The King of Torts,* John Grisham
81. *Timeline,* Michael Crichton
82. *A Walk to Remember,* Nicholas Sparks
83. *Conversations with God, Book 1,* Neale Donald Walsch
84. *Debt of Honor,* Tom Clancy
85. *Chicken Soup for the Teenage Soul II,* Jack Canfield, Mark Victor Hansen, and Kimberly Kirberger
86. *Rainbow Six,* Tom Clancy
87. *The Polar Express,* Chris Van Allsburg
88. *Angels & Demons,* Dan Brown
89. *Green Eggs and Ham,* Dr. Seuss
90. *The Client,* John Grisham
91. *The Purpose Driven Life,* Rick Warren
92. *The Lord of the Rings,* J.R.R. Tolkien
93. *Goodnight Moon Board Book,* Margaret Wise Brown; pictures, Clement Hurd
94. *The Bear and the Dragon,* Tom Clancy
95. *Executive Orders,* Tom Clancy
96. *The 9 Steps to Financial Freedom,* Suze Orman
97. *Ten Stupid Things Women Do to Mess Up Their Lives,* Laura Schlessinger

98. *The Giver,* Lois Lowry
99. *Message in a Bottle,* Nicholas Sparks
100. *Summer Sisters,* Judy Blume

INDEX

A

academic studies, 254–257

action adventure. *See* thrillers

Adams, John, 256

Adams, Scott, 25

adventure. *See* thrillers

Aeneid, 273

affliction fiction, 230–233

Against All Enemies: Inside America's War on Terror, 101

Agatson, Arthur

  The South Beach Diet, 16, 23, 28, 30

  The South Beach Diet Cookbook, 28

  The South Beach Diet Dining Guide, 28

  The South Beach Diet Good Fats/Good Carbs Guide, 28

Albom, Mitch

  The Five People You Meet in Heaven, 221

  For One More Day, 253

  Tuesdays with Morrie: An Old Man, a Young Man, and Life's Greatest Lesson, 11, 16, 53–56

Allen, Tim, 25

All I Need to Know I Learned from My Cat, 24

"All I Really Need to Know I Learned in Kindergarten," 48

All the President's Spin: George W. Bush, the Media, and the Truth, 109–110

American Best Sellers: A Readers Guide to Popular Fiction, 61

American Dynasty: Aristocracy, Fortune, and the Politics of Deceit in the House of Bush, 96, 110

America (The Book), 98, 107

Angela's Ashes, 15, 251

Angels & Demons, 263

  summarized, 1–3

animals, 24–25

Apocalypse, the, 195–207

Apollyon, 201, 204

Approval Addiction: Overcoming the Need to Please Everyone, 18, 184

Armageddon, 201, 205

Assassins, 198, 212

Atkins, Robert

  Diet Revolution, 27–29

  Dr. Atkins' New Carbohydrate Gram Counter, 27

  Dr. Atkins' New Diet Revolution, 16, 27

Austen, Jane, *Pride and Prejudice*, 12

Automatic Millionaire system, 35

B

Bach, David, Automatic Millionaire system, 35

Bad Cat, 25

Barzun, Jacques, *From Dawn to Decadence*, 8

Bear, John, *The #1 New York Times*

P

Winfrey, Oprah, 11, 30, 228–232,
  257–258. *See also* Oprah's Book Club
wisdom, folksy, 33
Women and Self-Help Culture,
  169–170
women, books for, 249–253
Woodiwiss, Kathleen E., *Season
  Beyond a Kiss,* 12, 148–149,
  153–154, 155, 156, 159
Woodward, Bob
  Bush at War, 109
  Plan of Attack, 109
  State of Denial, 109
*World is Flat, The: A Brief History of
  the Twenty-First Century,* 255
*World Made Safe, A: Values in
  American Best Sellers, 1895–1920,* 8
*Worse Than Watergate: The Secret
  Presidency of George W. Bush,* 94, 96

Y

Yaggy, L. W., *The Royal Path of Life,*
  134
*You: On a Diet—The Owner's
  Manual for Waist Management,* 31
You: The Owner's Manual, 31
*Your Best Life Now: 7 Steps to Living
  at Your Full Potential,* 18, 184–185

Z

Zone, The, 28
Zukav, Gary, *The Seat of the Soul,* 18,
  177, 186, 220

About the Authors

Lisa and John are lifelong book-lovers and smart alecs who now teach literature and writing. They have authored and co-authored such eclectic works as *Who Killed Homer?*, *S'mores: Gourmet Treats for Every Occasion*, *Bonfire of the Humanities*, *The Talking Greeks*, *Business and Marketing Writing*, and *Actaeon, the Unmannerly Intruder*.